手把手
教你申请美国商科名校硕士

Elite Master's Programs in US Business Schools:
Critiques, Analysis and Samples

张 旭 编著

U0731301

中国人民大学出版社
·北京·

图书在版编目 (CIP) 数据

手把手教你申请美国商科名校硕士 / 张旭编著. —北京：中国人民大学出版社，2011.9
ISBN 978-7-300-14250-0

Ⅰ.①手… Ⅱ.①张… Ⅲ.①留学生教育–申请–英语–写作–美国 Ⅳ.①H315

中国版本图书馆 CIP 数据核字（2011）第 182922 号

手把手教你申请美国商科名校硕士
张　旭　编著
Shoubashou Jiaoni Shenqing Meiguo Shangke Mingxiao Shuoshi

出版发行	中国人民大学出版社	
社　　址	北京中关村大街 31 号	**邮政编码**　100080
电　　话	010－62511242（总编室）	010－62511398（质管部）
	010－82501766（邮购部）	010－62514148（门市部）
	010－62515195（发行公司）	010－62515275（盗版举报）
网　　址	http:// www. crup. com. cn	
	http:// www. 1kao. com. cn（中国 1 考网）	
经　　销	新华书店	
印　　刷	北京市易丰印刷有限责任公司	
规　　格	185 mm × 260 mm　16 开本	**版　次**　2011 年 11 月第 1 版
印　　张	13.75	**印　次**　2011 年 11 月第 1 次印刷
字　　数	308 000	**定　价**　38.00 元

继《手把手教你写作美国名校申请文书》付梓之后，出版社几位老师和我合计了一下，觉得有必要写一本针对目前留美商科专业申请的指导书。回顾这些年商科专业申请的情况，仔细翻阅了自己写作和指导的商科专业选校名单、专业变化和文书，我发现确实有些地方值得与大家分享和借鉴。

我开始动笔写作的时候，已经是 2011 年 4 月 5 日，前一年度绝大部分的商科院校申请结果都已经出来了，这包括几个主要的专业，金融、人力、会计、物流、管理科学、信息工程管理、市场、媒体和其他几个非常小众的管理类交叉专业。MBA（工商管理硕士）和 DBA（商学院博士）出结果的时间也大致相同。在平时的咨询和辅导中，家长和同学们问得最多的就是商科学校的专业确定、选校和文书。这是除了法律和经济相关专业以外，我回答最频繁的专业类别，可以很郁闷地说，商科类的答疑占去了我大量的时间。最近在辅导高中生申请本科选专业的时候，商科专业的有关问题也经常出现。所以，我希望通过这本书，大家在咨询我或别的老师前，能对美国大学商科专业有准确和真实的了解。我也争取一次性地解决所有基本和重要的问题。

在高中生选择本科专业的问题上，我觉得本书可以起到一个前瞻性的作用，让大家了解一下商科研究生和工作到底是干什么的。这是很关键的问题，因为美国大学本科是可以转专业的，而且，我反复强调，大学本科生在基础还未打好、兴趣爱好仍未成型时不要贸然跟风选择热门的所谓商科专业。打好基础，在数理、逻辑、工程、计算机等专业领域先踏实学习，然后进一步到管理类和商科类专业课程，这才是硬道理。否则，一个小毛孩子，整天想着到了美国读一个金融衍生品，将来做巴菲特这样的人，或者做 CEO 管理几百人的公司，是特别幼稚的。如果家长在这方面没有正确引导，这是家长的教育失误。某些中介和辅导老师曲意迎合，这就是职业操守问题。回过头来，申请美国大学商科类硕士的几个基本和重要问题是什么呢？这里我简单列举一下，同时，这本书也是按照这个逻辑顺序来操作的。

首先，就业指导一切，毕业后的工作规划指导留学规划的全过程。毫不客气地说，现在的美国经济结构和社会，已经不是 5~10 年前中国留学生的黄金时代。我在美国念书和工作期间，就明显感觉到竞争越来越激烈，市场上优秀的外国人才越来越多。以往中国学生容易就业的经典职业或"避风港"，如会计和计算机编程，慢慢变得艰难，雇主的条件也变得苛刻，往往一个学生会面临巨大的竞争。我们的毕业时间是每年的 5 月份，在这个时间前的 15 天，即 4 月 15 日，就是申请工作签证 H-1B 的递交截止日。而这个递交必须是由你的雇主先填写美国劳工部的表格，SPONSOR（代表）你向移民局递交工作签证的申请，错过这个时间就要等到下一年了。这也意味着，在这个截止日前，中国学生必须确定和接受一个工作机会，而且雇主公司必须准时负担费用和递交申请，否则，OPT（留学生选择性实习期）就要开始计算了，过了这个实习期，你就必须离开美国。我能力有限，每一年辅导的学生数量不多，但是大家向我汇报找工作情况时，我都会想起自己在纽约刚开始工作时的同样经历，几万个工作签证几周甚至几天内一下就用光了，包括那两万个特别为获得美国硕士学位以上的申请者预留的名额也一扫而光。我提醒大家注意，在选择商科专业的时候，一定要考虑一下去年或毕业那一年的工作和市场情况。这个信息从什么地方能得到？网络上就有很多，自己不妨先看看，然后结合自己的情况，和你的辅导老师细细地敲定和规划好，这是商科申请成功的第一步。

其次，坚实的工作经历或优秀的实习背景和分数一样重要。每一年的 4、5 月份，我都要发一通同样的抱怨和议论，因为反反复复有学生在咨询我商科申请的时候，居然不知道自己要去实习或通过实习来加强自己的背景。也有太多的学生（这里也要批评一些胡乱指挥的家长）想通过家里的某些关系，随便弄一个银行或公司的实习证明来充数。任何一件事情，没有做过和没有经历过，都不可能给你一个最真实的感受和理解，最后即使是我亲自写的文书，也会变得了无新意。一般来说，本科在读的学生申请美国的商科时，最好有一个或两个相关的实习经历，例如，申请金融的学生，就必须知道学校对你的工作经历和实际操作经验是非常感兴趣的。很多学校不要求工作经验，但是都会说 PREFER（偏好）这样的经历。在辅导一些学生的过程中，我也经过审慎的考虑推荐他们到我的一些朋友和过去的学生工作的公司实习，这些公司基本上都是美国公司在华的代表机构（RO）或全资公司（WFOE）。这里也要注意的是，部分学生在面试后虽然录用了，但是用人单位的面试人员都对他们的表现颇有微词，这也反映了现在相当多的中国本科生在社会经验和基本商业礼仪方面的严重缺失。例如，面试时着装太过随意，虽然美国人都很随便，基本的商业轻松着装（BUSINESS CASUAL）也是需要的吧。还有，面试完后拍屁股就走，没要名片，甚至回来后也没有发一封信 (THANK YOU NOTE) 作为感谢，大大咧咧，自以为是北大、人大、外经贸、外交学院的学生就牛上天了。这样的学生毫无例外地都被我狠狠地剋了一顿。我认为有一个这样的职场惯例：过去有好工作的人，以后也会有好工作；细节上留心的人，别人也会对你留心。我们申请商科类的研究生，从现在开始，就要在礼仪、技能、人脉和经验上做好积累，甚至从大一开始，就应该规划这个事情，不要到了大三和研二，突然才考虑实习和经历，那时候就有些手忙脚乱了。

再次，就是基本考试的分数要拿得出手。每一年，由于申请留学日益便利和中国大学生就业形势的恶劣状况，申请美国商科类研究生的人数都在增加，据博创几位老师的估计，单单是在几个主要的北京高校内，2010—2011 年度申请商科各个专业的人数就有好几千人，实际提交申请的可能还不止这个数目，这里还不包括上海、广州、西安和武汉的学生。有学生问，老师，我的 GMAT 和 TOEFL 要考到多少分才算是 OK 呢？我觉得，从 GMAT 的分数上讲，700 分已经不是很稀罕的事情，要申请专业排名靠前的名校，这是一个大家在准备考试的时候应该设立的目标，当然，有丰富工作经验的学生例外。至于 TOEFL 分数，我觉得没有到 100 分基本就很难选择学校了。商科硕士和博士申请有一个特点，即不是在综合排名榜上的每个学校都有你想学的专业，很多专业都设立在综合排名稍微靠后的学校院系里。但即使是排名稍后的学校和院系，对 TOEFL 的要求也是很苛刻的，因为专业太热门，申请人数太多，学校不胜其烦，没有满足基本条件的学生很难进入第二轮的面试和筛选。我举一个简单的例子，有个大学叫 PACE UNIVERSITY，综合排名排到不知什么地方去了，我在纽约上学和工作的时候，有时候要到州法庭或市政厅去，出了地铁就会看到这个学校孤独地矗立在布鲁克林大桥边上，直到 2004 年我才知道这栋灰色大楼原来是一所大学。这个学校有金融相关专业，涉及投资和风险管理，由于地理环境优越，基本处于给华尔街看门的位置，大家可以发现，它对于申请金融的外国学生的 TOEFL 要求也是 100 分。当然，也有 85 分 TOEFL 的学生被这个学校录取，但是这个风险和代价你敢尝试和愿意付出吗？我举这个例子的意思很明显，在高度紧张和紧凑的商科学习课程里，学校要求你的听力和口语都要达到一定的水平，这和一些 ESL 和语言课程不一样，好的和差的商科项目基本都有一个标准考试的门槛，我也希望大家能够注意到这一点，提高警惕，别以为随便一个排名靠后的学校就降低了分数要求。

最后，就是申请文书的写作和申请时间节点的把握。商科硕士申请和 MBA 一样，分为好几轮，第一轮最早的，大家可以在书里看到，居然是 9 月 14 日。商学博士的申请截止时间可以晚些，和正常的 PHD 申请截止时间相差不大。大家要注意，递交申请要争取赶得早些，如果条件齐备了，最好能赶上前面两轮。我的经验是第三轮和以后录取的机会就很零星了，基本都是在前面两轮出了结果。今年 1 月 15 日有一位申请金融的学生突然找到我们三位老师，说拜托某国内著名的留学英语培训机构下属的中介办理申请（这里不点名，因为这样把留学当做附带产业的机构实在是太多），把材料给对方之后她也没继续留意（这个学生这种事关自己、高高挂起的做法也要严厉批评），结果负责的咨询顾问中途离职，另一个负责写作的人不知所措，她的文件也就无人问津了。1 月 15 日尚未写好文书和递交网申，金融这样的专业就基本很难申请到排名靠前的学校了。怎么办？只能硬着头皮重新调整选校和加急写作文书，虽然我们亲自操刀写作，但这样短的时间内做出的申请文书质量可想而知。结果一个条件很好的学生就只能委曲求全了。这里我要再次提醒大家，把握好时间的节点，预留足够时间和辅导老师沟通文书框架和内容，争取尽快递交，才能在申请中占据有利的位置。

这本书针对以上几个问题是这样安排的：首先把商科的专业细分，按照不同的专业先进行综合评述，对就业前景学科优势进行了分析；接着重点介绍几个中国学生申请最多、最频繁的院校，对课程、班级、学习时间、就业率和院系特点做点评；然后选取申请过这个学校并成功拿到录取和奖学金的几个学生作为例子，将他们的文书和我辅导时的一些感受和意见作为总结。MBA 类院校的文书更为复杂，这里就先不考虑，下一本书再说。我希望大家先看看商科硕士和博士到底应该如何申请，并了解如何操作才能达到最佳效果。所有的英文内容和学校信息都是各个美国大学的网站和公开出版物上取得的，有兴趣的学生和家长可以加以对照。

沿袭前面图书的习惯，和大家共勉：在做任何一件事情的时候，都要以最高的标准来要求自己。

张旭

2011-10

目　录

金融硕士
Master of Science in Finance

金融专业的简单介绍

我觉得有必要进行一个简短的说明，由于申请金融的学生很多，对金融没有很好了解和规划的学生，缺乏坚定信心的学生，我不建议申请，否则竞争如此激烈，花费如此之大，实在有些得不偿失。

通过几个主要的途径在美国大学可以获得金融类知识的学习，MSF（金融硕士）只是其中的一个。首先，经济学类的硕士、应用经济学、计量经济学和金融经济学的硕士都会涉及金融的知识。其次，美国学校中的商学院也有博士学位，这些博士学位里面，有金融方向的研究，例如金融商学博士（DBA of Finance Track）。金融博士的录取名额一般较少，是为了培养未来商学院老师而做准备的。再次，其他学科和金融、会计以及管理交叉的部分，都有金融知识方面的培训，如经济社会学、国际发展和研究、传媒管理和营销、精算和应用数学、统计专业等。当然，这些学科培养的是研究型人才，不是百分百针对金融市场的。最后一个，就是本章的重点，金融硕士教育。

美国的金融研究生教育，可以说经历了几个主要的发展阶段。最初的金融研究生教育方向，是从经济学的一个分支分出来的，这个分支叫计量经济学和统计经济学。可以说从这一刻开始，金融硕士就开始带上了强烈和深刻的数学烙印，这里也提醒数学不好的学生尽早打消这个念头，数学不好，你根本读不下来，读下来了也没有太大的实际意义，工作了也会很快被解雇。这个发展阶段的金融硕士教育有个延续至今的名字：数学金融（Mathematical Finance）。随着时间的推移，在 20 世纪 70 年代的时候，美国大学的金融教师发现，单纯的数学分析无论是在方法还是结论上都欠缺了一定的灵敏度和对日新月异市场信息变化的灵活度，可不可以加入一些针对不同市场及经济学和管理科学方法论的研究呢？由此衍生出另一个金融研究生的发展方向：分析金融学（Analytical Finance）。接下来的时间，全球金融市场经历了 1990 年代的持续震荡以及大量新的金融产品的涌现，分析和数学金融学单单依靠计量的方法已经很难进行复杂的交易模型和模拟盈利模式，难以满足因为股票交易的二级市场活动、极端复杂和多样化的投资组合以及房地产抵押等金融产品产生的问题和分析需求。金融工程（Financial Engineering）应运而生。毕竟没有计算机的帮忙，很多运算已经变得复杂得不可实现了。我们会在下一章节研究这个专业。在金融工程出现的同时，市场上分工开始高度地细化，咨询、销售、客户服务、计算分析、实时交易和风险管理等开始出现。可以很客观地说，市场需要什么，学校就应该培养什么，在这一点上，美国的学校目前是做得最好的。在这个高度细化的市场上，公司和银行不需要各个专业方向都有涉猎、了解和精通的全才，个别专业方向有所专长的人最好用。因此，金融硕士（MSF）就开始出现了。

MSF项目的学习时间不长，一般一年到一年半就可以读完，个别项目也可以在两年内读完，正好满足华尔街对于普通应用型人才的急切需求。项目学分的总数一般在36~48分。学生们在进入项目后，会经过一个系统而全面、但并不是特别精细的金融知识学习。在自主选课阶段，学校会要求学生专注于本项目比较擅长的几个方面，如房地产金融、组合投资分析、保险和理财、数学模型和金融衍生品的使用、国债和短期债券等。因而学生对于学校的选择，是万里长征的第一步，也是最为关键的一步。

下面，我们一起来先看看我们整理的金融专业的院校名录。需要注意的是，这个名录是依据金融专业的整体实力，因此包含了金融博士和管理科学博士的因素在内。大家也要看清楚，并不是每个列出的学校都开设并招收金融类硕士的项目。然后我们看看挑选出的几个开设金融硕士的项目情况来进行点评。英文部分我就不全部翻译了，但主要精神和意思我会进行扼要说明。

部分金融类院校名录

以下为我们中国学生申请最多的金融硕士项目，这里并非按照排名，更全的金融硕士列表数目太多，大约有50所，这里不一一列出，请关注我的博客和博创留学网页。

1. American University 美国大学
2. Boston College 波士顿学院
3. Brandeis University 布兰迪斯大学
4. University of Arizona 亚利桑那大学
5. Boston University 波士顿大学
6. Clark University 克拉克大学
7. Columbia University 哥伦比亚大学
8. University of Florida 佛罗里达大学
9. University of Delaware 特拉华大学
10. University of Denver 丹佛大学
11. University of Illinois Urban Champaign 伊利诺大学香槟分校
12. University of Maryland 马里兰大学
13. George Washington University 乔治·华盛顿大学
14. University of Houston 休斯敦大学
15. Illinois Institute of Technology 伊利诺理工学院

16. John Hopkins University 约翰·霍普金斯大学
17. MIT 麻省理工学院
18. Ohio State University 俄亥俄州立大学
19. Princeton University 普林斯顿大学
20. University of Rochester 罗切斯特大学
21. Rensselaer Institute of Technology 伦斯勒理工学院
22. Purdue University 普渡大学
23. Tulane University 杜兰大学
24. Syracuse University 雪城大学
25. Texas A&M University 得州农机大学
26. SUNY Buffalo 纽约州立大学水牛城分校
27. Washington University in St. Louis 华盛顿圣路易斯大学
28. Vanderbilt University 范德堡大学
29. Wake Forest University 维克森林大学
30. University of Wyoming 怀俄明大学

张旭老师点评名校

1. Boston College: Master of Science in Finance 波士顿学院金融硕士

http://www.bc.edu/schools/csom/graduate/msf/admission/requirements.html

○ 学校基本概况

波士顿学院建于 1863 年，位于马萨诸塞州的切斯纳特小镇。该校原来是由耶稣会教友所建立。这样的大学在美国还有几家，如纽约的 Fordham 大学，南方的 Loyola 大学等。历史上该学院共有 63 位诺贝尔奖得主。在波士顿学院，教授们最重要的责任是教学和研究，并且在最近十年都获得研究的奖励及授证认可，为学校创下新的纪录。最近几年，学校获得来自社会各界的自愿捐款达十亿美元之多，而学校也在着手利用这些资金整顿校务，改造校园形象。

该学院注册的学生在大学部有 8 900 人，研究所则有 4 600 人。主要学院（波士顿学院的各个专业学术领域部门可称之为"学校"，与一般大学的"学院"属同一概念）包括神学院、艺术与科学学院、艺术与科学研究所、管理学校、教育学校、护理学校、社会工作学校、波士顿学院法律学校、进修学院等。

○ 院系介绍和项目优势

An extensive review of fundamental tools and concepts in finance provides students with a foundation for advanced work in corporate finance, investments and financial institutions. There are eight required courses covering these areas, and two electives in such specialties as portfolio theory, international finance and the structure of corporations and markets, though students may take electives in a wide array of business disciplines.

这个项目的学习主要由 8 门必修课程组成，学习的主要方向为公司财务、投资学与金融机构研究。

The ten course program, which is accredited by the American Assembly of Collegiate Schools of Business, is designed to be completed in one year of full-time study or 22~24 months of part-time study, both of which include one summer.

项目在一年内可以完成 10 门课程学习。根据法律规定，获得 F-1 签证的中国学生在美国不能学习 Part-time 课程，因而这里说的两年的学习时间并不适合我们。

Electives can be taken in other appropriate disciplines outside of finance, and must be advanced (600- or 800-level) courses. A faculty advisor is available to assist students with his/her specific program.

学校内有导师可供学生选择，但我觉得没有必要，因为没有毕业论文的要求，一般不需要指定某一个导师来指导。

Classes meet once each week, Monday through Thursday, from 7:00 to 9:30 p.m. Occasionally a course may be offered from 4:30 to 6:50 p.m. During the two summer sessions, courses meet two nights per week from 6:30 to 9:30 p.m. on a Monday/Wednesday or Tuesday/Thursday schedule.

这里讲的是上课时间的安排。

Students following the self-paced option students take two courses per semester whereas cohort students take four courses per semester. All students are expected to take one course during each of the two summer sessions. In some cases, arrangements may be made with the director to adjust course loads to meet personal circumstances. Students are expected to complete all requirements for the MSF degree within three years, except for those with approved leaves of absence.

学校建议同学们每学期修 4~5 门课，其中最好有一门课在暑假学习。

○ 班级构成

Full-Time MSF September 2010 Enrollment

Applications Received	475
Class Size	53

Academic and Professional Background

Average GMAT Score	657
GMAT Score 80th Percentile Range	592~718

Average Undergraduate GPA	3.37
Average Full-Time Work Experience	2.8 years
Work Experience 80th Percentile Range	0~5.9 years

We now accept the GRE for admission to the MSF programs. Please reference ETS for GMAT comparison information.

这个表格说明了波士顿学院金融班级的构成与分数等要求，也暗示了录取委员会在申请审理过程中的偏好。这个方面是我们在调查学校时要注意的重要信息点。可以看到，GMAT 的平均成绩比较高，达到 660 分。我们中国学生实际的录取分数一般高出 30~40 分。这个项目从去年开始接受 GRE 的成绩。

Diversity Snapshot	
Women	42%
International	59%
Average Age	26
Age Range	21~39
	Chile
	Colombia
	Greece
	Guatemala
	Indonesia
Countries/region	Korea (ROK)
Represented	Mexico
	Morocco
	People's Republic of China
	Philippines
	Taiwan (China)
	United States of America
	Venezuela

从国际学生的比例来看，接近 60% 的学生是外国学生，是相当高的，加上台湾学生的数目，华人学生的数目估计会占到 30% 即国际生的一半以上。而且，学生的年龄跨度很大，学校对申请人有无相关工作经验还是有要求的。

○ 核心课程

Corporate Finance　公司金融
Investments　投资学
Financial Econometrics　金融计量经济学

Management of Financial Institutions　金融机构管理

Fixed Income Analysis or Portfolio Theory　固定收益与组合投资

Derivatives and Risk Management　衍生品与风险管理

Theory of Corporate Finance　公司金融理论

Financial Policy　金融政策分析

在这 8 门核心课程中，公司金融、投资学与金融机构管理最为重要，也是本项目的优势所在，另有 3 门是辅助性基础课程，即金融计量经济学、公司金融学理论与金融政策分析。应用性较强的课程有 2 门：固定收益与组合投资、衍生品与风险管理。

○ 申请的必备条件和要求

（1）先修课程：对于没有金融背景的同学，必须先修过数学、经济学和金融学理论的基本课程。对于课程是选修还是必修课，学校没有要求。

（2）Completed and Signed Application Form 申请表格

（3）Current Resume：

Please prepare a business resume that includes your educational and professional information. Professional information should consist of employment history in reverse chronological order with titles, dates, relevant information and an indication of part-time or full-time status. Please provide your Employment History separately from your resume. The Employment History should follow the following format: Name of Employer | Dates of Employment | Title | Starting Salary/Ending | Reason for Leaving. Please provide information regarding any gaps in employment and clearly indicate if you are still working at your most recent employer. If you are no longer employed, please indicate that on your employment history document. If you are a current student and therefore do not have any postgraduate work experience, you still must submit a work history document. Please write N/A for each of the categories.

这里学校对简历提出了很严格的要求，首先是需要单独不同于简历做一个 Employment History（工作经历）的列表。如果是短暂工作与实习经历，也需要写最近的时间、工作地点、雇主及工作内容等信息。这里也反映了波士顿学院对工作经历的偏好。如何提交？这个在下面就会提到。

（4）Two personal essays are required. Essays should be typed on separate sheets and numbered. A third essay is optional and you may use it to present any additional information you would like the Committee to consider.

三份申请短文，其中一份自选。

（5）Two Recommendations 推荐信要求最少两封。

（6）Transcripts must be submitted online. Applicants may either upload a self-reported transcript or scan a copy of each official transcript for every college or university in which you were enrolled in a degree granting program. If you are a current student please include your current classes even if you have not received your final grades. International students must submit an official English translation of academic credentials for evaluation. If admitted, you will be required to submit an official paper transcript from each institution you have listed. Official documents must bear the actual signature of the registrar and the official seal or stamp of the institution. All applicants who completed their undergraduate course work outside of the United States must have the equivalent of a US bachelor's degree. If you are uncertain about your educational equivalency with the US bachelor's degree, we recommend that you have your transcript evaluated by a credential evaluation organization such as World Education Services.

此处的成绩单要求和别的学校不一样，在网申系统自行汇报（Self-report）即可，不需要在申请时递交给学校。在录取以后，国际学生必须提交所有的正式成绩单，我们说的正式成绩单即为盖章而且有封印的正式大学成绩单。在申请季节开始前的每年9月份，申请人就应该开始准备中英文成绩单。

（7）GMAT/GRE/TOEFL 标准考试成绩
（8）$100 Application Fee

○ 国际学生要求

Academic Requirements 学术背景

In order to be eligible for any Masters or Doctoral graduate program, international applicants are required to hold a college or university degree equivalent to a four-year American bachelor's degree. We typically recommend that international applicants confirm their educational equivalency with a credential evaluation organization such as World Education Services. You may upload any verification report to your online application to demonstrate your educational equivalency to the admissions committee.

对于国际学生，BC 要求申请人首先具备大学四年的学历，同时，学校建议国际生通过 WES 对成绩单进行认证。

Transcripts 成绩单

All applicants must submit a self-reported transcript with their application. You may either upload a scanned copy of your official transcript or complete the self-reported transcript Excel document provided in the online application. All course names must be translated into English before submission. There is no need to convert your GPA to the 4.0 scale. If admitted, you will be required to provide an official paper transcript sent directly to the Carroll School of Management from each college or university attended. If available, your school should send a transcript in English along with the original language document. The School reserves the right to withdraw any offer of admission if there is a discrepancy between the self-reported transcript and the official transcript.

大学成绩单的提交是在网申时递交扫描件，这里学校对操作的要求是比较宽松的，也可以用自创的表格实现。一旦被学校录取，申请人必须将有学校盖章封印的正式成绩单邮寄过去。

Language Requirements 语言要求

All students whose first language is not English are required to take either the Test of English as a Foreign Language (TOEFL) or the Pearson Test of English (PTE). The minimum required score on the TOEFL is 100 on the Internet-based test, 250 on the computer-based test, and 600 on the paper-based test. The minimum required score on the PTE is 68. TOEFL and PTE scores are valid for two years. Those candidates required to take the TOEFL or PTE must at least report their unofficial scores prior to submitting their application. Both overall and component test scores must be reported on the application form.

Only the self-reported test score is required at the time of your application. If admitted, please request official test scores from ETS (TOEFL) and/or Pearson (PTE) to be sent to the Carroll School of Management. You may select school code 3033 for the TOEFL. To obtain information about these tests, visit the ETS website or the Pearson website.

PTE 考试在中国并不盛行，但学校对 TOEFL 的分数要求一般会在 100 分以上，这是必须的。不满足条件的申请人，除非委员会特别认可，一般会在第一轮甄选就被直接删去或拒绝。根据我的经验，也有个别运气很好的同学在分数没有达到的时候被录取。注意，这一般是从等待名单（Waiting List）上获得的，时间都在 5、6 月份，别的学校已经接受，而且签证的预约也来不及了。

○ 截止日期

PROGRAM	DEADLINE	NOTIFICATION BY
MSF Full-Time	February 15, 2011 （2 月 15 日）	April 15, 2011
MSF Part-Time (January 2011)	October 15, 2010	December 1, 2010
MSF Part-Time (September 2011)	May 1, 2011	June 15, 2011

○ 学习费用和支出

Estimate of Student Expenses for the 2010—2011 Academic Year

Tuition and Fees	$38,100
Room and Board	$9,900
Books and Supplies	$1,650
Medical Insurance	$1,898
Personal Expenses	$4,200
Summer living	$4,200

Graduate Assistantships and Scholarships

The Carroll School of Management offers a number of graduate assistantships and scholarships to Full-Time Masters candidates. Assistantships and scholarships are merit-based awards, and therefore awardees have exceptionally strong application materials and profiles above the class profile. These awards are made only at the time of admission and vary in amount. Graduate assistantships involve research or administrative duties in exchange for a stipend. Assistantships can be offered in combination with academic scholarship awards.

学校的奖学金发放类别只有优秀奖学金（merit-based），国际生是可以申请的，在奖学金发放上，学校并不要求申请人去写作或者提交特别的文件或材料，只需要在申请材料中说明或注明即可。

2010—2011 Academic Year Full-Time MSF Expenses

Tuition Fee Per Credit Hour	$1,270
Tuition – 30 Credits	$38,100
Room and Board	$9,900
Books and Fees	$1,650
Medical Insurance	$1,898
Personal Expenses	$4,200
Summer Living Expenses	$4,200

由于学校的地理位置处于波士顿这样的城市，这个学校的金融项目费用较贵，在每个学时的收费上，1 270 美元属于比较高的档次。可以说在波士顿地区，这个学分的收费丝毫不比哈佛低。那么存款证明需要准备多少呢？根据这个费用的总数，换成人民币，以一年的时间计算，同时生活费用按照美国学生的一般支出计算，加起来就可以得到存款证明需要的数字。注意，这是必须填写进申请表格中的一项，所以在递交时，心里要有准备，否则容易出现前后矛盾。

2. Vanderbilt University: Master in Finance 范德堡大学金融硕士

http://www.owen.vanderbilt.edu/vanderbilt/admissions/ms-finance-admissions/

○ 学校基本概况

范德堡大学由海军将领范德比特于 1873 年出资建立，位于田纳西州的首府纳什维尔 (Nashville) 市，是一所以本科教育为主、研究院发展较快的综合性大学。全美大学综合排名第 18。该大学的所有机构设施都位于主校区，它同时拥有数个优秀的附属研究机构，包括：戴尔天文台（Dyer Observatory）、公共政策研究院和范德堡大学医学中心等。该校历史上人才辈出，是美国两位副总统以及诸多州长和参议员的母校。宋美龄的父亲宋嘉树先生 1882 年亦在此就读神学院。学校景色迷人，从 1988 年开始在此设置国家植物园，被誉为全美"最美丽校园"。

范德堡大学在校学生约为 10 500 人，其中研究生大约 5 000 多人。学校设有四个本科学院和六个研究生学院。本科学院包括文理、工程、音乐和神学院。专业设置有心理学、人体发展、经济、英文、政治科学、语言文学、数学、物理学、工程技术等学科。

○ 院系介绍和项目优势

The Vanderbilt MS Finance is a rigorous, accelerated program designed for recent college graduates seeking careers in asset management, investment research, sales and trading, insurance, corporate finance and risk management. Students complete a core curriculum in quantitative finance and can pursue tracks in either Quantitative or Corporate Finance. Along the way, students master advanced skills in financial databases, portfolio management, financial modeling, firm valuation, econometric forecasting and asset allocation.

You'll learn how to be a well-rounded leader. You'll learn not only the fundamentals of finance, but also how to apply critical thinking, problem solving and communication strategies to realistic business situations. The program helps you get ready for the Chartered Financial Analyst (CFA) exams.

这个项目的主要方向是公司金融和金融市场交易，课程设置很紧凑，结合了很多计量经济学和金融数据库管理的内容。但这也是相当多业内人士对这个学校项目课程有看法。很多人认为学校的课程设置有些铺得太开，一些重点的方向如资产管理方法和案例、公司估值和股东权益分析等，反倒轻描淡写，失去了项目多年来积累的传统。但是，有一点是这些年没有改变的，即这个项目的内容很适合准备参加注册金融分析师考试的同学。

○ 核心课程

必修课有两种模式，同学们可以选择 Mod Ⅰ 或 Mod Ⅱ 在秋季上学。

Required Courses—Mod Ⅰ

Number	Course Title	Credits
MGT 311	Introduction to Financial Accounting　金融会计	2
MGT 402	Financial Economics II (MSF)　金融经济学	2
MGT 403A	Econometrics (MSF)　计量经济学	2
MGT 405	Financial Modeling (MSF)　金融模型	2

Required Courses—Mod Ⅱ

Number	Course Title	Credits
MGT 403B	Econometrics (MSF)　计量经济学	2
MGT 432A	Corporate Valuation　公司估值	2
MGT 435C	Derivatives Markets　衍生品市场	2

Suggested Electives 建议选修课

Number	Course Title	Credits
MGT 411A	Financial Reporting 金融报表	2
MGT 411B	Financial Reporting 金融报表	2
MGT 425	Game Theory and Business Strategy 博弈论与商业策略	2
MGT 432B	Corporate Financial Policy 企业金融政策	2
MGT 433A	International Financial Markets and Instruments 国际金融市场与工具	2
MGT 433B	International Corporate Finance 国际公司金融	2
MGT 435A	Equities Markets 流动资本市场	2
MGT 435B	Bond Markets 债券市场	2
MGT 436	Financial Institutions 金融机构	2
MGT 437	Real Estate Financial Analysis 地产金融分析	2
MGT 438	Real Estate Investment and Development 地产投资	2
MGT 448	Negotiation 谈判与交易	2
MGT 536	Active Portfolio Analysis 投资组合分析	2
MGT 539F	Special Topics in Accounting: Federal Income Taxation of Mergers and Acquisitions 金融并购与联邦收入所得税	2
MGT 630A	Asset Pricing Theory 资产定价理论	2

○ 申请必备条件和要求

In addition to the completed application and application fee, you will be required to provide the following:

（1）Unofficial transcripts 非官方成绩单

（2）Self-reported GMAT or GRE scores 自行报告的标准考试成绩

（3）Resume 简历

（4）Comprehensive work history 工作经历记录

（5）Essays 申请文书

（6）Two letters of recommendation 至少两封推荐信

（7）Self-reported TOEFL or IELTS scores (international only) 托福或雅思考试成绩

Transcripts and Test Scores

We require a separate transcript from every college or university you attended.

Official transcripts are required from each institution only if you accept an offer of admission. If you cannot calculate your cumulative GPA or convert it to a four-point scale, leave the field blank; we will evaluate your academic record accordingly.

范德堡的 MSF 项目申请所需文件大同小异，唯一值得特别关注的是其申请审理分为两轮。第一轮初步筛选，大部分的申请人在这一阶段将会被划分，因此，国际生提交的成绩单与 TOEFL 或雅思成绩，只需要在网申时如实汇报即可。也就是说，只需上传与扫描，等到学校正式录取后再补交这两份重要文件，即大学成绩单和托福或雅思成绩。

Essays

Your essays give us great insight into your personality and your other unique qualities. You will submit the two required essays with your online application.

In the first of the two essays you should explain your short-term (post-MSF) and long-term career plans as specifically as possible. Each essay is limited to no more than 500 words.

文书题目共有 4 个，但最主要的是这里所点明的前面 2 个关于职业规划和学习计划的题目。

Your recommenders can submit your recommendations securely online to us along with your other application materials. Recommenders will also have an option to download a PDF recommender form if they choose not to complete an online recommendation. Instructions will be included in an email sent to each recommender after you enter the person's contact information in the Recommender section. All paper-based recommendations must be submitted in unopened envelopes, with the recommender's signature across the sealed flap. We require two recommendations from managers who can evaluate your personal qualities, ability to succeed in a top MSF program and potential for success in management and leadership roles. Acceptable recommenders include current or former professors, current and former employers, clients and individuals with whom you have worked regularly as long as they can provide a meaningful evaluation in a professional context.

推荐信可以提交两至三封，这里学校对推荐信作了明确要求。一般来说，基本上所有金融项目的学校都要求教授或老板使用电子系统在网上提交推荐信。纸张的推荐信已经越来越少见，大家也注意到，推荐人可以是老师、老板，甚至是工作中的同事或客户，如何安排好这些人，就需要同学们与辅导老师仔细商量。

○ 截止日期

Deadlines

Round	Apply	Decision	Deposit
1st	Nov 29, 2010	Jan 21, 2011	Feb 14, 2011
2nd	Jan 31, 2011	Mar 18, 2011	Apr 11, 2011
3rd	Mar 14, 2011	Apr 22, 2011	May 20, 2011

○ 就业情况分析

借这个机会讲讲金融硕士专业毕业生的几个主要工作领域。一般来说，金融工作分为三大块：买方、卖方和中间服务方，简单地说几乎所有的金融人士都可以归到这三大块。至于具体操作的领域，按照以下的分析，大家可以对将来金融硕士毕业生从事什么样的工作有个大概了解。

1. Quantitative Finance 计量金融学

（1）Trading and Principal Investments 交易与主体投资，这是最主要的一个领域。

Sales and trading are the investment bank's distribution arm. This group is responsible for selling all of the financial products (stocks, bonds and their derivatives) developed by the investment banking area. As such, they serve as the vital link between the sellers (corporations, government entities) and the buyers (investors).

（2）Investment Research 投资研究

（3）Proprietary Trading 财产交易

（4）Private Equity/Merchant Banking 私募和商业银行

这个领域的工作是"卖方市场"工作，也是大部分 MSF 毕业生首先会获得的工作。

2. Risk Management 风险管理

Risk Analysts weigh the probability of profits and losses and make recommendations to senior management on acceptable strategies. Entry-level job titles for these positions include derivatives risk analyst, market risk analyst, and portfolio risk analyst. Duties include developing and managing risk management methodologies; providing financial reporting and risk analytics; and evaluating and testing pricing models.

风险管理是初级分析员必须担当的工作。主要做衍生品、市场风险与浮动及投资组合收益分析。

3. Corporate Finance 公司金融

（1）Corporate/Industry Finance 公司和行业金融

Corporate finance includes two key functions: accounting and finance. Accounting concerns itself with day-to-day operations—bookkeeping. Accountants balance the books, track expenses and revenue, execute payroll, and pay the bills. They also compile all the financial data needed to issue a company's financial statements in accordance with government regulations. Finance professionals analyze revenue and expenses to ensure effective use of capital.

企业金融服务应属于金融市场上最为活跃的活动。这个行业的初级工作是做公司财务、会计与金融策略以及金融报表。

（2）Divisional Financial Analysis—In this area, you work with each division's business team to prepare financial plans, make forecasts and compare actual financial results to forecasts. 分行业金融分析

（3）Treasury—The treasury department is responsible for all of a company's financing and investing activities. This department works with investment bankers who help the corporation raise capital through stock or bond issuances, or to expand through mergers and acquisitions. 财务部门工作

（4）Cash Management—This is a company's piggy bank. The cash-management group ensures the company has enough cash on hand to meet its daily needs. The group also invests excess cash in overnight short-term investments. 现金流管理

4. Private Wealth Management 私人理财

Private banking and wealth management are the coordinated delivery of banking, asset management, insurance and fiduciary and tax services to high net worth individuals through a network of highly trained private bankers, investment managers and other specialists. Private wealth managers interface with multiple divisions of investment firms and are able to offer clients resources and services that sophisticated institutional investors have traditionally enjoyed. Offerings include investments in initial public offerings (IPOs), new issues, derivatives and proprietary products. Private wealth managers also deliver an institutional level of research, advisory services and execution to investors. Entry-level job titles for this position include Financial Analyst and require CFA designation for advancement.

私人理财服务的工作人员需要 CFA（注册金融分析师）资格。这种考试分三级，第一级较为简单，大部分 MSF 同学在三个月准备后，在已学课程基础上均能通过，第二和第三级的考试比较难，提供的工作是资产管理、保险、信托与普通银行服务，工作中对于投资组合与税务问题也有广泛涉及。

3. University of Rochester: Master of Science in Finance 罗切斯特大学金融硕士

http://www.simon.rochester.edu/programs/full-time-ms/admissions/index.aspx

○ 学校基本概况

罗切斯特大学创建于 1850 年，原先是一所教会学校，后来各种不同来源的资本进入，促使学校逐渐改制成为一所宗教色彩不太重的偏理工的学校。学校位于纽约州西部的工业城市罗切斯特。罗切斯特大学的图书馆约有 330 万藏书，分散在 11 所图书馆，其中 Rush Rhees Library 是最大的图书馆，建筑古色古香。在该校教师和校友中有 5 名诺贝尔奖金获得者、9 名普利策文学奖获得者、7 位全国科学院院士、18 位美国文理研究院院士。美国国防部每年向其赞助超过一亿美元的科研费。该大学曾被 2007 年 Kaplan/Newsweek "How to Get into College Guide" 提名为 25 所新常春藤院校之一，该名单列举了能以自身的教学与学生质量与传统常春藤学校竞争的后起之秀。而在《华盛顿月刊》大学排名中该大学排在第 21 位。《美国新闻与世界报道》在 2008 年美国最受欢迎大学排名中将罗切斯

特大学排在第 35 位。

罗切斯特大学大约有 4 500 名全日制注册本科生，3 900 名研究生以及终身教职人员 1 200 多名。该校主要有 7 大学院：文理学院 (College of Arts and Sciences)、伊斯曼音乐学院 (Eastman School of Music)、华纳教育及人文发展学院 (Warner Graduate School of Education and Human Development)、工程及应用科学学院 (School of Engineering and Applied Sciences)、赛门企业管理学院 (Simon Graduate School of Business Administration)、护理学院 (School of Nursing)、医学院 (School of Medicine and Dentistry)。

○ 院系介绍和专业优势

In one year, the Simon School's M.S. in Business Administration with a concentration in Finance can teach you what you need to know to enter the world of global finance. We are best known for our research and scholarship in the area of finance. This concentration provides students with state-of-the-art techniques for financial analysis. Students learn to formulate and solve important corporate finance problems and to obtain information from the many databases on financial markets. This concentration prepares students for careers in banking, corporate finance, risk management and investment management.

罗切斯特大学的金融专业排名，尤其是 **MBA** 方向下的金融研究，在美国排名一直非常靠前，主要的优势就在于企业金融与投资管理，风险管理与银行业务倒不是它最为人所知的两个专业方向。注意这个学校的要求并不是特别高，但每一年申请入学的同学基本都会选择这个学校，因而竞争激烈。

○ 班级构成

Full-Time M.S. Class of 2011 Profile
Successful Simon M.S. candidates come from a variety of backgrounds, from the humanities to business and economics. To find out more about the qualities of a successful applicant, please review our selection criteria.

Class Characteristics:	
Enrolled M.S. Students	131
Average Age	24
Countries of Origin (non-U.S. citizens)	10
Undergraduate Majors:	
Business & Commerce	45%
Economics	16%
Engineering	6%
Humanities & Social Sciences	8%

Math & Science	25%
Undergraduate GPA:	
Average	3.4
Middle 80% range	2.9 ～ 3.8
GMAT:	
Average	662
Middle 80% range	580 ～ 740
GRE:	
Average	1289
Middle 80% range	1090 ～ 1450
TOEFL:	
Average	102
Work Experience (Years):	
Average	1.2
Middle 80% range	0 ～ 3.2
Gender:	
Male	51%
Female	49%
M.S. Degree Enrollment:	
Accountancy	23
Finance	73
Marketing	24
Information Systems Management	11
Financial Aid:	
Enrolled students awarded merit scholarships	80%

　　从专业背景上来说，罗切斯特大学的金融硕士班级招收的大部分是金融、商业和理工背景的本科生。对于工作经验，可以从班级构成图上看出，学校对于工作经验并无特别要求，也无明显的偏好，学校最喜欢的看来是已经有 MBA 学位的申请人。罗切斯特的班级构成反映的另一个重要的信息，是学校对标准考试分数及本科学术表现特别看重。按照惯例，如果在 GMAT 录取平均分上增加 30~40 分的话，一般中国学生有竞争力的分数应为 700 ～ 720 分左右，本科学分绩也是，3.4 对于部分理工同学来说有些困难，但

对于复旦、外经贸和人大的同学来说，这个平均分应该不成问题。

○ 核心课程

Classes are taught by a faculty internationally known for financial expertise. The degree is offered to two distinct groups:

Students who have already earned an M.B.A. with a non-finance focus, and need additional training in finance and/or are considering a career change. Students with a completed Bachelor degree and a demonstrated quantitative aptitude.

Required Core Courses (for those without a prior M.B.A.)

Students who do not hold an M.B.A. start in July and complete 43 credits to receive the degree:

GBA 461 Core Economics for M.S. Students (Foundations Course)

GBA 462 Core Statistics for M.S. Students (Foundations Course)

ACC 401 Corporate Financial Accounting (plus 1 credit lab)

FIN 402 Capital Budgeting and Corporate Objectives

STR 403 Economic Theory of Organizations

ACC 410 Accounting for Management and Control

FIN 411 Investments

FIN 413 Corporate Finance

之前没有获得 MBA 学位的同学，必须先学经济学、统计、会计、资本预算、企业运营目标、管理学和投资学等课程。

Required Core Courses (for those holding an M.B.A.)

Students who hold a prior M.B.A. start in September and complete 36-39 credits:

FIN 402 Capital Budgeting & Corporate Objectives (may be waived by area coordinator)

STR 403 The Economic Theory of Organizations

ACC 410 Accounting for Management and Control

FIN 411 Investments

FIN 413 Corporate Finance

已经获得 MBA 学位的同学，仍然要完成近 40 学分的课程，包括经济学理论、管理会计、投资学与企业金融。

Electives for the M.S. program include 选修学科

(6 required electives for those without an M.B.A. and 8 electives for those holding an M.B.A.)

ACC 411 Financial Statement Analysis　金融报表分析

ACC 423 Financial Reporting Ⅰ　金融报表制作Ⅰ

ACC 424 Financial Reporting Ⅱ　金融报表制作Ⅱ

ACC 431 International Financial Statement Analysis　国际金融报表分析

APS 420 Applied Time Series Analysis　时间序列分析

BPP 426 Macroeconomics　宏观经济学

FIN 423 Corporate Financial Policy and Control　企业金融政策与内控

FIN 424 Options and Futures Markets　期货与期权

FIN 425 Banking in Financial Markets　银行业务

FIN 430 Financial Institutions　金融机构

FIN 433 Cases in Finance　金融实操案例

FIN 434 Investment Management and Trading Strategies　投资管理与交易策略

FIN 442 International Economics and Finance　国际经济与金融

FIN 446 Financial Information Systems　金融信息系统

FIN 448 Fixed-Income Securities　固定收益

FIN 511 Advanced Financial Economics　高级金融经济学

FIN 532 Advanced Topics in Capital Markets　金融市场研究

FIN 533 Special Topics　专项研究

FIN 534 Advanced Topics in Corporate Finance　公司金融研究

MTH 515 Mathematical Finance　数学金融

STR 440 Organizational Governance and Control　组织架构与管理

以上选修课包含已经获得 MBA 或未获得 MBA 的同学的所有选修课程。在众多的选修课程中，各项设置比较均匀，涵盖了金融实物的三大主要领域，同时也可以看出来，对于金融、会计课程，罗切斯特大学没有过多设置，交易模型类的课程也没有设置。

○ 申请必备条件和要求

The Simon School uses a self-managed online application. This requires the applicant to accumulate the necessary documents to complete the process. Applications will be processed when they are submitted, although an application cannot be reviewed for a final decision by the Admissions Committee until all materials are received and the application is complete. Once submitted, academic records, essays and recommendations may not be copied, borrowed or returned.

学校的申请系统为自行汇报方式，即重要文件和指标如学分绩、成绩单、GMAT 和 TOEFL 成绩等，包括财产证明都是自行上网传送。

申请材料 Application Checklist

（1）Online application form　表格

（2）Current résumé　简历

（3）One required essay (double spaced, 12-point font, 500 word limit)　500 字申请文书

（4）Unofficial transcripts, scanned and uploaded for each college attended (admitted students will be required to submit official transcripts at a later date)

（5）Test-taker results for GMAT, scanned and uploaded (M.B.A. or M.S. applications; optional for M.S. Medical Management and M.S. Marketing applicants) 非官方成绩单扫描

（6）Test-taker results for GRE, scanned and uploaded (M.S. applications only; optional for M.S. Medical Management and M.S. Marketing applicants) 标准考试成绩

（7）Test-taker results for TOEFL, scanned and uploaded (all international candidates except those who received a degree from an English-speaking institution) 纸质托福成绩单扫描

（8）One online letter of recommendation (submitted electronically); a second letter of recommendation is optional 两封推荐信

（9）$125 application fee 申请费用

申请材料清单也显示了这个学校申请系统的快捷、明了与科学。我觉得越是优秀的项目，在申请过程上就越是便捷与简单，这也是一种气魄与文化。大家注意，在提交 GMAT 与 TOEFL 成绩时，需要扫描正式成绩单，在以往的辅导过程中，部分学生在考了 TOEFL 后往往忘了索要纸质的成绩单，结果在这一环节就出了问题，学校虽然不要求 ETS 寄官方成绩，却需要你扫描并上传纸质官方成绩单。同时，成绩单只需要一份。

○ 国际学生要求

Admission Requirements

Notarized English translations are required for all official documents and transcripts. In most cases, international students are required to take the Test of English as a Foreign Language (TOEFL). The TOEFL will be waived only for candidates who have completed a degree at an English-speaking instruction. Please note that the TOEFL is the only test that the Simon School will accept for the application. The IELTS can not be substituted for the TOEFL. 学校不接受雅思，只认 TOEFL。

Funding Graduate Study

We strongly recommend that each student secure financing prior to submitting the application for admission. While the Simon School offers partial tuition, merit-based scholarship assistance to some of our incoming M.B.A. and M.S. students each year, competition for these awards is intense. International applicants should not count on receiving any financial assistance unless it is awarded at the time of admission. We recommend that international candidates identify personal or external funding options while simultaneously pursuing admission to the program, as the process to secure loans may sometimes take longer than expected.

In 2009, the Simon School introduced the International Student Loan Program (ISLP) to offer access to U.S. based education loans to our international students. Students seeking access to this loan need not have U.S. credit history or a U.S. citizen as a co-signer. Please visit here to learn more, and all necessary information is provided at the point of an offer of admission to the Simon School.

一般来说，罗切斯特大学或多或少会给录取的学生一定的经济资助，即奖学金，但同学们不要指望学校给全奖，至少我还没见到过，同时，学校提供 ISLP 的贷款机会，这里也可以仔细看看。

○ 截止日期

Program	Application Deadline	Notification Date By
Full-Time MS—August and September 2012 Entry	October 15（第一轮）	January 15
	November 19（第二轮）	February 15
	January 5（第三轮）	March 31
Final Application Deadlines	March 15	May 15
	May 15	July 15

Final Application Deadline for International Students: March 15, 2012（最终截止日期）

○ 就业情况

M.S. students focusing in Finance may be interested in working in positions such as:

Corporate/Industry Finance 企业金融（分析）

Financial Analyst within a company division, Treasury department or Cash Management group

Risk Management 风险管理

Derivatives Risk Analyst 衍生品风险分析师

Market Risk Analyst 市场风险分析师

Portfolio Risk Analyst 组合投资分析师

Investment Management 投资管理

Financial Analyst 金融分析师

Investment Research 投资研究

Sales & Trading 销售

Merchant Banking 商业银行

这里可以看到金融硕士就业的几个主要领域。

MS Finance New York City

Program Highlights

The Simon School's Master of Science degree in Finance New York City is a 13-month graduate program designed for working professionals who seek an advanced finance degree on an accelerated part-time basis from a world-class finance institution.

The lock step program consists of twelve courses of 3 credit hours each. Ten courses will be conducted at a midtown Manhattan location on alternate weekends commencing March 2011.

These courses will be arranged in modules of two courses with four weekends of instruction. The remaining two courses are week-long programs conducted off-site, one at the main campus at the University of Rochester in the summer of 2011 and the other at a European location at the end of the program. Travel and accommodations will be provided for week-long courses. World-renowned Simon faculty in the fields of Finance, Accounting and Economics will lead the program instruction.

　　这是罗切斯特大学在纽约城中开办的金融班，注意，这个课程是给正在工作的职业人士准备的，十次课，其中有两次是在学校的罗切斯特校区上课。卡耐基梅隆大学与加州大学伯克利分校也在曼哈顿开办类似的班级，但没有金融工程专业。

4. University of Illinois at Urbana-Champaign: Master of Science in Finance 伊利诺伊大学香槟分校金融硕士

http://www.business.illinois.edu/msf/

○ 学校基本概况

　　伊利诺伊大学香槟分校成立于 1867 年，多年来被业界公认为全美最优秀的理工大学之一，理工类专业排名和麻省理工学院等校不相上下。在公立大学中，从总体研究和师资力量来看，该校与加州大学伯克利分校、密歇根大学、俄亥俄州立大学、弗吉尼亚大学和威斯康星大学等均为其中的领军学校。校内学生众多，学校设备完善且先进，该校属下的学院多达 20 多所，有逾 80 个研究中心、实验室及研究所，提供的主修课程超过 150 种。学校也因安排的课程多次被评为全美提供多元化课程的最佳大学。截至 2007 年，该大学共有 24 位教授或校友荣获过诺贝尔奖，2 位荣获过普利策奖，共有 22 位美国国家科学院院士、28 位美国国家工程院院士。伊利诺伊大学香槟分校的图书馆藏书量高居全世界公立大学的第 1 名，以及所有大学之第 3 名，仅次于私立的哈佛大学和耶鲁大学。

　　伊利诺伊大学香槟分校有本科生约 32 000 人，研究生 10 500 多人。该大学由 18 个学院和研究所组成。本科专业主要有：会计、广告学、农学、企业管理、工商管理、生物学、生物工程、化学、化学工程、土木工程、计算机工程、计算机科学、经济学、环境工程、电子工程、工程力学、工程物理、环境经济和政策、金融、综合管理、历史、信息系统、国际商务、市场营销、材料工程和科学、数学、机械工程、媒体学、保险统计、音乐、哲学、物理、心理学、统计学、技术系统管理、房地产、旅游管理；研究生专业主要有：艺术、生物化学、生物工程、生物科学、生物、化学工程、化学、音乐、土木工程、会计学、广告学、教育学、经济学、心理学、社会学、统计学、法学、自然资源和环境科学、哲学、系统工程等。

○ 院系介绍和专业优势

Established in 1958, the Illinois MSF is among the longest running programs of its type in the world. The curriculum, which can be completed after 12 months of rigorous, full-time study, is taught by internationally recognized finance faculty and provides an opportunity to study with an international peer group at one of the premier public research institutions in the world.

The College of Business is proud to provide MSF students with a new home beginning in Fall 2008. The Business Instructional Facility is a sustainable, environmentally efficient building. The Market Information Lab within the new facility, sponsored in part by the Chicago Mercantile Exchange, provides students with state-of-the-art tools and software products, bringing real-world exposure to their academic experience.

UIUC 的这个项目是一个老项目，也是金融界享有盛名的项目，学校为 MSF 班级安排了新的教学地点并提供了新的设施。

Illinois MSF Program: a CFA Program Partner

The ILLINOIS Master of Science in Finance program has been officially named a CFA Program Partner. As such, the MSF curriculum covers more than 70% of the CFA Body of Knowledge and teaches students the tools they need to prepare for and be successful with the CFA exams. The Chartered Financial Analyst (CFA) certification is a professional designation awarded by CFA Institute. The professional investment community recognizes the value of the CFA certification to support hiring and promotion decisions. For more information, visit the CFA Institute and CFA Review Program websites.

UIUC 项目所讲授的课程与 CFA（注册金融分析师）所测试内容有相当大的重合，学生们在完成这个项目的学习后，基本上不用再上 CFA 的培训即可参加第一级的考试。

One Year to a Brilliant Career

MSF Career Services provides a suite of products and services for students and recruiting firms, including personalized coaching on job strategy and negotiation, as well as access to top recruiters, alumni, and career resources. ILLINOIS MSF graduates are sought after by hundreds of companies who recruit students from the College each year. Your interest in Illinois MSF shows that you recognize excellence, not only in our program, but in yourself. Apply today and join our network of successful alumni and faculty.

UIUC 的职业服务办公室也是在业界比较出名的，在芝加哥地区校友圈子内影响力巨大。

○ 核心课程

The MSF program begins in June with an intense, core summer curriculum. Over summer term, students master fundamental techniques in financial statement analysis, financial modeling, stock and firm valuation, statistical analysis, regression analysis, and time series analysis. The two summer core classes are Corporate Finance and Valuation and Quantitative Methods for

Finance. Moving beyond the traditional lecture format, students practice technique applications through the use of software tools during regular class meetings and in weekly review sessions.

核心课程是由暑期开始的，暑期两门课程为企业金融与估值、金融计量方法。

Key content features of the summer curriculum are:

Corporate Finance and Valuation—introduces students to fundamental tools in corporate finance such as:

（1）Financial statement analysis 金融报表分析

（2）Estimating a firm's cost of capital 企业资本成本预估

（3）Project analysis and the use of investment decision rules 项目分析与投资决策

（4）Stock and firm valuation techniques 股票与公司交易

（5）Monte Carlo simulations analysis 蒙特卡洛模型分析

（6）Quantitative Methods for Finance—introduces financial applications of quantitative techniques covered in areas such as:

Analysis of time series data on stock returns and bond yields 时间序列分析

Analysis of cross-section firm or bank data 跨行业分析

（7）Applications of the Capital Asset Pricing Model (CAPM), and the Fama-French model in investments and corporate finance in-class teaching of financial modeling techniques with Excel 资本资产定价模型和多因素模型

（8）Forecasting financial statements 金融报表评估

（9）Project analysis and the use of NPV and IRR decision rules 项目分析和净现值与收益率

（10）Valuation techniques (Discounted cash flow valuation, multiples valuation, adjusted present value) 估值方法和技巧（包括现金流分析、多指数分析和调整现值方法等）

（11）In-class teaching of Monte Carlo techniques with Crystal Ball software

Applications of Monte Carlo techniques in project analysis, stock, and firm valuation 蒙特卡洛模型课堂讲授和操作实例

The core curriculum is completed in the fall semester with two additional courses in investments and financial economics. These courses have been structured to provide a strong foundation for advanced study in corporate finance, investment, risk management, commercial or investment banking, insurance and real estate.

秋季的两门附加课程侧重于投资和金融经济学。

（1）Investments—provides an introduction to modern investment theory and its application to investment management. Topics include:

Historical analysis of equity market returns 流动资本市场数据

Portfolio analysis and asset pricing models 投资组合与资产定价

Equity portfolio management, stock analysis, portfolio performance evaluation 投资组合管理、股票分析、投资组合评估

Efficient market hypothesis 市场假设

Active portfolio management and predicting portfolio returns 投资组合管理

（2）Financial Economics—emphasizes microeconomic concepts related to:

Consumers, producers and how markets work 消费、生产和市场运作

Capital markets, risk and choice under uncertainty 资本市场、风险和不确定因素

Strategy and decision tree analysis 投资策略和决策

Financial markets and the role of information 信息和资本市场

Financial system and the macroeconomy 金融系统和宏观经济

Required Courses：

Finance 580 QM: Quantitative Methods for Finance 计量金融数学方法

Finance 580 CF: Corporate Finance and Valuation 企业金融与估值

Finance 511: Investment 投资

Finance 580 FE: Financial Economics 金融经济学

Areas of Specialization 专业领域：

Corporate Finance 企业金融

Finance 521: Advanced Corporate Finance 高级企业金融

Finance 522: Cases in Financial Strategy 金融策略

Finance 524: Mergers and Acquisitions 合并收购

Finance 551: International Finance 国际金融

Finance 580 PE: Private Equity 私募资金

Finance 580 TBM: Turnaround and Bankruptcy Management 交接与破产管理

Finance 580 BF: Behavioral Finance 行为金融学

Finance 490 EQP: Equipment Leasing and Financing 租借设备与融资

Accounting 517: Financial Statement Analysis 金融报表分析

Asset Management 资产管理

Finance 419: Real Client Managed Portfolios 真实客户资产组合

Finance 515: Fixed Income Portfolios 固定收益组合

Finance 580 AM: Asset Management 资产管理

Finance 580 BF: Behavioral Finance 行为金融学

Finance 580 EMI: Empirical Methods in Investments 投资实证方法

Finance 580 HF: Hedge Funds 对冲基金

Quantitative Finance 计量金融

Finance 512: Financial Derivatives 金融衍生品

Finance 513: Financial Engineering Ⅰ 金融工程Ⅰ

Finance 514: Financial Engineering Ⅱ 金融工程Ⅱ

Finance 515: Fixed Income Portfolios 固定收益组合

Finance 580 ERM: Enterprise Risk Management 企业风险管理

从课程设置上看，非常明显，UIUC 的数量化倾向非常明显，在课程设置上比别的项目更加专注于数量分析、流动资产与投资组合中的收益分析等。这都需要比较扎实的数学基础方可申请。

○ 申请必备条件和要求

申请材料 Application checklist

Complete an online application (registration required) 申请表格

Pay application fee ($70 domestic/$90 international) 申请费用

Provide transcripts and academic credentials 成绩单和证书

Provide official GMAT or GRE scores (taken no earlier than June 2006) 标准考试

Provide 3 letters of reference 三封推荐信

Provide resume (with exact dates of employment) 简历

Provide written statement (in 300 words or less describe your area of interest in finance and what your goals are upon completion of the MSF program) 申请文书

○ 国际学生要求

Additional requirements for international students:

Official TOEFL or IELTS score (taken no earlier than June 2009) 外语成绩

Provide evidence of financial support for duration of program 财产证明

很多同学问，在读的大三学生没有毕业怎么提供毕业证和学位证？我认为这是个显而易见的问题，在读生直接提供成绩单即可证明你的在校资格。学位证等你拿到了再提供也可以。注意，这就要求我们在准备成绩单时，最好请教务处在成绩单的注解部分写明你的毕业时间、所要拿到的学位和时间等。相当多的中国大学教务处开具的成绩单没有这些信息。

○ 截止日期

Application Deadline	Notification Sent	Deposit Deadline
November 10, 2010(第一轮)	December 8, 2010	January 5, 2011
January 26, 2011（第二轮）	February 16, 2011	March 2, 2011
February 23, 2011（第三轮）	March 18, 2011	April 6, 2011
March 31, 2011（第四轮）	April 8, 2011	April 15, 2011

○ 就业情况

Many reputable firms come to the U of I campus to recruit MSF students. These recruiters attend job fairs, hold company presentations, and schedule interviews. Please visit the MSF career services website for a complete list of such companies.

For US citizens and permanent residents, 70% of students actively seeking employment accepted positions in the United States within 3 months of graduation. By 6 months after graduation, 100% accepted employment. By 3 months after graduation, 56% of the MSF students actively seeking employment (including international students) accepted positions in the US or abroad. By 6 months after graduation, 80% of the MSF students actively seeking employment (including international students) accepted positions in the US or abroad.

Salaries for positions vary greatly based on the industry, country of employment, and work experiences of the individual prior to admission to the program. These factors make it difficult to report a fair salary figure. For those graduates working in the United States, an average salary of $63,000 was reported excluding bonus and incentive compensation, which in some cases makes up the majority of annual compensation. MSF graduates find their jobs through a variety of tools including networking, on-campus recruitment, jobs postings, headhunters, and individual contacts.

UIUC 在毕业生就业率方面很有自信，我辅导的学生在 UIUC 就读金融硕士后，如这里的数据显示，在毕业的 6 个月内基本找到工作。工作的地点除了就近的芝加哥、库克郡和大伊利诺伊地区，也有相当多的学生前往纽约州。至于工资，学校提供的数据是平均的税前工资，一般投资银行和基金公司的入门阶段工资都会在 7 万美元以上，所以说 UIUC 给的数据还是稍微保守了一些。

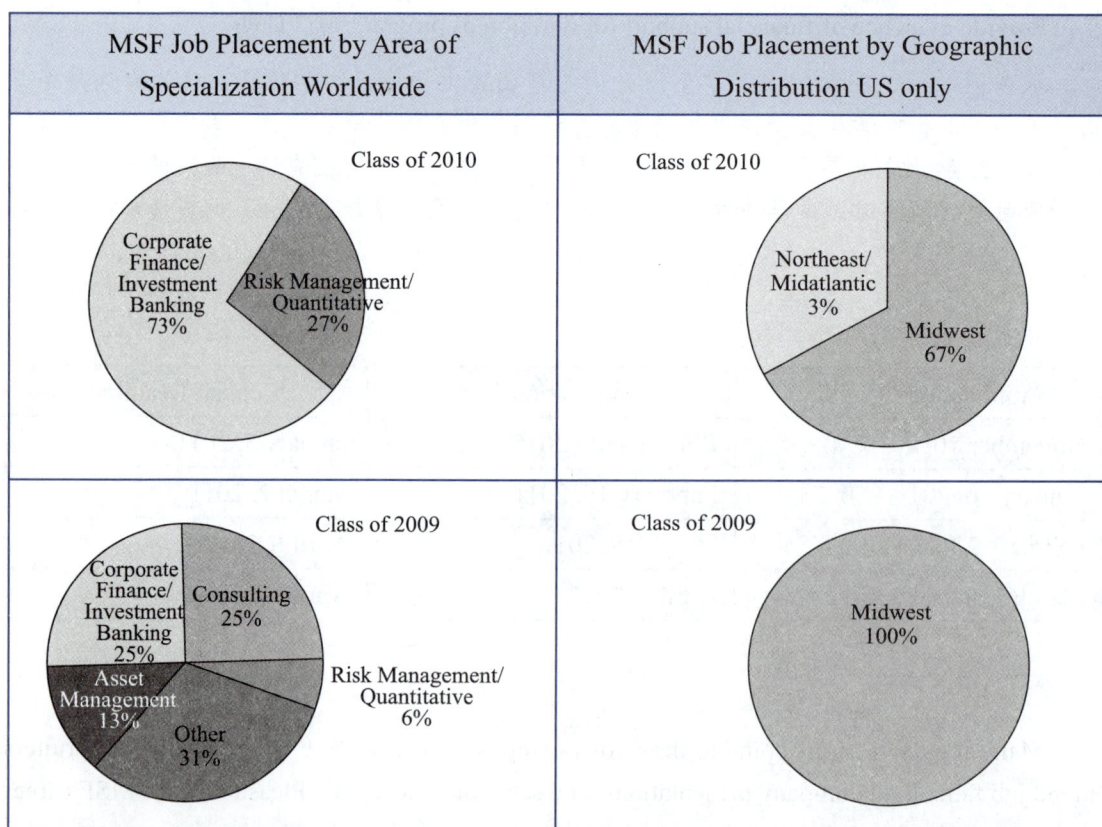

MSF Job Placement by Area of Specialization Worldwide	MSF Job Placement by Geographic Distribution US only
Class of 2010 Corporate Finance/Investment Banking 73% Risk Management/Quantitative 27%	Class of 2010 Northeast/Midatlantic 3% Midwest 67%
Class of 2009 Corporate Finance/Investment Banking 25% Consulting 25% Asset Management 13% Other 31% Risk Management/Quantitative 6%	Class of 2009 Midwest 100%

Class of 2008

Consulting 32%
Risk Management/Quantitative 24%
Other 10%
Corporate Finance/Investment Banking 24%
Asset Management 10%

Class of 2008

Southwest/West 11%
Northeast/Midatlantic 22%
Midwest 67%

Class of 2007

Consulting 22%
Risk Management/Quantitative 21%
Other 11%
Corporate Finance/Investment Banking 27%
Asset Management 19%

Class of 2007

Southwest/West 22%
Midwest 45%
Northeast/Midatlantic 33%

Class of 2006

Consulting 38%
Risk Management/Quantitative 5%
Other 10%
Corporate Finance/Investment Banking 37%
Asset Management 10%

Class of 2006

West 8%
South 17%
Midwest 75%

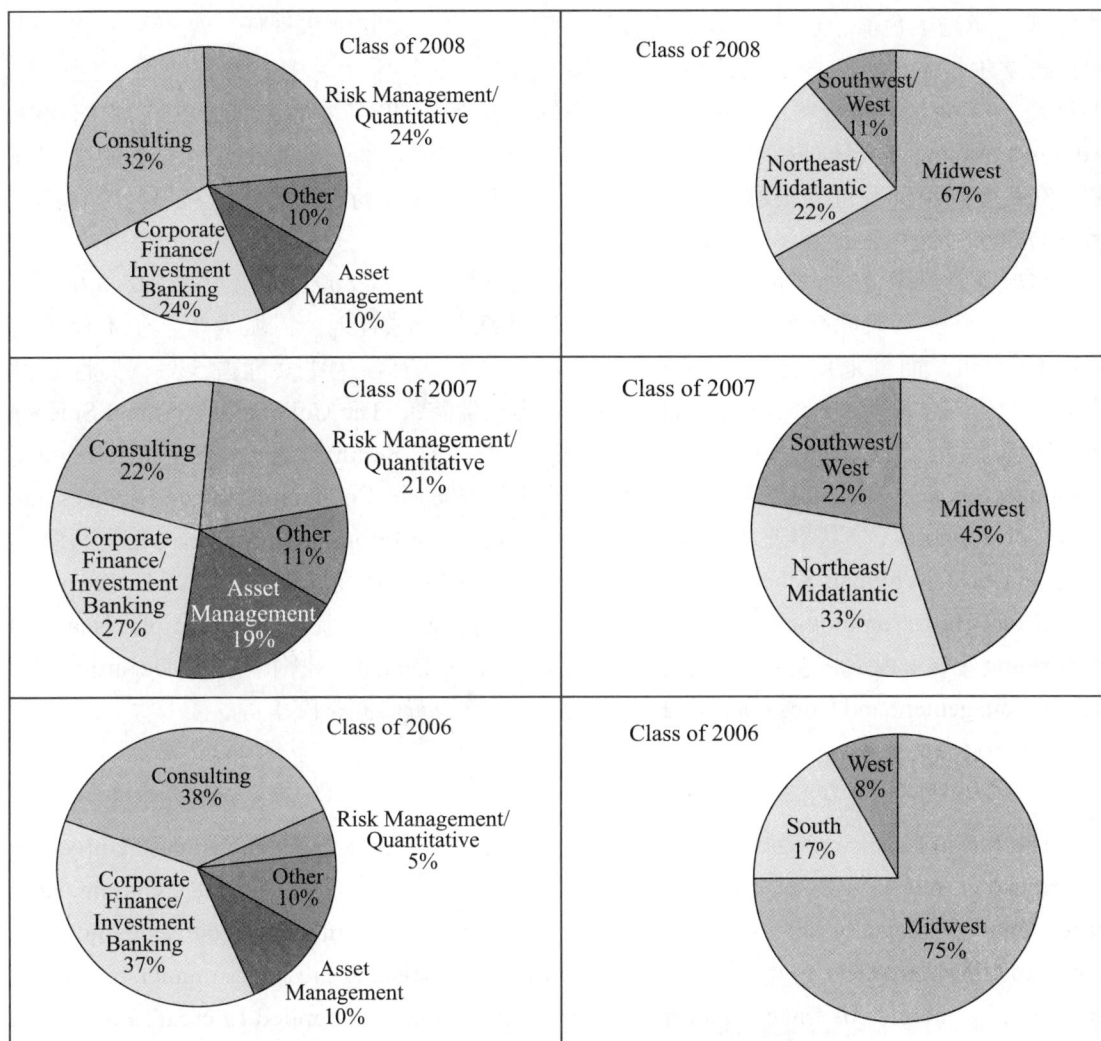

　　主要的毕业生去向和工作领域，集中在咨询、公司金融、投资组合研究和分析、支持管理、风险管理和分析及普通商业银行业。大家可以对比一下这几年 UIUC 毕业生的去向和领域。

5. Syracuse University: MS in Finance 雪城大学金融硕士

http://whitman.syr.edu/MS/Finance/requirements.asp

○ 学校基本概况

　　雪城大学（Syracuse University，或译叙拉古大学）位于素有 Central New York 之称的纽约州中部城市——雪城，是一所历史悠久的著名综合性私立大学。这里治安良好，环境优美，湖光山色。该学校致力于使教师、学生、职员共同承担责任，让三方一起工作而促进学生学术成长、职业成长和个人成长，从而成为以学生为中心的著名研究性大学。近年来，雪城大学在全美 3 000 多所大学中综合排名为 40 名左右，其公共管理（Public Administration）、信息研究学院和纽浩思公共传媒学院的一些专业均在专业排名中名列前茅。在《美国新闻及世界报道》公布的美国最新综合大学排行榜中，该校被评为综合排名最好的 50 所大学之一。

雪城大学现有 15 所学院，200 多个专业。雪城大学现有 800 多名正式教师，3 000 多名职员，600 多名兼职教师，并有 20 多万校友活跃于全球各地。雪城大学学生不仅来自美国 50 个州，而且来自全世界 90 多个国家和地区。现有学生中女性占 54%，男性比例为 46%。主要学院有：School of Architecture（建筑学院）、The College of Arts and Science（文理学院）、School of Education（教育学院）、L.C. Smith College of Engineering and Computer Science（L.C. 史密斯工程与计算机科学学院）、College of Human Services and Health Professions（公共事业和健康职业学院）、School of Information Studies（信息科学学院）、Martin J. Whitman School of Management（马丁·J·惠特曼管理学院）、S.I. Newhouse School of Public Communications（S.I. 纽豪斯公共交流学院）、College of Visual and Performing Arts（视觉和表演艺术学院）、Department of Drama（戏剧学院）、Department of Retail Management and Consumer Studies（零售管理及消费研究学院）等。

○ 院系介绍和专业优势

The MS in Finance program in the Whitman School of Management at Syracuse University is a rigorous, one year curriculum that prepares students to be leaders in the dynamic, fast-paced, and intellectually challenging world of finance. The program's core courses explore the nature of capital markets as they relate to organizational goals and provide an understanding of how broad principles of finance and quantitative methods can be applied to create investment strategies.

The MS in Finance program is flexible and allows students to customize their degree by taking elective courses in any of the following areas: statistics, accounting, economics, risk management, real estate, and corporate finance. With a state-of-the-art trading room, Whitman MS in Finance students have personal access to current market data, live news feeds, software for analysis, and other resources used by professionals in the field, including Bloomberg certification terminals and Factset terminals through Whitman's Ballentine Investment Institute.

据雪城大学 Whitman 管理学院来访的老师介绍，这个学校的金融项目在培养实际操作技能上，属于美国金融研究生教育内比较敢于创新的，学校的学分要求大约在 30 分左右，给学生提供了很多的实际操作与实习的机会，如巴伦汀投资研究所商学院的命名教授 Prof.Whitman 一直活跃在学校内，每年给 MSF 的学生讲授他创立的"Valve investing"金融投资理论。由于学校与纽约众多银行与投资机构关系密切，大部分学生在暑期实习时都有很大的益处与便利。

○ 核心课程

Program Requirements 毕业要求课程

The Whitman MS in Finance can be completed with 30 credits (typically one year) by students with academic backgrounds in finance, economics, accounting, and business. Students without academic backgrounds in these areas should expect to take up to an additional nine hours of foundation courses as part of the program. The MS Finance program advisor reviews each student's academic background and designs a program personally suited for the student.

没有金融学习与实操背景的同学，学校建议多修 3~6 学分来弥补金融经济学、会计等方面的背景。

<u>MS in Finance：Total Credits Required 30</u>

1. Finance Courses（18~21 credits） 金融课程

Theory of Finance 金融学
Investment Analysis 投资分析
Corporate Financial Policy and Strategy 公司金融政策与战略
International Finance 国际金融
Portfolio Analysis 投资组合分析
Securities Markets 证券市场
Equity Valuation 流动资产分析
Derivatives 金融衍生品
Distress/Value Investing 价值投资
Real Estate Finance 地产金融
Credit Risk Management 信用风险管理
Operational Risk Management 运营风险管理
Institutional Trading 机构交易
Investment Banking 投资银行业务
Financial Planning 养老和保险投资
Financial Modeling 金融模型
Commercial Bank Management 商业银行管理
Applied Financial Management 应用金融管理
Thesis (optional) 论文

2. Courses from Related Fields（9~12 credits） 相关领域课程

Regression and Time Series Analysis 回归分析与时间序列分析
Accounting 会计
Economics 经济学
International Business 国际商务

○ 申请必备条件和要求

MS Finance application

1. Official transcripts of academic credentials 成绩单

One official transcript from each postsecondary educational institution for which nine credit hours or more of course work was taken. All transcripts (academic records) must be official documents. If not issued directly by the college or university as original documents, they should be notarized, full-sized photocopies.

注意，这里我们说 notarized（公证）就是学校教务处认证盖章的成绩单，不是说要到公证处去办理。

2. Equivalency of U.S. Bachelor's Degree 学历

Applicants who studied at colleges and universities outside the U.S. should have a degree or diploma that is the equivalent of the U.S. bachelor's degree or higher. International credentials are assessed in terms of the educational pattern of the country, the type of institution attended, and the level of study completed before the expected date of enrollment in the Graduate School. In general, the degree should represent a minimum of four years of college-level study which follows at least 12 years of schooling at the elementary and secondary level.

申请人必须具备大学本科四年的学位与学历。

Other Asian countries—A university degree requiring four years of study. 亚洲（含中国）

3. Two letters of recommendation 推荐信两封

We suggest that both recommendations be professional references from those individuals who know you in an occupational setting, and that at least one of the recommendations is written by a current or previous supervisor. For those who do not have work experience academic recommendations are accepted.

4. Resume 简历

Please prepare a business resume that includes your educational and professional information. Professional information should consist of employment history in reverse chronological order with titles, dates, relevant information and an indication of part-time or full-time status.

5. Graduate Management Admission Test (GMAT) 标准考试

Applicants are required to take the GMAT. Please arrange for official reports to be sent directly to Syracuse University (Program Code: NGO-SB-94).

We do not accept the GRE score in place of the GMAT.

学校不接受 GRE 作为 GMAT 的替代。

6. Test of English as a Foreign Language (TOEFL) 托福考试

The Test of English as a Foreign Language (TOEFL) is required for all applicants for whom English is not the primary language. An iBT minimum score of 100 is required. Scores are valid for two years. The TOEFL is administered by the Educational Testing Service.

Note: Applicants who are citizens of the following English-speaking countries are not required to submit TOEFL scores: Australia, Bahamas, Barbados, Canada, Ireland, Jamaica, New Zealand, Trinidad and Tobego, and the United Kingdom. Applicants who have studied for a minimum of two full years at an institution in the U.S., U.K., or English speaking province in Canada may waive the TOEFL requirement. If you have studied in the U.S. for less than two years, you will be required to submit a TOEFL score.

在英语国家学习超过 2 年的申请人不需要提供 TOEFL 成绩。

We do not accept the IELTS in place of the TOEFL test.

学校也不接受雅思考试分数。

7. Non-refundable US$75 application fee 申请费用

All applicants must pay a non-refundable application fee of $75. Application fee waivers are not available.

8. Two Essays 申请文书

The essay questions can be found on the online application.

应该是三篇 Essay，有一篇为 optional（选择性的）题目。

❍ 截止日期

Fall 2011 Application Deadline:	Expect a decision after: (Decision mailing date)
1st Round: November 30	December 21
2nd Round: January 1	February 1
3rd Round: February 15 Final deadline for international applicants	March 15
4th Round: April 19 Final deadline for domestic applicants	May 17

❍ 学费和花费

Financial Support Documents 财产证明文件

The United States Department of State requires that international students admitted to an academic program in the United States have a student visa to enter the country and remain here for the duration of the program. Most students will attend the program on an F-1 visa. To be issued an F-1 visa you must first obtain an I-20 document from Syracuse University. To receive an I-20 from Syracuse University, you are required to submit proof of sufficient funding.

You may show funding from a number of different sources as long as the total funding available meets the University's guidelines for minimum funding for one full academic year of study for a graduate student (see chart below). The funding provided to the University to issue your I-20 does not necessarily need to be the same funds that you will actually use for your program.

雪城大学的录取，根据这些年的经验，一般不大会给予国际生奖学金，个别学生被录取后根据 GPA 与 GAMT 成绩的优秀与否，会获得 8 000~12 000 美元的奖学金。

Individual	Funding Required
Student	$45,334
Spouse or First Dependent	add $8,330
Spouse plus 1 Child	add $12,507
Spouse plus 2 Children	add $17,839

Acceptable proof of funding for privately sponsored applicants is a certified current bank statement on official bank letterhead, signed by an authorized bank official, indicating that sufficient funds exist to meet at least first-year expenses in U.S. dollars. An explanation of the relationship of the account holder to the applicant (ex. self, spouse, parents, other relatives) should accompany the funding documents.

具体财产证明文件的开具请大家和辅导老师商量。一般来说，不需要初始户口本等东西来证明资金提供人或赞助人和被资助者（申请人）的关系，没必要这么做，因为无论谁出钱，学校不关心。在签证的时候，I-20 上会写明资金来源和数量，因此，大使馆也不会特别索要学生和资助人的关系证明。

就业情况

Career Center 职业规划中心

The Whitman Career Center team is passionate about its work. With more than 40 years of collective experience in business and career counseling, the group offers services that prepare Whitman students for a competitive career search.

The professional team at the Whitman Career Center focuses on the career and professional development of Whitman students, with their long-term career success our number one priority. Using a variety of means, Whitman students are well prepared to launch an effective job search that leads to long-term career satisfaction. Through executive speaker series, students learn how to build a career path, and through "office hours with corporate recruiters," students can ask important questions about the recruiting process and how to differentiate themselves from their peers. Our team provides group career classes along with personal coaching sessions, which provide a strong foundation for Whitman students.

For our corporate recruiters, the Whitman Career Center creates strategies that support their ability to effectively and efficiently hire Whitman students. Through classroom presentations and career fairs, corporate partners can share insights about their corporation and career opportunities. Our campus interviewing program allows corporations to meet with students in a personal meeting to assess compatibility between the student and corporation. The Whitman Career Center has a reputation for providing exemplary services, which creates a positive recruiting outcome.

从就业的情况来分析，学校没有给出具体的行业与学生的去向及薪酬。从我辅导的几个学生的情况来看，基本都在毕业后3个月内找到工作，主要是投资银行、风险管理与金融行业分析等领域。这也和雪城大学的课程设置和培养重点有关，课程并不太过偏重数理和项目能力的培养，而是在尽可能多的金融实际业务领域进行培养，这也和商学院几位教授的一贯观点是相符的，即 MSF 应该培养具备广博与扎实的金融基础知识与能力的人才，而非专门从事计算与分析的专家，这是大家在递交简历和选择公司时要注意的。

第二章

金融工程、计算金融和金融数学专业硕士
Master of Financial Engineering, Master of Computational Finance, Master of Mathematics in Finance

金融工程专业的简单介绍

如前所述，金融工程专业完全不同于金融硕士专业，也不完全等同于计算金融专业。美国大学的研究生教育，尤其是商科相关的专业，一贯紧跟市场需求，投资人、银行和客户需要什么，学校就会调整课程提供相应的培训。随着大量新型金融产品的应用，尤其是投资组合产品的应用，投资公司和理财专员必须向客户解释清楚自己的决定和判断。举个简单的例子，无论是投资煤矿，还是买几只股票，为什么 A 类的投资组合和目标比 B 类的收益更高，风险更低，操作更简单？请用模型和数据说明，过往历史数据的参考意义已经逐步降低，市场上需要的是根据单独客户的投资意向、风险接受程度、流动性偏好等纷繁复杂的指标，来量身定做一套市场推销和实际操作工具。那么谁来制作或运行这样的工具？当然最好是金融工程专业的毕业生。

我认为金融工程专业申请成功的三大要素，大家已经都很清楚了，即金融知识和背景、数学分析能力、计算机编程和模型。但是这几个要素如何排列呢？我认为首要的是数学，其次是计算机，最后才是金融背景。所以，一个在外经贸大学或复旦大学学习金融本科的学生，和另一位清华大学或同济大学毕业的电子工程的学生同时竞争一个名校的金融工程专业录取，我觉得后者反倒会占据优势。金融知识的学习和培训，可以通过考试和课程来解决，而且这不是主要的难点，因为一年学习的时间足矣。难点在于，如果没有扎实的数理背景，没有学过微积分、概率、线性代数、偏微分、函数和随机过程，是根本不可能完成金融工程专业的课程学习的。另外，C++ 编程、算法与数据结构，这些计算机的能力倒是可以短期掌握，但是深层次的理解，仍需要大量的时间。这也是为什么说我国国内大学录取制度的一个弊病就是，大一新入学的金融专业学生居然大部分都是文科生。

美国大部分的金融工程院系，都是设置在数学系、工程学院下面，有一部分院校是联合设置在商学院下，但主要的任课老师仍然是工学院和理学院的教授。例如普渡大学的金

融工程专业方向，主要有三个入口，其一是商学院下面，另外两个入口分别是数学系和统计系。所以，我提醒大家注意，金融工程这个专业，应该反过来叫工程金融，这样就不会混淆认为申请时金融比工科背景要更吃香。有一部分学生比较盲目，没有考虑好自己的专业取向，误认为金融工程就是需要GMAT，然后就闷着头考试，考完了才发现原来学校更青睐GRE。很多金融工程项目都接受GMAT，但是从我辅导申请的经验来看，GRE更为合适，也更有竞争力。

可以毫不夸张地说，国内很多学生对金融工程专业毕业后能找到什么样的职位和工作有较大的误解。绝大部分的学生毕业后都会先从最基本的职位开始，即金融分析员（Financial Analyst）。至于操盘手和咨询师，那是不同方向的细化和工作两年以后的事情。职务头衔可能会变化，但是最直接和最基本的工作就是对市场上的固定收益、股票投资、流动性和金融产品进行分析、做报表和提供意见。主要的行业包括投资和保险业，其中有证券行和商品经纪行、银行投资部门和信贷机构、保险公司、社保基金、大型的私募基金和部分风险投资公司。每天的工作就是和数字和程序打交道，工作强度相当大，当然，工作中得到的个人收益也是成正比的。

下面我们来看几个学校，以此为样本来分析一下这个专业在不同学校的设置和特点以及我们需要注意的地方。

金融工程专业院校名录

以下为金融工程的学校中，我们中国学生申请最多的，也是实力最强的，但这里没有列出全部的近百所金融工程学校，请大家注意我的博客、博创网页和美国计算金融学会的项目列表。

1. University of California Berkeley 加州大学伯克利分校
2. Columbia University 哥伦比亚大学
3. NYU 纽约大学
4. Cornell University 康奈尔大学
5. University of Chicago 芝加哥大学
6. Carnegie Mellon University 卡耐基梅隆大学
7. Stanford University 斯坦福大学
8. Princeton University 普林斯顿大学
9. Massachusetts Institute of Technology 麻省理工学院
10. University of Michigan Ann Arbor 密歇根大学安娜堡分校
11. Purdue University 普渡大学
12. Georgia Institute of Technology 佐治亚理工学院
13. Kent State University 肯特州立大学
14. Claremont University 克莱蒙大学

15. University of Illinois Urbana Champaign 伊利诺伊大学香槟分校
16. Boston University 波士顿大学
17. University of Southern California 南加州大学
18. University of Waterloo 滑铁卢大学
19. SUNJ, Rutgers 新泽西州立大学罗格斯分校
20. University of Wisconsin—Madison 威斯康星大学麦迪逊分校
21. Worchester Polytechnic Institute 伍斯特理工学院
22. Rochester Institute of Technology 罗切斯特理工学院

张旭老师点评名校

1. Columbia University: Master of Financial Engineering 哥伦比亚大学金融工程硕士

http://www.ieor.columbia.edu/pages/admissions/Application/index.html

○ 学校基本概况

哥伦比亚大学位于美国纽约市曼哈顿，于 1754 年根据英国国王乔治二世颁布的《国王宪章》而成立，属于私立的常春藤盟校，由 3 个本科生院和 13 个研究生院构成。哥伦比亚的校友和教授中一共有 87 人获得过诺贝尔奖，包括奥巴马总统在内的 3 位美国总统是该校的毕业生。

该校下属学院有哥伦比亚学院、普通教育学院（成人学院）及工程与应用科学学院。其他学院有：商学研究生院、图书馆服务学院、法学院、艺术学院、艺术与科学研究生院、社会工作学院、内科与外科医学院、公共卫生学院、牙科与口腔外科学院和护理学院。哥伦比亚大学的教育学、医学、法学、商学和新闻学院都名列前茅。其新闻学院颁发的普利策奖是美国文学和新闻界的最高荣誉。

○ 院系介绍和专业优势

Financial Engineering is a multidisciplinary field involving financial theory, the methods of engineering, the tools of mathematics and the practice of programming. The Financial Engineering Program at Columbia University provides a one-year full-time training in the application of engineering methodologies and quantitative methods to finance. It is designed for students who wish to obtain positions in the securities, banking, and financial management and consulting industries, or as quantitative analysts in corporate treasury and finance departments of general manufacturing and service firms.

在介绍这个一年的项目时，金融工程的四大基本知识构成也很明显地列举出来，即金融理论、工程技能、计算机编程与应用数学。

The first half of our program is devoted to the tools of the trade and their use in modeling financial markets and instruments. Students take courses in stochastic processes, optimization, numerical techniques, Monte Carlo simulation, and data analysis. They also study portfolio theory, derivatives valuation, and financial risk analysis, making use of the methods they have learned.

第一部分的课程将学习行业内的基本技巧和金融模型，随即过程、最优化、数量化技巧、蒙特卡洛模型及数据分析均有涉及。

The second half of the program gives students the opportunity to take more advanced courses or study specialized topics. We offer a selection of more detailed courses on current subjects of interest, ranging from models of the term structure of interest rates to a study of the implied volatility smile, as well as a course on applications programming for financial engineering. Students can also choose from a variety of courses on particular markets and their models, for example mortgage-backed securities or credit-risk modeling.

第二部分的学习将侧重于个别金融领域的知识学习与技能培训，使大家有机会运用所学来进行实践。可以选择的领域可参考哥伦比亚大学在金融工程这个专业所设置的核心课程。

In addition to courses within the engineering school, students can also take electives from various schools within the university, such as the Graduate School of Business, the Graduate School of Arts and Sciences, the School of Law, and the School of International and Public Affairs. Our program also hosts a popular Financial Engineering Practitioners Seminar on Monday nights, at which Wall Street and industry practitioners present seminars on their recent research or particular specialty, and where students can hear firsthand about life in the financial world. The Department suggests a number of elective courses and four optional concentrations depending on areas of interest.

学生可以到别的学院进行选课，这也算在 36 分的总学分内。

○ 核心课程

MSFE Curriculum 2011—2012

For the class of 2011—2012, the MSFE Program requires the completion of 36 points on a full time basis only. Students start with an 8 week part I summer session (July 5- August 26, 2011), and continues through the 2011—2012 academic year. Students may complete the program in May 2012, August 2012 or December 2012.

All courses are for 3 credits, unless stated otherwise.

The curriculum below assumes that the student will complete the degree by May 2012.

以下是 2011—2012 样本的课程设置。

Sample curriculum for:

August 2012 completion

December 2012 completion

这是两个不同的毕业时间。

Summer Part I: Required Core, 9 points

IEOR E4701: Stochastic Models for Financial Engineering 金融工程的随机过程模型

IEOR E4702: Statistical Tools for Financial Engineering 金融工程的统计工具

IEOR E4706: Foundations of Financial Engineering 金融工程基础

IEOR E4729: Financial Markets, Institutions and Risk 金融市场、机构与风险

The Department requires that students achieve grades of B– or higher in each of the four fundamental core courses offered in the first summer. Poor performance in these courses is indicative of inadequate preparation and is very likely to lead to serious problems in completing the program. As a result, students failing to meet this criterion will be asked to withdraw from the program.

哥伦比亚大学要求每门课至少 B– 以上，否则会对不良学术表现作出相应处理。

Fall: Required Core Courses & Electives, 15 points

IEOR E4007: Optimization Models and Methods for Financial Engineering 最优化模型与金融工程

IEOR E4707: Financial Engineering: Continuous Time Models 延续时间模型

IEOR E4709: Data Analysis for Financial Engineering 金融工程数据分析

Two electives (6 points) 选修课

IEOR E4403: Advanced Engineering and Corporate Economics (S. Kachani) 公司经济学与高级工程

IEOR E4500: Applications Programming for Financial Engineering (D. Bienstock) 金融工程中的编程

IEOR E4720: Topics in Quantitative Finance: Commodity Derivatives (M. Higgins) 计量金融学中商品衍生品

Spring: Required Core Courses & Electives, 12 points

IEOR E4703: Monte Carlo Simulation 蒙特卡洛模型

Choose from the electives below, plus one other course in consultation with faculty adviser.

DRAN B8835: Security Pricing Models (C. Moallemi) 证券定价模型

IEOR E4602: Quantitative Risk Management (M. Haugh) 量化风险管理

IEOR E4630: Asset Allocation (G. Iyengar) 资产分配

IEOR E4710: Term Structure Modeling (M. Haugh) 期限结构模型

IEOR E4718: Introduction to the Implied Volatility Smile (E. Derman) 引申波幅初步

IEOR E4721: Topics in Quantitative Finance: Computational Methods in Derivatives Pricing (A. Hirsa) 衍生品定价的计算模型

IEOR E4722: Topics in Quantitative Finance: Algorithmic Trading (I. Kani) 交易金融

IEOR E4723: Topics in Quantitative Finance: Foreign Exchange & Related Derivatives Instruments (D. DeRosa) 外汇交易与相关衍生品工具

IEOR E4724: Topics in Quantitative Finance: Introduction to Structured & Hybrid Products (I. Kani) 结构及混合投资产品

IEOR E4726: Topics in Quantitative Finance: Experimental Finance (M. Lipkin & A. Stanton) 实验金融学

IEOR E4731: Credit Risk Modeling and Credit Derivatives (X. He) 信用风险建模与信用衍生品

○ 申请必备条件和材料

The following materials must accompany the application:

Completed application form

One (1) official transcript from every post-secondary institution attended, sent from the institution, issued in English in a sealed envelope.

Three (3) letters of recommendation

Official Graduate Record Examination (GRE) General Test scores, sent from ETS. Scores are valid for five (5) years. Institution code is 2111; there is no department code.

Personal statement

Resume or curriculum vitae

Non-refundable application fee ($80)

从录取的要求材料上看，哥伦比亚大学的要求很普通，甚至没有多个单独的申请文书（Essay），只要求了一份个人陈述。结合学校的特点及项目侧重，才能写出满意的文书。从课程设置上看，哥伦比亚大学的 FE 更侧重于衍生品的研究、交易模型的使用及引申波幅的学习。

○ 国际学生要求

In addition, applicants whose undergraduate degree was received in a country in which English is not the official and spoken language must meet the following requirements:

Test of English as a Foreign Language (TOEFL) or International English Language Testing System (IELTS). Official scores from ETS are required of all students whose undergraduate degree was received in a country in which English is not the official and spoken language.

One (1) official transcript from every post-secondary institution attended, sent from the institution, issued in English in a sealed envelope.

Translation of the official transcript(s) is required if the institution(s) you attended does not issue transcripts in English. The transcript translation must be conducted by a reputable service and must be sent in addition to the official transcripts. Personal transcript translations will not be accepted.

对于成绩单，哥伦比亚大学不要求外国学生做特别认证，同时也接受雅思成绩。

○ 截止日期

Each program has specific deadlines. We urge all applicants to submit all application information by the deadline so the admissions committee can inform you of a decision in a timely manner.

Program	Admission	Deadline
MS&E	Fall only	February 15 秋季入学
MSFE	Summer only	December 1 夏季入学
MSIE	Fall/ Spring	February 15 (Fall); October 1 (Spring)
MSOR	Fall/ Spring	February 15 (Fall); October 1 (Spring)
PDIE	Fall/ Spring	February 15 (Fall); October 1 (Spring)
PhD	Fall only	December 1

○ 就业情况

Located in the financial center of the world, the Columbia MSFE Program provides its graduates with both a strong theoretical and a practical foundation in all aspects of financial engineering, from knowledge of financial markets and instruments through financial modeling in a variety of areas, programming and data analysis. The Program commences in July and is flexible, allowing students to graduate within one academic year by May, the end of the summer or December, based on their educational and career objectives. The first half of the program focuses on core courses and fundamental skills; the second half provides in electives in a wide variety of areas on both the buy-and sell-sides of the financial industry.

Columbia University is dedicated to assisting students in professional development, providing resources that include not only education but also resume and cover letter writing, developing professional appeal and interview/networking skills.

The Columbia MSFE Program has had a good track record placing graduates in full time positions and internships. The full-time placement statistics for students who started in July 2009 (completed the Program in 2010) are listed below. The July 2008 career information and July 2007 career information is also available.

我觉得哥伦比亚大学就不必多说了，当年我念书的时候就有 3 个学金融工程的朋友还未毕业就已经工作 offer 在手了，优越的地理环境及超强的课程设置使得 FE 的毕业生备受欢迎。

Class Size: 48

Total number of graduating students: 48（学生人数）

(6 students did not respond to the survey)

Students with employment: 38（班级中毕业时获得工作人数）

Percentage of students placed:（90% 就业率）

Range of Annual Base Salary: $50,000~$125,000（薪资范围）

Sign-on Bonus: $5,000~$40,000

First Year-End Bonus: 10%~150% of Base Salary

以下是毕业生就职后的工作方向及职务。注意，在美国的金融机构中，刚开始的职务（Entry-level）一般为分析员，或者顾问（Associate），工作 2~3 年后提升专门领域内的 SA（Senior Associate），然后是 VP（Vice President），再往上就应该是总监（Director）。再往上走就是职业生涯中比较高的级别管理总监 MD（Managing Director），或者某个领域或行业的代表（Representative）。

毕业生工作岗位

Analyst　分析员

Global Market Analyst　全球市场分析员

Assistant Trader　交易员

Junior Trader　交易员

Associate　咨询顾问

Market Risk Analysis Associate　市场风险分析员

Business Consultant　商业顾问

Market Risk Analyst　市场风险分析员

Developer—Order Execution Algorithms　数据和模型研发员

Market Risk Group Associate　市场风险顾问

Equities Structuring Associate　股票投资分析员

Quantitative Risk Analyst　风险量化分析员

Quantitative Research Analyst　量化分析员

Financial Services Management Consultant　金融服务管理行业咨询顾问

Risk Management: Market Risk　风险管理：市场分析

Financial Software Developer　金融软件开发员

Software Developer　软件开发员

Fixed Income Analyst　固定收益分析员

Transaction Services Associate　交易服务咨询顾问

Fixed Income/Structured Products Associate　固定收益和组合投资顾问

Valuation and Risk Control Associate　估值和风险控制指导

Global Financial Risk Management Analyst　金融风险管理分析员

2. University of California Berkeley: Master of Financial Engineering 加州大学伯克利分校金融工程硕士

http://mfe.berkeley.edu/admissions/requirements.html

○ 学校基本概况

加州大学伯克利分校为世界知名学府，在众多权威大学里名列前茅，学术声望享誉全球。它地处旧金山东湾伯克利市的山上，是美国久负盛名的一所综合性公立大学。加州大学伯克利分校拥有雄厚的师资，有 8 名诺贝尔奖金获得者、3 名普利策奖获得者、140 名 Guggenheim 奖获得者、22 名 MacArthur 奖获得者、120 多名美国科学院院士。学校优秀的教学质量和良好的声誉吸引了众多优秀的学生，并在很大程度上提高了学校的声誉，为该校吸引了大笔的科研资金，每年用于科研的经费高达 6 亿美金，足以证明其强大的科研实力。2009 年的诺贝尔奖中有 4 位得主与该校有关。伯克利加大图书馆共有 3 座主图书馆，藏书超过 1 000 万册，是北美地区第四大的图书馆。在 2004 年英国的 The Times Higher World University Rankings 中，该校曾被评为"世界第二"的大学。

加州大学伯克利分校在校全日制学生约 35 409 人，其中本科生 25 151 人，研究生 10 258 人，教授和高级研究人员约为 1 900 人。该大学以传统的多学科综合的文理学院为主，新兴学科和专业学院为辅。伯克利分校拥有全美最大的研究生部，提供了近 110 个专业的学位项目。全校共有 3 个法学院，5 个医学院，14 个其他学院，大多数学院下面还设有系。主要学院如下：商学院：金融工程、工商管理、法学与工商管理、管理学；文理学院：生物学、基因学、免疫学、艺术学、戏剧学、法语、德语、意大利语、天文学、地质地理、数学、统计学、历史、政治、心理学、社会学、环境科学、法律制度、大众传媒、发展研究等；工学院：电子工程、计算机科学、工业工程、运筹学、材料科学、采矿工程、机械工程、海上建筑、海岸工程、核技术工程等；化学学院：化学、化工机械；教育研究学院：语言文学文化教育、政策、组织、衡量和评价；新闻研究院：法律、亚洲研究、拉丁美洲研究；法学院：法学、JD（高级职业学位）、LLM（法律速成）、法律和社会政策；信息管理和系统学院：信息管理和系统、信息用户和社会、信息组织的管理和服务、信息经济学、信息检索、信息技术、系统分析和设计、信息政策等；自然资源学院：农业和资源经济学、环境科学、营养科学、植物科学；眼科学院：视力学；公共保健学院：卫生统计、环境卫生科学、传染病研究、健康服务和政策分析、免疫学、微生物学、健康和药学、基因咨询；社会福利学院：社会福利；公共政策学院。

○ 院系介绍与专业优势

The Berkeley MFE curriculum prepares you to work as a financial engineer immediately after graduating. MFE courses are designed exclusively for MFE students, and are seamlessly integrated with one another.

This cooperation between course material allows the mathematical, statistical, and computer science methods to be integrated with the theoretical framework and institutional settings in which they are applied. For example, macroeconomics is taught in relevant context in the fixed income markets course, during the discussion of term structure, and during the equity and currency markets course, in the context of exchange rate determination. Similarly, insurance concepts are introduced in the advanced derivatives courses where students can easily understand their relation to similar products.

The MFE requires only one year of study, which is ideal for motivated students with strong quantitative skills and focused career interests.

伯克利分校的金融工程教学有些与众不同，我们可以看到，项目的教学是由实际的金融分析环境决定的。教学的模式并非单个的学科分支，而是按照问题、市场环境与具体项目来组织安排所有相关金融工程的三大核心技能学习：数学、统计与编程等科目。

整个项目的学习时间持续一年，学分总数大约为 30 分。

○ 班级构成

MFE Class of 2011—2012 (graduating in 2012)

Applicant Pool & Class Size	
Applications Received:	404
Number of Admits:	88
Enrolled Students:	68

录取率大约为 20%

Academic Profile	
Average GRE/GMAT Quantitative Score (in percentile)	92.6
Average GRE/GMAT Verbal Score (in percentile)	82.6
Average GRE/GMAT Analytical Score (in percentile)	55.2
Average Undergraduate GPA (US only):	3.5
Undergraduate Institutions Represented:	55
Graduate Institutions Represented:	28

申请人的 GRE/GMAT 成绩均在 90% 的比例（即比当次考试 90% 的考试者要高），GPA 学分绩也在 3.5 以上，研究生并不比本科生要多。

Undergraduate Majors	
Business	6%
Computer Science	7%
Economics	13%
Engineering	44%
Mathematics	22%
Natural Sciences	4%
Other	4%

很明显工程类专业的申请人要比商科与经济学的更受偏好，在中国，经济学的学习、计量经济与统计的方法教授不是很全面，因而更加没有优势。

Locations of Undergraduate Institutions	
US	19
International Schools	36
Argentina	1
Canada	3
France	3
Germany	2
Hong Kong	5
India	7
PR China	7
Republic of Korea	2
Russia	2
Singapore	5
Thailand	1
United Kingdom	2

亚洲学生占了相当一部分，当然 19 个美国学生内也有一部分是在美攻读别的学位的中国研究生。

Previous Job Experience	
Finance	43%
Engineering	12%
Research & Development	23%
Information Systems	7%
Consulting/Management Services	7%
Project Management	2%
Other	6%
Average Years of Work Experience	3.44

从工作经验的偏好上讲，平均 3、4 年的工作经验意味着超过 70% 的申请者至少具备 1~2 年的工作经验。在我辅导学生申请的过程中，伯克利老师反馈的意见也相同，而 10 份申请材料中，在读本科生只占大约 3 份左右。

○ 核心课程

Designed by a world-class business school, the MFE Program's curriculum challenges you to think of innovative ways to integrate quantitative methods with the theoretical framework and institutional settings in which they are applied. Taught by a renowned faculty comprised of prominent scholars and industry luminaries, MFE courses are anchored in cutting-edge research and best practices in financial engineering.

The Berkeley MFE Program is a one-year program beginning in March, with an internship period from October to January, and graduation the following March.

MFE students must successfully complete 28 units of coursework (1 unit = 15 class hours), including an Applied Finance Project, plus an internship or on-site project. The 10- to 12-week internship project is a required condition for graduation.

项目开学的日期较为特别，每年 3 月份开学，直至次年 3 月结束，中间穿插了学校安排的在华尔街或银行的实习，大约 3 个月的时间，总学时为 420 个小时。

○ 申请必备条件和要求

The MFE can be completed in 12 months of full-time coursework. Applications are accepted year-round on a rolling deadline, and 60 students are enrolled each year. The program begins and ends only in the spring (March), and is not available part-time. The goal of the application review process is to identify those candidates who are the strongest fit with our program. Applicants should possess:

学校接受流动申请，即招生日期开放，先到先得，班级招满为止，大约 60 名学生一个班。

（1）A valid degree from an accredited institution, comparable to the 4-year Bachelor's Degree from UC Berkeley 大学本科学历

（2）Recommended post-university work experience. Preferred but not required. The MFE also admits undergraduate students with strong academic background with little to no experience 工作经验的要求

（3）Prior exposure in computer programming (C, C++) and familiarity with computers as a computational and management tool 编程语言的学习即 C、C++ 等方面技能的准备

（4）Experience with statistical and econometric applications (Examples: SAS, Gauss, RATS, S-Plus, and Garch) 对 SAS 等统计软件的熟悉与使用经验

（5）A strong quantitative background including linear algebra, multivariate calculus, differential equations, numerical analysis and advanced statistics and probability (see our prerequisite course chart). Experience with mathematical tools (Examples: MatLab, Mathematica, or MathCad) 数量能力背景，包括线性代数、微积分、微分方程、数字分析、概率及有 MatLab 等数学工具的使用经验

（6）Excellent writing, speaking, and presentation skills (in English) 英语语言能力优秀

○ 申请材料清单

To apply to the MFE Program, applicants must submit an online application. The MFE

Program no longer has a paper application. To be considered for admission, an applicant must have successfully completed the following:

（1）Online Application 申请表格

（2）$225 Application Fee 申请费用

（3）English Language Proficiency 托福和雅思成绩

（4）Please note that there is NO LONGER a video requirement. You may disregard this portion of the application instructions. 申请人不能再递交录像材料，这个要求取消

（5）University Transcripts 大学成绩单

（6）GMAT or GRE Score Reports 标准考试成绩

（7）Two Letters of Recommendation 至少两封推荐信

Interviews

注意：伯克利分校需要对申请学生进行面试。

○ 国际学生要求

English Proficiency

○ 截止日期

For the academic year beginning March 2012:

Round	Online application submitted by	Application will be reviewed by
One	January 20, 2011 第一轮	March 30, 2011
Two	March 31, 2011 第二轮	June 3, 2011
Three	June 22, 2011 第三轮	August 26, 2011
Four	September 1, 2011 第四轮	November 1, 2011

Slots are held open until applications from the September 1, 2011 deadline are considered and processed. Late applications will be accepted through November 1, 2011. Late applications will take 4-6 weeks to process from the day that they are marked "complete".

每年9月1日开始审理下一年3月1日开班的学生申请。

To apply to the MFE Program, applicants must submit an online application. The MFE Program no longer has a paper application. Please remember that there is no fall admission; the MFE Program begins in March of every year.

○ 就业情况

When you join the Berkeley MFE Program, you are one year away from turning your specialized training in hedge funds, risk management, derivatives, and commodities investments into a successful career in finance, strategy, or risk assessment. Haas has an unrivaled history of helping students secure top jobs—Berkeley MFE graduates received job offers in each of the previous four years at the highest average starting salary of any similar program. Berkeley MFE alumni are well established members of premier firms in the world's top financial markets, such as New York, London, and Tokyo.

The Haas School's resources, its deep ties to global firms, and its highly personalized services will provide you with the tools and connections you need to launch the next stage of your career. Employers seek out Berkeley MFE students because they demonstrate not only a mastery of powerful financial engineering tools, but also a solid understanding of the best practices for the changing technological, global, and human dimensions of finance. Your entire Berkeley MFE experience is designed to give you the knowledge, experience, and connections you'll need to immediately launch a successful career in financial engineering.

The Berkeley MFE Program at the Haas School of Business provides a depth of study in finance that is not available in traditional MBA programs, reaching beyond basic business concepts to teach you how to combine modern portfolio theory with computational methods. It also provides many opportunities to learn firsthand how to apply these theories and methods to real-world situations. You will also benefit from the quality of students, breadth of activities, and network of impressive alumni contacts inherent to a top-ranked business school and a world-class university.

哈斯商学院在美国西部及纽约均有很高的声望，亚洲的香港及东京市场也对哈斯毕业生青睐有加，毕业生主要的就业方向为金融分析、对冲基金、银行/公司风险管理、衍生品设计与运用及商品期货交易领域。这个项目与别的 MFE 项目不一样，混合了金融理论学习与计算机编程的知识。在某种意义上讲，金融方向的 MBA 学习比不上哈斯的 MFE 项目学习的广度和深度。

3. Carnegie Mellon University: Master of Computational Finance 卡内基梅隆大学计算金融硕士

http://www.tepper.cmu.edu/master-in-computational-finance/admissions/application-process/index.aspx

○ 学校基本概况

卡内基梅隆大学（简称 CMU）位于宾夕法尼亚州的老工业城市匹兹堡市，一桥之隔就是在同城的另一所大学匹兹堡大学，是一所偏重数理研究的实力较强的私立大学。该校由安德鲁·卡耐基于 1900 年创建，专门培养技术人才，学校慢慢开始由本科和技术培训向以研究为主的大学转变。越南战争爆发后，学校与附近的梅隆学院合并为卡内基梅隆大学。曾被《美国新闻与世界报道》评为全美明星级大学第 24 名，并获得《纽约时报大学指南》四颗星的学术评分。如今，卡内基梅隆大学已从一所纯技术性学校，逐步发展成为享誉世界的顶级研究型大学。

卡内基梅隆大学拥有在校学生超过 10 000 名，大学部学员基本上占一半比例，教职员工 1 300 多名。该大学下设 7 个学院分别如下：卡耐基工程技术学院——该院由 6 个系组成：化学工程系、民用工程系、电子学和计算机工程系、工程和公共政策系、系统工程系、金属工程和材料科学系；艺术学院——它培养的学生涵盖建筑设计到表演艺术和视听艺术等广泛领域，由建筑系、艺术系、设计系、戏剧系、音乐系组成；计算机科学学院——该院只设计算机科学系；工业管理研究生院——下设工业管理系；人文和社会科学学院——该院下设经济系、英语系、历史系、哲学系、心理学系、社会和决策学系、统计系；梅隆理学院——该院下设生物科学系、化学系、数学系和物理系；城市与公共事务学院。

○ 院系介绍和专业优势

Introduced in 1994, Carnegie Mellon's pioneering Master of Science in Computational Finance (MSCF) is considered by many today to be the top quantitative financial engineering program in the country.

The MSCF program is the joint venture of four colleges on our campus-the Tepper School of Business, the Mathematical Sciences Department, the Department of Statistics, and the Heinz College. Administered by the Tepper School of Business, the MSCF student enjoys the advantages of the business school environment, including the full resources of the School's placement services. As a result of the collaborative efforts of these four colleges, MSCF's twenty-five courses are both balanced and deep. Designed expressly for the MSCF student and the needs of the industry, the curriculum seamlessly integrates instruction in probability, statistical analysis, numerical methods, computation and simulation methods, stochastic processes, economics, and their application in today's quantitative financial markets.

The MSCF program is intense and extremely demanding—recruiters know the students graduating from MSCF are bright, highly motivated and keenly interested in the financial engineering industry. Our employment rates remain high—even in these challenging times.

卡内基梅隆大学的金融工程专业实际上称为计算金融学，这个专业由四个学院合力组成并由商学院监管：商学院、数学学院、汉斯学院、统计学院。可以说，在学院设置这个专业的 25 门课内，数学课程与统计课程占了相当大的部分，当然，也有金融学、工程学、组织学及计算机编程内容。

○ 班级构成

Entering Class of:	2008	2009	2010
Class Size	97	70	94
Full-time Pittsburgh	42	31	40

Part-time Pittsburgh	0	1	1
Dual MBA/MSCF	2	3	1
Full-time New York	37	25	38
Part-time New York	14	10	13
Math Certificate	2	2	1
International	60%	53%	69%
Average years of full-time professional experience	2.0	2.6	2.6
Percent with full-time professional experience	64%	69%	61%

班级分为 2 个，一个在匹兹堡上课，另一个在纽约的曼哈顿上课，纽约班级大约为 92 人，匹兹堡为 35 人左右，其中国际生均占 65% 左右，同时注意平均工作年限只有 2 年，这意味着有相当一部分学生无工作经验。

Academic & Test Information

GPA Average	3.61	3.62	3.62
Avg. GRE Quantitative Score	792	793	792
Avg. GRE Verbal Score	587	594	581
Avg. GMAT Total Score	723	702	715
Avg. GMAT Quant	49	48	49
Avg. GMAT Verbal	39	38	38

按照中国学生申请时分数提高 20% 的比例，同时从往年申请这个专业的录取情况来看，GRE 分数 ≥ 1300 分，GMAT ≥ 720 分。

Undergraduate Majors

Business/Economics 商科	19%	23%	16%
Computer Science 计算机	24%	16%	27%
Engineering 工程	28%	33%	23%
Math/Stat 数学	20%	20%	22%
Science 科学专业	9%	8%	7%
Other 其他	0%	0%	5%
Bachelor's Degree	64%	71%	71%
Master's Degree	27%	26%	20%
Doctoral Degree	7%	3%	9%

对于相应专业的申请人，大家可以对比一下。

○ **核心课程**

Full-Time Course Sequence

Earning the MSCF degree requires the satisfactory completion of twenty-five MSCF courses (150 units). (The MSCF program reserves the right to change course times and offerings at any point during the academic year.)

要完成学位，需要 150 个单元、25 门课的学习。

Fall 1: August 29 to October 22, 2011

MSCF Finance 金融学

Financial Computing Ⅰ 金融计算Ⅰ

Probability 概率论

Macroeconomics for Computational Finance 计算金融学与宏观经济学

Presentations for Computational Finance 计算金融学讲座

Fall 2: October 26 to December 21, 2011

Fixed Income 固定收益

Options 期权

Statistical Inference 统计推论

Multi-Period Asset Pricing 多期资产定价

MSCF Deutsche Trading Competition（德意志银行）交易竞赛

Spring 3: January 16 to March 7, 2012

Financial Products and Markets 金融产品与市场

Financial Computing Ⅱ 金融计算Ⅱ

Linear Financial Models 线性金融模型

Stochastic Calculus for Finance Ⅰ 随机微积分Ⅰ

Spring 4: March 19 to May 9, 2012

Financial Time Series Analysis 时间序列分析

Financial Computing Ⅲ 金融计算Ⅲ

Stochastic Calculus for Finance Ⅱ 随机微积分Ⅱ

Simulation Methods for Option Pricing 期权定价的模拟方法

Fall 1: August 27 to October 20, 2012

Advanced Derivative Modeling 高级衍生品模型

Studies in Financial Engineering 金融工程研究

Statistical Arbitrage 统计套汇／套利

Numcrical Methods（工程）数值方法

Fall 2: October 24 to December 20, 2012

Choose four of five 5 选 4

Financial Computing Ⅳ 金融计算Ⅳ

Quantitative Asset Management 量化资产管理

Topics in Quantitative Finance 计量金融课题

Credit Derivatives 信用衍生品

Financial Economics for Computational Finance 金融经济学

Course of Study 学习的基本安排构架

Over the fall and spring semester of the first year, students are taught traditional finance theories of equity and bond portfolio management, the stochastic calculus models on which derivative trading is based, computational methods including Monte Carlo simulation and finite difference approximations of partial differential equations, and statistical methodologies including regression and time series. Also provided is a "Presentations" course which provides one-on-one assistance in helping students better communicate their ideas before their peers, and the Deutsche Trading Competition which uses CMU's FAST software to emulate a trading environment with cash prizes awarded to the top traders at a special reception at Deutsche Bank. During the semester following the summer internship, students take courses in asset pricing, statistical arbitrage, risk management and dynamic asset management. The program concludes with a sophisticated financial computing course, an algorithmic trading competition, and a case-based presentation course in financial engineering. In addition to VBA, Matlab and S+ packages, C++ is incorporated into the curriculum and students create software in several courses.

秋季与春季的学习，更侧重于金融基本理论与投资组合理论，另外，随机模型也是学习的重点，还有蒙特卡洛模型。卡内基 FAST 软件以及在讲座课程中一对一的个性化指导，都使得参加德意志银行交易大赛的学生享有实际交易与操作的经历。每年表现优秀的学生还会获奖。在接下来的学期内，学习更侧重于资产定价、统计学应用、动态资产评估等更为精细化的专业方向学习。同时，VBA、Matlab、C++ 等信息工程与计算科目也会学到。

Exclusively for MSCF

Each of our twenty-five courses has been designed expressly for the MSCF program. For example, "Stochastic Calculus for Finance," taught by the Math Department, is not the stochastic calculus course offered to students in the Math Department, but rather a course that develops stochastic calculus within the context of models drawn from the financial services industry. "Credit Derivatives," "Statistical Arbitrage", "Simulation Methods of Options Pricing," "Linear Financial Models"—every one of our courses has been similarly designed.

学校设置的每门课均为卡内基梅隆大学四大学院为金融工程专业特别设计。

Center for Computational Finance

Research in quantitative finance at Carnegie Mellon is a campus-wide activity. This is fostered in part by the Center for Computational Finance housed in the Department of Mathematical Sciences. The research of Carnegie Mellon faculty affiliated with the Center brings them in contact with industry practitioners and facilitates updating the MSCF curriculum with the latest knowledge in quantitative finance.

该校还设有一个专门的计算金融研究中心，全校的努力与资源都朝这方面倾斜，条件得天独厚。

○ 申请必备条件和材料

1. Completed online MSCF application form (available starting in early September 2011)

2. Unofficial transcripts of all academic work (Admitted students will be required to submit official transcripts at a later date)

3. Resume

4. Work history (as detailed in the online application)

5. Two required essays (only one is required for certificate applicants)

6. Three letters of recommendation (not required for certificate applicants)

7. Official GRE from ETS or GMAT scores from Pearson VUE

8. TOEFL score from ETS (only for students whose native language is not English)

9. $100 application fee

10. Graduate Student Financial Forms and supporting documents (only for students who are not U.S. citizens or permanent residents)

具体说明

（1）TRANSCRIPTS 成绩单： Through our online application system, candidates are required to upload legible, scanned/digitized copies of their transcripts and degree certification from all academic institutions attended, even if a degree was not conferred. Please scan an official copy of your transcripts. Internet printouts will not be accepted. Transcripts should clearly indicate the name of the institution, student's name, degree earned (if applicable) and date the degree was completed (if applicable). If the original documents are not in English, official translations must be included. If admitted, you will be required to send in original, official transcripts to verify the unofficial transcripts submitted through the online application system.

学校只要求扫描正式成绩单上传。

（2）RECOMMENDATIONS 推荐信: At least three Letter of Recommendation forms must be completed by individuals who are able to provide specific and relevant information about your qualifications for MSCF study. If you are currently a full-time student or a recent graduate (within the past three years), please submit at least one recommendation from an academic source. If you have completed more than one year of full-time, post-undergraduate work experience, you should submit at least one evaluation from a supervisor or professional source. If possible, please submit at least one letter of recommendation from an individual who can speak directly to your mathematics and/or quantitative ability. Recommendations from friends, family members, acquaintances and other sources not able to evaluate applicants on an academic or professional basis are unacceptable.

这里是个特例，要求 3 封推荐信，而且明确要求必须是有学术与职业背景的推荐人才能写推荐信。

（3）GRE/GMAT 标准成绩：The Graduate Record Examination (GRE) or the Graduate Management Admissions Test (GMAT) is required of all applicants. Test scores must be forwarded directly to Carnegie Mellon by ETS in the case of the GRE or Pearson VUE in the case of GMAT. GRE is preferred. If you hold a PhD at the time of application in a related discipline AND you are able to submit a photocopy of the GMAT/GRE that was part of your original PhD application, you may request a waiver of the GMAT/GRE test requirement.

（4）TOEFL 托福：The Test of English as a Foreign Language (TOEFL) is required of applicants whose native language is not English. The only exception is for applicants who have earned a degree at a university where the language of instruction is English in which case we ask for documentation from the university of such. You should take the TOEFL no later than January in order to assure prompt delivery of your scores. All official TOEFL scores must be forwarded to Carnegie Mellon by ETS.

学校已经接受过 IELTS 成绩，需要特别申请才会同意，一般情况下，要求的基本上是 TOEFL 成绩。

（5）APPLICATION FEE 申请费用：A non-refundable application fee of $100 is required of all applicants.

（6）FINANCIAL FORMS 财产表格：International applicants who are admitted to the MSCF Program must submit formal bank certification evidencing sufficient resources to complete the program. More information for international students can be obtained through the Office of International Education.

这是一个财产证明与金融信用表格，申请时必须填写递交。过去有的学生反映交了材料学校没反应或老说材料不全，问题就出在漏了这个表格。

MSCF Merit Scholarship 卡内基梅隆学习优秀奖学金

Many people ask, are scholarships available? And the answer is, yes!

In fact, all full-time students admitted to the program are automatically considered for an "MSCF Merit Scholarship". No additional application is required to qualify for this award. The criteria for selection is based on the strength of the student's candidacy relative to the overall applicant pool for the year. Scholarship decisions are made at the time of admission and are announced in the admission letter.

MSCF Merit Scholarships are valid only for the year in which the admission offer is made and dependent on your status remaining in the full-time program. All merit scholarships are partial awards.

有奖学金，没什么说的，大家努力吧。

○ 截止日期

Fall 2011 MSCF Application Deadlines

Application Complete by	Decision to applicant on
November 01, 2010	January 24, 2011
January 03, 2011	April 04, 2011
March 07, 2011	May 23, 2011
April 25, 2011	June 20, 2011
After April 25, 2011	Decisions released on a rolling basis

○ 就业情况

The MSCF program is housed in the Tepper School of Business which provides the MSCF students with the many resources of Tepper's "Career Opportunities Center (COC)." Located in both our New York and Pittsburgh campuses, the staff of the COC is dedicated not only to bringing recruiters and students together but also to helping students decide upon various aspects of their finance careers, craft good resumes, and develop valuable interviewing and networking skills.

除了有职业办公室，卡内基梅隆大学的商学院每年均有大量的就业与面试机会可供所有在 COC 登记的同学利用。

Graduates from MSCF work exclusively in the financial engineering industry. Careers vary but usually revolve around derivatives pricing and trading, risk management, research, structured products, quantitative portfolio management and analytics software development. MSCF's recruiter relations are broad and deep, and our students enjoy a strong employment record:

92% of the class of 2011 (graduating Dec. 2010) had offers as of January 18, 2011;

88% of the class of 2010 (graduating Dec. 2009) were employed within three months of graduation;

83% of the class of 2009 (graduating Dec. 2008) were employed within three months of graduation;

96% of the class of 2008 (graduating Dec. 2007) were employed within three months of graduation.

从就业率的数据看来，MCU 就业还是很好的，这个项目的时间比较久，而且在美国金融界名声很好，同哥伦比亚大学、加州大学伯克利分校一样，号称是在曼哈顿最受重视的数理金融专业，这也是我选取这三所学校的最大理由。

第三章

人力资源管理硕士
Master of Arts of Human Resource, MS in Human Resource and Labor Relations

人力资源管理专业的简单说明

首先说明的是，人力资源管理专业不是我们说的单位里管管人事的专业，在美国学校和职场里，这个专业包涵的内容很多，主要有以下这么几个部分：劳工关系和工会组织、企业咨询和管理咨询、薪酬体系、业绩核算考核与激励、动员机制和人力解决方案、员工培训和招聘（包含猎头）以及公司架构和管理层搭建等等。在美国，劳工法和移民法在公司用工方面的应用、组织行为学、组织心理学、行为研究等方面也是人力资源管理的重要组成部分。

我们发现，大多数提供人力资源管理专业研究生和本科课程的院校，都不把这个专业设置在商学院里面，而是单独地放在人力资源及劳动关系学院下面。当然，录取标准也是借鉴了商学院的标准，接受 GMAT 成绩。大家注意，有一个规律就是，凡接受 GMAT 成绩的人力资源项目，大多数授予理学硕士（Master of Science）学位，而只接受 GRE 的项目，往往授予的是文科硕士（Master of Arts）的学位，如位于华盛顿特区的乔治·华盛顿大学即是如此。当然，商学院的 MBA（工商管理硕士）项目的两年课程中，也会安排人力资源管理的课程，并提供这样的方向研究。另一个获得人力资源管理课程学习的途径是到美国读经济学硕士，主攻劳动经济（Labor Economics）方向，由于篇幅限制，关于这个方向的讨论暂不在本书涉及。

那么在美国的人力资源管理学习中，会涉及什么课程呢？主要就是我们在上面说到的几个研究方向：管理学、劳工法、公司管理、绩效考核、招聘环节、沟通和危机处理、统计学、公共关系等。尤其值得大家关注的是，由于这个专业的学习和量化工作有很大关系，大家以后到了工作岗位上从事这个工作，大量时间要花在报表和数据处理上，学校在录取时，会比较看重你的统计和量化的能力和准备。另外，人力资源管理课程的学习以研究生研讨会为主，课堂上的讨论也很重要，学校也会考虑你的相关工作背景和交流能力。在最近的两年申请过程中，我发现越来越多的学校开始在筛选申请人时偏好与要求申请者具备一到两年的工作经历。例如，明尼苏达大学的人力项目设置在卡森商学院内，以往是不要求工作经验的，但在最近两年的申请辅导过程中，我发现它们开始提出工作经历的要求，因而在校生申请者必须格外注意实习的安排和在文书中的表现。

人力资源管理专业对本科学习的专业背景不是特别看重，这两年申请这个专业的学生逐渐增多，尤其是本科学习英语专业的学生开始瞄准这个专业。该专业的学习时间为一年半到两年，毕业后从事的工作大多数是在咨询行业。这一点大家必须看到，美国的人力资源毕业生的就业方向和国内大学劳动人事专业毕业后的工作方向有很大不同。国内的路径和美国的正好相反，举例说，一个在宾州州立大学毕业的人力资源学生，首先会考虑在几家主要的人力和企业咨询公司工作几年，然后跳槽到某个生产企业或大公司任人力经理或总监，而在国内毕业的这个专业的学生，很多人直接就被某企业或公司的人力部门或管理部门招聘。我觉得这个路径的差别反映了中美人力市场的成熟度不同和对人力资源管理这个专业的不同看法。随着国外专门从事人力资源管理咨询的公司进入中国开展业务，以及知名企业开办的人力资源管理理念的培训，大家会慢慢看到，人力资源管理这个专业在中国的前景是比较不错的，优秀的人力资源管理人也会得到更加理性的重视。

下面我们看几个学校样本来了解一下。人力资源管理这个专业没有专门的排名，所以我们列举了主要的学校并挑选了一些设置这个专业且排名尽量靠前的院校。

人力资源专业院校名录

1. Cornell University 康奈尔大学
2. University of Minnesota at Twin Cities 明尼苏达大学双城分校
3. University of Illinois at Urbana Champaign 伊利诺伊大学香槟分校
4. Michigan State University 密歇根州立大学
5. Rutgers, The State University of New Jersey 新泽西州立大学罗格斯分校
6. Purdue University 普渡大学
7. Ohio State University 俄亥俄州立大学
8. University of South Carolina 南卡罗来纳大学
9. Pennsylvania State University 宾夕法尼亚州立大学
10. Georgia State University 佐治亚州立大学
11. Texas A&M University 得克萨斯农工大学

这里也必须列举一下未在排名中体现的不错的几个学校。
12. Georgia Southern University (Georgia) 佐治亚南方大学
13. Depaul University (Illinois) 德保罗大学
14. Hofstra University (New York) 霍夫斯特拉大学
15. Indiana University of Pennsylvania (Pennsylvania) 宾州印第安纳大学
16. Loyola University Chicago (Illinois) 莱奥拉芝加哥大学

17. Marquette University (Wisconsin) 马凯特大学
18. New York Institute of Technology (New York) 纽约理工学院
19. The Catholic University of America (District of Columbia) 美国天主教大学
20. University of New Haven (Connecticut) 纽海文大学
21. Utah State University (Utah) 犹他州立大学
22. West Virginia University (West Virginia) 西弗吉尼亚大学
23. Claremont Graduate University (California) (Master of Science in Human Resources Design) 克莱蒙研究大学
24. Temple University (Pennsylvania) (MS-HRM) 坦普尔大学
25. University of Tennessee—Knoxville (Tennessee) 田纳西大学诺克斯维尔分校

张旭老师点评名校

1. University of Illinois Urbane Champion: Master of Arts of Human Resource 伊利诺伊大学香槟分校人力资源管理硕士

http://www.ler.illinois.edu/prospectivestudents/mp_overview.html

○ 学校基本概况
请参见本书前面该校的简介。

○ 院系介绍和专业优势

A Master of Human Resources and Industrial Relations (M.H.R.I.R.) from the School of Labor and Employment Relations will prepare you for professional responsibilities in business, union, and government organizations and give you tremendous flexibility for specialization. The School has an aggressive and effective Career Services Center that will provide you with one-on-one career counseling, workshops on career development, and access to major Fortune 500 corporations that recognize the quality of the School's program.

这个项目应叫人力资源与工业关系，毕业生大都会进入专门的人力资源公司，还有相当一部分人到工会、政府部门工作，香槟分校的人力资源毕业生就业率一直排在最前列。

Typically, about 170 students are enrolled in the master's program. Generous financial aid packages are available that are extremely competitive with those offered by other universities.

Most students take three semesters to complete their program requirements for a master's degree. There are several program options, however, including part-time enrollment and a joint degree program with the College of Law or College of Business that can extend this timing. Most of our students use the summer months to apply the knowledge and skills that they have learned at the School by working as an intern. The LER program is 48 hour of 12 courses, completed usually in 3 semesters.

项目共 48 个学分课程，就读学生需要 3 个学期即一年半完成。绝大部分中国学生，由于语言能力与学习方法的适应问题，需要 2 年时间，我辅导的学生到了学校后也如此反映。同时，UIUC 提供联合项目的授课，与商学院和法学院共同设置课程与学位。

○ 班级构成

In 2009—2010, LER students came from 94 undergraduate institutions, 18 states and 13 countries. The class was 69% female, 18% minority, and 28% international. Thirty-six percent of students had at least one year of work experience and the average age at entrance was 24.

从班级上看，近 100 名学生中，只有大约 1/3 的学生有一年左右的工作经验，其余大部分为本科毕业生。由于不限制本科就读专业，因而这里没有列出。

申请必备条件和要求

(1) Completed application form submitted online. All supporting materials must be uploaded and submitted online with the application. 申请表格

(2) Application fee: $70 domestic and $90 international. 申请费用

(3) Transcripts of all academic work submitted online with application. 大学以及研究生成绩单

(4) Three letters of recommendation from people who can speak to your ability to do graduate level work and/or your commitment and interest in the field of human resource management and industrial relations—submitted electronically. 三封关于学术、工作和人力领域的推荐信

(5) Your GRE test scores (no subject test required) reported electronically to Institution Code 1836 OR request your GMAT scores be sent to code VKR-TK-05 标准考试成绩，学校接受 GRE

(6) For international applicants, minimum TOEFL score of 590 PBT, 243 CBT, or 96 iBT reported electronically to Institution Code 1836. IELTS also accepted. 托福成绩和最低要求，接受雅思成绩

(7) Declaration of Finances (International applicants only) with Program Code 10KS0364MHRI on the form 财产证明表格

(8) Statement of purpose submitted online with your completed application 学习计划和陈述

大家注意，在申请条件上，UIUC 接受 GRE 或 GMAT, 也接受雅思成绩。但学校对本科在读 GPA 要求很高，3.5/4.0 为准入标准。对于 GMAT 与 GRE 考试的数学与数学分析，分数要求较高，GMAT 分数一般在 680~720 分之间。对于文书，学校只要求一份个人学习计划，在网申系统中还会有学习计划的描述。从经验来看，这个学校录取和发给奖学金的学生，在本科或研究生阶段获得的学分绩在 3.5~3.6 分左右。

○ 截止日期

Fall application deadline is February 1 and November 1 for spring admission. Applicants will be notified around March 15 for fall and around December 1 for spring admission.

秋季学期申请的截止日期是 2 月 1 日，春季是 11 月 1 日。

○ 核心课程

LER 530 Foundations of Industrial-Organizational Psychology 工业组织心理学基础

LER 548 Topics in Personnel Management 人力管理专题

LER 561 Compensation Systems 薪酬系统

LER 562 Human Resources Planning and Staffing 人力规划与配备

LER 563 Human Resource Information Systems 人力管理信息系统

LER 564 Human Resource Training and Development 人力训练与发展

LER 565 Human Resources Management and Strategy 人力资源管理与战略

LER 567 Negotiation in Human Resource Decisions 人力管理决策与谈判

LER 568 Firm Performance and Human Resource Management 公司绩效与人力资源管理

LER 597 Managing Employee Performance 员工绩效管理

LER 598 Designing High-Involvement Workplaces 设计高效工作环境

○ 就业情况

Human Resources and Industrial Relations is a business function with a focus on developing and maintaining an organization's human capital. This includes hiring the right people; keeping those hires well-paid, motivated and satisfied; complying with government regulations; and dismissing employees who are not performing well. In today's economy it includes attracting the right mix of people to make an organization competitive, which has sparked the field of human resource management to grow as a profession as it helps organizations of all sizes succeed. HR/IR requires more human interaction than other business functions such as accounting, finance and IT. You will notice that the focus of the job descriptions below is not solely on job duties but on personal and professional qualities: leadership, communication, maturity, integrity, business savvy and problem-solving skills.

Graduates from LER are highly sought for internship opportunities and full-time employment. The descriptions below will give you some idea of the jobs available to human resource professionals. It is not uncommon for our graduates entertain more than one job offer and most accept a position before they graduate. As Rob Chavarry says above, there is no guarantee of employment, but LER will provide the resources, the access, and the opportunity to maximize your education and convert it to a well-paid and exciting job. The average private sector starting salary for LER graduates in 2009—2010 was approximately $70,578, with different ranges depending on location. On top of that, most students added an average $6,967 signing bonus. Over 80 employers accessed LER Career Services during 2009—2010 looking for good hires, and many of those came on campus to recruit LER students. You can read more about our students' success, the companies that recruit at LER, and the career services offered to LER students by checking out our placement statistics.

In 2010—2011, 90% of domestic candidates who were eligible for and searching for full-time employment in the US were placed in positions by May graduation. For full-time entry-level hires, the average private sector salary was $73,093. Signing bonuses averaged $8,207 ranging between $3,000~$35,000. Ninety-two percent of graduates found their positions through LER Career Services. Interns received an average salary of $4,824 per month (private sector), with a range of $1,920~$6,800 per month. Ninety-eight percent of eligible domestic LER students were placed in internships and 47% of graduating domestic LER students accepted a full-time position with the company at which they interned the previous summer. Eighty-eight percent of students found their positions through LER Career Services.

Salary Acceptance by Region, 2010—2011

(Full-time, Private-sector)

Regional Locations	Salary Average	Salary Range
West	$68,871	$38,500~$83,000
South	$73,738	$58,000~$89,000
Northeast	$73,600	$70,000~$75,000
Greater Midwest	$69,570	$47,664~$78,000
Illinois	$67,087	$55,000~$89,000

Companies hire our graduates in full-time positions that are either "direct hire" or "rotational." Direct hire positions enable you to go into a position and immediately begin contributing in that particular location. Rotational programs typically are broad-based development programs designed to give your career a boost by providing a high level of visibility within an organization, broad-based skill development, and a wide understanding of the business operation.

从就业数据上看，大约 80% 的毕业生会在毕业后 3~6 个月找到工作。UIUC 的 HR 毕业生有相当一部分人到劳资与关系（IR）这个领域，每年的校内面试环节也有大约 80 家企业到校园内招聘。按照 2009—2010 年的毕业生平均年薪来看，7 万美元的年薪在人力资源管理的初级职位来说已经是比较高的了。我辅导的学生在 UIUC 反映，近年来在美国毕业后，部分美国公司会对移民资格（即工作签证）产生疑惑或不愿招收外国学生。但这种公司只占一部分，而且随着经济形势的好转，UIUC 的专业声誉与优秀的企业人力资源课程设置都会给毕业生在找工作的过程中加分。

2. Ohio State University: Master of Arts of Human Resource 俄亥俄州立大学人力资源管理硕士

链接：http://fisher.osu.edu/mlhr/

○ 学校基本概况

俄亥俄州立大学建于 1870 年，是一所综合的公立研究型大学，发展至今已成为全美第三大的公立大学，被《美国新闻与世界报道》评为俄亥俄州最好的州立大学。它由哥伦布的主校园和位于利马、曼斯菲尔德、马里恩、直布罗陀岛、纽瓦克和渥斯特的分校组成。其中哥伦布校园有四幢建筑目前被评为国家历史文物保护建筑：Ohio Stadium、Orton Hall、Enarson Hall 和 Hayes Hall。

俄亥俄州立大学哥伦布分校共有 19 个学院、170 个科系。其主要院系如下：教育学院、工程学学院、食物学院、农业和环境科学、研究生院、人的生态学院、人文学科学院、新闻事业和通信学校、法律、Moritz 学院、数学和物理学学院、医学和公共卫生学院、音乐学校、自然资源学校联盟的医疗业学校、奥斯汀 E. Knowlton School、建筑艺术学院、生物科学学院、商业 Fisher 学院、牙科医科大学护理学院、Optometry 学院、药学院、社会和行为科学学院、社会工作学院、大学学院、兽医学院。

○ 院系介绍和专业优势

Human resource practices are essential components in developing and executing organizational strategy. Fisher's Master of Labor & Human Resources（"MLHR"）program will help you set the pace with the changing business environment by continually offering innovative programming and courses that reflects and taps into the knowledge of HR practitioners and corporate leaders.

Fisher's MLHR program is one of the very few HR graduate programs in the United States taught within a college of business. In addition to learning from leading HR and organizational theorists, your focus while enrolled in the program will be to take HR theories and apply them in real-world settings.

The Fisher MLHR program provides you with: a generalist's perspective; experiential learning opportunities, including an optional internship; expanded career opportunities, regardless of whether you are looking to make a career change or advance in your current organization; the ability to complete the program on a full-time or part-time basis. As a Fisher MLHR student, your degree has official certification from the Society for Human Resource Management （"SHRM"） and adheres to its required 2005 curriculum guidelines.

俄亥俄州立大学的劳动与人力管理专业是美国不多的几所放置在商学院内的课程。这样的设置课程与学位有以下几个特点：

首先，商学院管理学的课程会加入到人力管理的学习中，尤其是在领导力、组织力、国际合作精神几个方面有着重点培养；其次，课程与专业的学习会偏重于组织行为研究等学科方向。对于投资者关系与并购产生的人资配备问题等课题学习也会涉及；但数学与统计能力方面的培训可能会稍微弱一些。不过总体的就业方向和学习领域与其他人力资源管理方向是一样的。

○ 班级构成

Class of 2011 Profile
Students enrolled: 47
Women: 72 percent
Minority: 19 percent
International: 21.2 percent
GRE:
Average Verbal: 475
Average Quant: 593
GPA:
Average: 3.33
2.78~3.82 middle 80 percent
Percentage Enrolled Part-Time: 28 percent
Class of 2012 Profile
Students enrolled: 52
Women: 73 percent
Minority: 11.5 percent
International: 19.2 percent
GRE:
Average Verbal: 475
418~600 middle 80 percent
Average Quant: 593
494~672 middle 80 percent
GPA:
Average: 3.33
3.10~3.65 middle 80 percent

学校也接受 GMAT 成绩，当然以 GRE 为最受欢迎的分数，这也是 OSU 一大特点。每年大约有 10~14 名外国学生进入这个 50 人左右的班级，其中平均成绩都在 3.5 分左右，这也对本科学习表现提出了极高的要求。

○ 申请必备条件和材料要求

(1) Applicants must submit two official, unopened, original and certified copies of transcripts from every college or university they have attended. You are not required to submit official transcripts for any grades earned at The Ohio State University. 两份成绩单，而且要寄送到不同的地址。每年申请都会有学生寄错。

(2) All applicants are required to take the Graduate Record Examination (GRE) or Graduate Management Admission Test (GMAT). Be sure to take it as soon as you are well prepared. 标准考试成绩，同样接受 GRE 成绩。

(3) If you are an international applicant, you will also need to demonstrate proficiency in English by taking the Test of English as a Foreign Language (TOEFL), the Michigan English Language Assessment Battery (MELAB), or the International English Language Testing System (IELTS) test unless you are from an English-speaking country. 也接受雅思成绩，从托福分数来看，学校招生办老师明确表示托福 iBT 应在 100 分以上。

(4) Detailed Resume 简历

This is your opportunity to showcase your employment history, extracurricular and/or community activities, language skills, and military record, if applicable.

(5) Letters of recommendation 最少两封推荐信

When deciding whom to ask for letters of recommendation, you will want to choose individuals who can attest to your scholarship, professional development, personal character, and overall potential to succeed. Be sure to make your requests in plenty of time to allow respondents to prepare thoughtful, detailed letters on your behalf.

(6) Original essays 三份文书

We cannot overstate the importance of the essays as an opportunity to present yourself to us in a meaningful, in-depth way. We encourage you to invest time in your essays, be genuine, and include examples with the points you make.

(7) Nonrefundable application processing fee.The application fee is $60 (U.S. Dollars) for United States citizens, permanent residents, or asylees, and $70 (U.S. Dollars) for International students. 申请费用

○ 截止日期

If you are...	Entering	Application Deadline
International Applicant	Autumn Quarter	November 15 (for fellowship nomination consideration)
Domestic Applicant (full time only)	Autumn Quarter	December 31 (for fellowship nomination consideration)
International Applicant	Autumn Quarter	March 1 秋季入学
Domestic Applicant (full-time or part-time)	Autumn Quarter	June 1* *Applications received after this date will be considered on space available basis
Domestic Applicant (part-time only)	Winter Quarter	October 1
Domestic Applicant (part-time only)	Spring Quarter	January 1

○ 就业情况

Fisher will add unparalleled value to your career. Three months after the Class of 2009 graduated, 87.9 percent of the new graduates had accepted a full-time position. Fisher is consistently ranked among the nation's best business schools for providing outstanding employment opportunities for our students.

At Fisher, 13 percent of students enrolled in the MLHR program are international students. Consequently, Career Management places a great emphasis on meeting the special challenges and unique needs of international students. For example, Career Management includes a consultant who specializes in developing personalized plans for global job searches and helps international students searching for jobs in the United States, as well as students looking for international job opportunities.

每年有近90%的毕业生找到全职工作。为了帮助外国学生，商学院在就职服务上格外注意，有几位顾问专门帮助国际学生制订找工作的计划，协助简历修改和参与面试。俄亥俄州立大学在美国东部及中部有较高的声誉，费舍尔商学院更是以培养应用型人才著称，因而在人力与劳动关系学院的就业记录上，毕业生就业率一直较高。

3. Cornell University (MILR) 康奈尔大学工业和劳工管理

http://www.ilr.cornell.edu/gradDegreePrograms/degrees/MILR/index.html

○ 学校基本概况

康奈尔大学是常春藤盟校中较为年轻的一所学校，建于 1865 年，创建人是实业家康奈尔，学校因此得名。学校主校区位于纽约州的伊萨卡（Ithaca），其他两所分校分别位于纽约市和卡塔尔教育城。主校区位于山顶，可以远眺城市和卡尤加湖，一派辽阔气象。校园面积有 3 000 多英亩，与美国东北部典型的较为拥挤的大学相比，呈现出一派宏大气度。康奈尔大学的大多数专业排名均处于全美领先的位置，其酒店管理学院曾被希尔顿酒店创始人康拉德·希尔顿称赞为"全世界最优秀的学院"。依据美国"国家科学研究委员会"（National Research Council）的最新排名，康奈尔大学的师资水平位居全美前列，历史上共有 41 位诺贝尔奖得主是本校师生，创下了全美大学多项第一。

学校现有在校生 19 000 人左右，其中本科生 13 510 人，其余均为研究生。康奈尔大学目前设有下列 13 所学院，每个学院都自主制订学术计划，分别为：农业和生命科学学院，兽医学院，人类生态学院，工业和劳资关系学院（以上四个学院为合同学院 Contract College），法学院，约翰逊管理学院，建筑、设计和规划学院，文理学院，工程学院，研究生院，旅店管理学院，医学院（校址在纽约市区内），医学研究生院（校址在纽约市区内）。此外还有大学图书馆、营养科学部、生物科学部、暑期班及校外学习部等机构。

○ 院系介绍和专业优势

The ILR School is the premier institution for the study of employment and workplace issues. We were the first school to develop a graduate degree program in this field and our advanced degrees are considered among the best in the world. ILR is recognized internationally by the International Labor Organization, the European Union, international intergovernmental organizations and numerous Fortune 500 Companies as a top producer of student talent and relied upon for the highest level of inter-disciplinary research in work-related fields.

ILR graduate programs develops dynamic individuals who are driving positive change in work worldwide. Our five top-ranked and highly regarded graduate degree programs provide a broad-based foundation with a specific, intense focus on the interaction between people and organizations in the workplace and are unlike any other programs in the world. The strength of the program is well known and ILR graduates are always in demand. Our graduates have positions in the private and public sector in business, financial services, manufacturing, consulting, technology, government, not-for-profits, labor unions and non-government organizations. Cornell and ILR's alumni hold senior and influential positions in numerous businesses and labor organizations and serve as mentoring and networking resources.

康奈尔大学这个项目全称应为工业组织关系硕士。它是美国研究生院中历史最为悠久的几个项目之一，开创了三大方向的研究：组织行为学与个人发展、国际劳动关系研究、科技企业管理与人力资源。这个专业的毕业生大多进入政府部门、劳工组织与咨询公司工作，少量学生进入跨国企业和金融公司的人事或战略规划部门。康奈尔大学这个项目除了在众多人力资源管理领域都十分擅长与精专之外，其中组织管理与战略咨询领域最为令人注目，这也是康奈尔大学这个项目的最大优势所在。

○ 班级构成

Current MILR Class Profile
Average Class size: 56 students
Average age: 26
Average years of work experience: 3 years
Mean GRE: 562 Verbal; 677 Quantitative; 4.2 Analytical
Mean GMAT: 35 Verbal; 42 Quantitative; 5.1 AWA
Mean TOEFL: 106
International Population: 36%

班级近 60 名学生中，平均年龄 26 岁，平均工作经验在 3 年左右。这个值得大家注意。超过 1/3 的学生是国际学生，对 GMAT 成绩的要求也比较高，同时对 TOEFL 成绩的要求应为人力资源专业学校中最高的一个。

○ 核心课程

MILR students choose from one of the following five areas of concentration and select a Special Committee Chairperson (advisor) in their area:

Human Resources & Organizations 人力资源与组织关系
Collective Representation 集体谈判与协商
Dispute Resolution 争端解决
Labor Market Policy 劳工市场政策
International and Comparative Labor 国际劳动研究

Students have a great deal of flexibility in choosing their courses in addition to the required core courses. Courses offered by the ILR School and the 13 other colleges at Cornell provide opportunity for cross-disciplinary work. Entering first semester students are required to take ILRHR5600, ILROB5200, and ILRHR6910 in a bundled format. This bundled course set contains a large case study that cuts across the three classes requiring students to address the case from an integrated HR, organizational design, employee motivation, and finance perspective.

6 core courses 六门核心课程

混合课程即 blended course，三门课一起上并进行统一的考核。要求学生用混合课程中所学的多种知识与技能来解决一项大的案例作业。这种教学方式不同于单独案例教学，更加具有难度与挑战性，无论是人力资源理论、金融知识、组织行为学与员工激励方案设计等方面知识均要综合运用。

ILRLR 5000 Collective Bargaining（集体谈判与协商）—A comprehensive introduction to the industrial relations system of the United States. The negotiation, scope, and day-to-day administration of contracts; union and employer bargaining structures; implications of industrial relations issues for U.S. competitiveness and public policy; industrial conflict; and U.S. industrial relations in international and comparative perspective.

ILRLR 5010 Labor and Employment Law（劳工与雇用法）—A survey and analysis of the law governing labor relations and employee rights in the workplace. The first half of the course examines the legal framework in which collective bargaining takes place, including union organizational campaigns, negotiations for and enforcement of collective bargaining agreements, and the use of economic pressure. The second half of the course surveys additional issues of rights in employment, including such topics as employment discrimination, the developing law of "unjust dismissal," and union democracy. Also serves as an introduction to judicial and administrative systems.

ILRST 5110 Statistical Methods for the Social Sciences（社科统计方法与工具）—A second course in statistics that emphasizes applications to the social sciences. Topics include: simple linear regression; multiple linear regression (theory, model building, and model diagnostics); and the analysis of variance. Computer packages are used extensively.

ILROB 5200 Organizational Behavior（组织行为学）—Survey of concepts, theories, and research from the fields of organizational and social psychology as these relate to the behavior of individuals and groups in organizations. Job attitudes, motivation, performance, leadership and power, group formation, perception, and organizational climate. A preliminary course for advanced work in organizational behavior.

ILRLE 5400 Labor Economics（劳动经济学）—A course in labor market economics for prospective managers in the corporate, union, and governmental sectors. The course begins with demand and supply in labor markets, presenting the tools of decision analysis for workers and firms. It then goes on to consider various topics for managers including deciding on the optimal mix of capital and labor to employ; attracting and retaining talent; pay and productivity; hiring and training investments; and pensions and retirement. The final section of the course covers other important labor market issues including unemployment, discrimination, poverty and inequality, and analysis of public policies.

ILRHR 5600 Human Resource Management（人力资源管理）—A survey course covering the major areas of the management of human behavior in work organizations. Consideration is given to aspects of strategic human resource management such as staffing, training and development, performance management, compensation, and employee relations. Emphasis is on exploring these issues from both strategic and tactical levels to increase organizational effectiveness.

6 elective courses from one of the following concentrations:

Human Resources and Organizations

Labor Market Policy

Collective Representation

Dispute Resolution

International and Comparative Labor

选修课从以上5个领域内其中一个领域选取。同时，已经获得美国大学 JD/MBA 学位的申请人，可以向学校申请一年内完成这个硕士项目，但6门核心课程必须要完成。

○ 申请必备条件和材料要求

Admission to ILR is competitive, but each application is considered in its entirety and in comparison with other applications for the same class. The admissions committee, composed of faculty members from all concentrations, review the applications carefully and consider many factors in admissions decisions.

(1) **Areas of study**—Successful applicants have undergraduate (and graduate) degrees from a wide variety of majors including: the social sciences, humanities, psychology, business, history, law and others. 康奈尔大学这个项目录取学生不拘一格，各个本科专业都有。但从比较往年本科学生的经历看，社会科学和商科专业的学生轻易占上风。

(2) **Work experience** —Work experience is not required, but a majority of applicants for the professional masters programs (MILR and MPS) have spent a few years in the workplace. The MILR program is intended for students with 1-4 years of work experience, but we also admit a small group of outstanding students directly from strong undergraduate programs. 大部分申请人都有工作经验。

(3) **Transcripts** —From all colleges or universities you've attended must be submitted. There is no specific minimum grade point average used as a cut-off, although undergraduate coursework and grades are a factor in the admission decisions. 本科学分不作要求，但 3.3 分是必须的。

(4) **Recommendations** —2 academic recommendations are required. Some applicants may want to submit professional recommendations instead of academic ones, which is permitted, but bear in mind that the admissions committee will want to know how you are likely to function in an academic setting. More than 2 letters of recommendation may be submitted. 可以递交超过两封推荐信，但我建议 3 封就足矣。

(5) **Interviews**—Official admissions interviews are not offered, but informal visits are welcomed. Please see the Visiting ILR page for more info on scheduling a visit to ILR. 面试不是必须的。

(6) **Resume**—MILR applicants are required to submit a resume with their application. 学习

和工作简历

(7) **Statement of Purpose**—MILR applicants are required to submit a statement of purpose with their application. 个人陈述和学习计划

(8) **Writing Sample**—MS/PhD applicants are strongly encouraged to submit a writing sample. Applicants who have already completed a Master's degree should submit a copy of their Master's thesis. 这个写作样本最好在辅导老师指导下完成选题与初稿。文章要求在 10~20 页，英文双倍行距格式，按照美国学术论文标准即可。

(9) **Required tests**—All applicants are required to submit test scores. Applicants may take either the Graduate Record Exam (GRE) or Graduate Management Admissions Test (GMAT). The GRE is our preferred test and is taken by the vast majority of applicants. Applicants to the MILR/MBA dual degree program must take the GMAT, which is required by the Johnson School. **The LSAT is not accepted in place of the GRE or GMAT.** 标准考试成绩，接受 GRE，但不接受法学院入学考试。

○ 国际学生要求

TOEFL is required for international students from countries where the native language is not English. Applicants must meet set minimum category scores in order to be admitted to Cornell University under the Cornell Graduate School policy. According to Cornell Graduate School requirements, applicants with TOEFL scores below the following minimums in any of the four categories cannot be admitted to Cornell University:

Listening: 15

Reading: 20

Speaking: 22

Writing: 20

这个 TOEFL 要求基本可以忽略，学校只是写出了最低水平，所以应满足接近 105 的分数。

ILR recommends applicants have a minimum total score of 100 on the TOEFL with recommended sectional scores of 25 in each category. Applicants who score below 25 in any TOEFL category may be asked to complete Cornell's summer English for International Students and Scholars (EISS) program prior to enrolling in ILR classes in order to assure admitted students of the best chance of success in the program.

康奈尔大学可以接受雅思成绩，但不鼓励学生们使用。

○ 截止日期

Spring 2012—October 15, 2011 (Please know the application will not be available until mid-summer.)

Fall 2012 Admissions

Round 1—January 1, 2012 第一轮

Round 2—February 15, 2012 第二轮

这里要注意，康奈尔大学这个项目不接受春季入学，只有秋季入学。

○ 就业情况

ILR graduates work in every region of the United States and around the world. Graduates have taken positions in the business, high-tech, financial services, manufacturing, and not-for-profit sectors. Their job titles range from Recruiter, HR Manager, Labor Relations Specialist, and Senior Consultant in the corporate world, to Field Examiner with the NLRB to Research Analyst with a union. Because ILR alumni hold senior and influential positions in numerous businesses and labor organizations, the strength of the program is well known around the country, and even the world.

Cornell ILR graduate students are in great demand. ILR's Office of Career Services (OCS) is particularly effective at helping MILR students find positions, and also works closely with students with targeted job needs to identify job leads. Graduate students in the MPS, MS, and PhD programs work closely with their professors to find employment, and are encouraged to use OCS services. The staff in OCS can also facilitate networking with ILR alumni, an excellent resource.The OCS offers a full schedule of programs and informative workshops, and provides individualized assistance including resume preparation, practice interviews, developing career networks, creating a job-search strategy, and evaluating offers. The office hosts a corporate career fair each fall, a social-justice career fair each spring in conjunction with ILR's Union Days activities, a winter internship program, and career forums.

Summer internships can help hone skills, clarify the specific work and identify the kind of organization students will choose for their careers. Most masters students earn between $500 and $1,732 a week during a summer internship. Many students eventually accept full-time offers from their summer internship sponsors. (For example, 39% of 2009 MILR graduates took this opportunity). International students should see the ISSO website for regulations with regard to internships in the US and full-time employment upon graduation.The Office of Career Services manages an active on-campus recruiting program that brings representatives from many of the country's foremost human resources programs to campus, and other career forums representing careers in labor, policy, and other fields. Interviews for both full-time and summer internship positions are held during the fall and spring semesters. The Office sponsors job postings throughout the academic year. Many students (85% of MILR graduates) accept positions before graduation. In 2009 the average starting salary was $78,262, with a range from $51,871 to $120,000. The average signing bonus in the corporate sector was $10,611.

康奈尔大学的职业辅导办公室提供讲座与培训，积极为大家提供实习机会。

Cornell dual MILR/MBA students are highly regarded in the job market. In 2009 the average starting salary was $105,667, with a range from $93,000 to $120,000.

康奈尔大学的 MILR 项目在美国东部享有盛名，一直都在人力资源项目中位列榜首。除了得益于之前我所说的首创几个领域的专门研究，还有其灵活、实用与创新的混合式课程。一般来说，康奈尔大学 MILR 毕业生首先会得到以下几个工作职务，因其有一定的代表性，我简单讲讲。HR Manager（人力经理），这是进入企业或特定组织担任人事管理的工作，传统意义上的人力资源，HR Specialist 与 Senior Consultant 则为人力资源专家与高级顾问，一般是在专门的第三方咨询公司与服务公司工作，为客户提供人力资源相关的问题和解决方案、策划与战略解决出路。Field Examiner（调查员）与 HR Analyst（人力研究专员）则是归属于美国劳动部、多个州自己的劳工委员会与各大工会的专业人员。当然，最后这个工作一般不会给中国学生，由于身份的问题，外国学生刚开始找工作时不大可能进入这些部门，但实习机会却是异常的多。

市场营销硕士
Master in Marketing

市场营销专业的简单介绍

　　市场营销硕士专业是美国大学商科研究生教育的一个重要分支，基本上所有的商学院都有这样一个研究方向，同时市场营销也是一个边缘和交叉专业，与传媒研究、公共关系学和管理学都有关联，部分美国大学在院系设置时就会同时在商学院以外单独设置一个市场研究的研究所或院系，具有单独招生的能力，例如密歇根州立大学。同时需要注意的是，市场营销专业在美国大学研究生教育系统里，这些年有两个发展趋势：（1）市场营销硕士逐渐并入工商管理硕士（MBA）专业的课程和专业设置，很多传统上设置市场研究硕士学位的学校，逐渐将相关研究转入 MBA 之下，不再单独设置市场营销的硕士学位，如密歇根大学罗斯商学院、UCLA 安德森商学院等；（2）和美国现代经济学发展一样，部分学校的市场营销专业开始撤销硕士专业，改为网络的硕士课程，主要的教学和研究精力开始转成博士课程。

　　大家在看到下面所列市场营销排名和学校时要注意，并不是每个排名表上的学校都是仍然设置硕士学位，即使是仍然授予硕士学位，我估计很多都是设置在 MBA 方向下。

　　那么剩下的市场营销课程呢？现在仍然设置市场营销专业硕士学位的学校，教授的课程也发生了很多改变，从以往单一的研究市场变动、市场数据、战略研究、消费心理学、客户管理和沟通、消费经济学等基本方向，变成加入大量的国际市场营销策略、新兴市场准入、广告研究、整合营销、网络媒体研究、物流和供应链管理等。可以说，现在的美国市场研究硕士教育，完全就是朝综合和国际方向发展，从学科交叉上说，已经和工程管理、物流研究、传媒经济等更加紧密结合在一起。

　　从招生的角度来说，市场营销专业对申请人本科或已获研究生所读专业不太限制，同时对工作经验也不是特别要求。有几个主要的因素是在申请过程中格外重要的，也是我觉得在国外申请中被大家经常忽略的。我前面说到，这个专业的发展方向就是和别的主要相关学科更加紧密结合，因而，市场营销的申请制作，必须紧紧围绕这一点来突出自己的特点：多元化、广博度、灵活性和适应性。这也是几位过去我辅导过的学生轻而易举地拿到名校项目录取和奖学金最为核心的一点。其次，要很好地规划自己的职业生涯和未来就业，尤其是毕业后的工作计划。这一点，也是被很多学生忽略，同时也是需要学生和辅导老师仔细沟通清楚的一点。我们发现，在申请市场营销的过程中，学校会特别关注这一点，因为大部分的项目均在一年内即可完成，部分项目需要两年，而且一般国际学生毕业后找到很合适自己的市场或咨询工作岗位，比读会计或金融的学生找到适合自己专业的岗位要难许多。

下面我们来看几个样本学校，了解一下市场营销硕士专业在申请中的一些关键点，也对这些学校和这个专业有一个最为直观的认识。

金融工程专业院校名录

以下为有市场营销硕士专业的学校，注意，很多学校都有市场研究、市场分析和MBA下的市场营销方向，但最直接的还是市场营销学的硕士专业。更加齐全的名录，请大家看看美国市场营销学会推荐的项目列表。

1. Northwestern University 西北大学
2. John Hopkins University 约翰·霍普金斯大学
3. New York University 纽约大学
4. Rochester University 罗切斯特大学
5. University of Florida 佛罗里达大学
6. University of Georgia 佐治亚大学
7. Clemson University 克莱姆森大学
8. Worcester Polytechnic Institute 伍斯特理工学院
9. Texas A&M University 得州农机大学
10. Virginia Polytechnic Institute 弗吉尼亚理工学院
11. Denver University 丹佛大学
12. Bentley University 本特利大学
13. CUNY Baruch 纽约城市大学巴鲁克学院
14. Temple University 坦普大学
15. University of Nebraska Lincoln 内布拉斯加大学林肯分校
16. Loyola University of Chicago 芝加哥洛约拉大学
17. Kent State University 肯特州立大学
18. Emerson College 爱默森学院

张旭老师点评名校

1. University of Georgia: Master of Marketing Research 佐治亚大学市场营销硕士

http://www.terry.uga.edu/mmr/

○ 学校基本概况

佐治亚大学（The University of Georgia, 缩写为 UGA）建于 1785 年，是全美历史最悠久的研究型大学。该大学的总校区位于美国佐治亚州雅典市，分校区在亚特兰大。在 2009 年，美国《新闻与世界报道》的全美大学综合排名中将其列于第 58 位，全美公立研究型大学排第 20 位,其传播学院与公共行政学院更为全美最顶尖的五所学校之一,并为美国电视花生人奖 (Peabody Awards) 的主办大学,被誉为美国南方三所公立常春藤大学之一。

佐治亚大学主要由以下 16 个学院组成:商学院、教育学院、景观设计学院、农学院、文理学院、家庭与消费科学学院、森林与环境资源学院、研究生院、新闻与大众传媒学院、法学院、制药学院、公共卫生学院、公共与国际事务学院、社会工作学院、兽医学院、生态学院。研究生专业设置:企业管理、中学教育、细胞生物学、保险、音乐教育、信息管理、公共行政、微生物学、戏剧、比较文学、人力资源、会计、英语、社会学、统计学、生物学、经济学、运动科学、金融、历史、非洲研究、人类学和天文学。

○ 院系介绍和专业优势

The Terry College is the leading specialized program for developing skilled marketing research professionals and executives. The program offers a unique blend of academic coursework, practical applications and projects, industry speakers, and seminars. The benefits of the MMR are unmatched: Exceptional Career Placement Record.

项目的优势是混合了理论学习和实践操作的技能培养,在市场营销理论、传媒研究、经济学和统计学方面都有课程安排,在夏、秋和春季课程安排上比较平均。这个项目是由研究项目发展来的,因而对数理统计方面的课题格外看重,项目的另一个优势是毕业生就业率较高。

○ 班级构成

Individual Attention to Students

MMR class sizes of 30 or fewer students enhance faculty attention to individual student learning and personal development. MMR faculty, Advisory Board members, and alumni develop first-name professional relationships with students and provide the individual coaching and mentoring essential for career development.

班级人数为 30 人左右。

○ 核心课程

Summer	Fall	Spring
Introduction to Statistics Methods 统计方法3.0 Credit Hours	Introductory Econometrics 计量经济学3.0 Credit Hours	Applied Multivariate Methods 多变量分析3.0 Credit Hours
Data Collection Methods 数据收集方法3.0 Credit Hours	Applications of MR Techniques 市场研究方法应用3.0 Credit Hours	Applications of MR Techniques Ⅱ 市场研究方法应用3.0 Credit Hours

续前表

Summer	Fall	Spring
Qualitative Research 数量分析3.0 Credit Hours	Consumer Behavior 消费行为学3.0 Credit Hours	Discrete Choice and Conjoint Analysis 离散模型和联合分析3.0 Credit Hours
Executive Seminar Series 管理学研讨会	Executive Seminar Series 管理学研讨会	Marketing Research Project Ⅱ 市场研究项目1.5 Credit Hours
Marketing Research Project I 市场研究项目1.5 Credit Hours	Special Topics in Marketing Research 特别市场研究项目3.0 Credit Hours	Executive Seminar Series 管理学研讨会
	Marketing Research Project I 市场研究项目1.5 credit hours	Customer Relationship Management 消费者关系管理3.0 Credit Hours

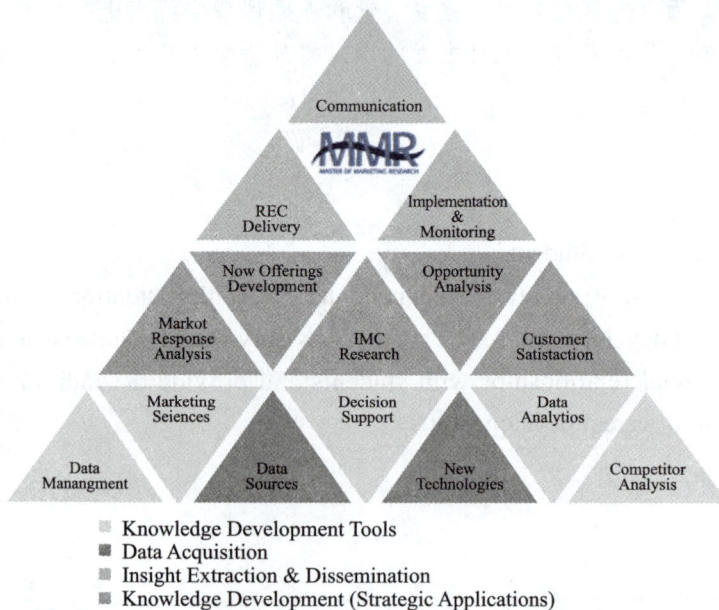

- Knowledge Development Tools
- Data Acquisition
- Insight Extraction & Dissemination
- Knowledge Development (Strategic Applications)

以上图形是说明佐治亚大学市场研究项目对于市场营销学研究逐步构成的看法和观点。在金字塔图形的最下方是数据分析和处理能力，中间是结合传播和市场理论的研究角度，继续往上到了接近顶端的位置是市场行为和机会的分析。

○ 录取条件和必备材料

（1）Candidates average a strong undergraduate grade point average in a quality degree program. The average GPA for students entering the MMR program is 3.4. 大学平均学分绩要求

（2）Excellent verbal and mathematical skills, candidates have competitive GMAT and GRE scores. The average GMAT score for students entering the program is 630 and the average GRE is 1350. Candidates should submit either the GMAT or GRE score—not both. 学校接受 GRE 成绩

（3）Faculty references 至少两封推荐信

（4）Although relevant work experience prior to entering the program is common among many new MMR students, candidates are also encouraged to apply to the MMR program for enrollment straight after completing their undergraduate studies. 对于工作经验不做硬性要求，鼓励应届本科生直接申请

（5）TOEFL scores for international applicants 外语能力成绩

佐治亚大学的市场营销硕士申请录取不是特别看重工作经验，但录取的学生基本都有一年左右的工作经验或显著的实习经历。另外，学校对本科成绩非常看重，一般 GPA 低于 3.5 分的学生在申请这个学校时会遇到一些困难，同时，GRE 分数在申请这个项目时更为普遍，而 GMAT 成绩不能按照 630 分的指导分数，而应是 680 分以上。注意，学校也接受雅思考试的成绩。

大家要注意，申请材料中有三大部分的材料必须寄送到研究生院和市场研究系办公室。

Component Ⅰ 第一部分	
Submit To:	UGA Graduate School 研究生院
Submission Method:	Online 在线提交
Submission Address:	http://www.applyweb.com/apply/ugg/
The following materials should be submitted to this location: An application to UGA Graduate School A non-refundable application fee submitted via credit card or e-check—the fee for domestic applicants is $75—the fee for international applicants is $100. 在线提交申请表格并支付申请费	

Component Ⅱ 第二部分	
Submit To:	UGA Graduate School 研究生院
Submission Method:	Mail 邮寄
Submission Address:	UGA Graduate School 320 E. Clayton St., Suite 400 The University of Georgia Athens, GA 30602

Component Ⅱ　第二部分

The following materials should be submitted to this location:

Two official transcripts from each college and university attended. (International applicants: Send two sets of official academic records and official proofs of degree.) Please note that official transcripts for transfer credits must also be supplied; transfer credit posted on the records of other institutions is unacceptable. The Registrar from your schools must seal the documents in an envelope and sign their name across the seal of the envelope. Transcripts should be sent directly to UGA Graduate School. One official copy of your GMAT or GRE scores sent by Educational Testing Service directly to UGA Graduate School. Candidates should submit either the GMAT or GRE score—not both. International Students: Please submit one official copy of your TOEFL or IELTS scores sent directly from the testing agency to UGA Graduate School. (Helpful tips for international applicants) 邮寄内容：（1）两份官方的大学成绩单，信封及成绩单本身必须盖章；（2）官方由ETS寄送的GRE/GMAT成绩；（3）官方的TOEFL成绩单。

Component Ⅲ　第三部分

Submit To:	
Submission Method:	Mail 邮寄
Submission Address:	Jamese Meyer, Coordinator：研究生申请协调员Coca-Cola Center for Marketing Studies, Terry College of Business, The University of Georgia Athens, GA 30602

邮寄内容:

• A resume

• A letter explaining the reasons you are interested in a career in marketing research

• Three letters of recommendation. When you complete the online application, you must list three recommenders and their email addresses. The Graduate School will send your recommenders the form to submit their letter of recommendation online. Your recommenders can choose to submit their recommendation online or mail a letter to Jamese Meyer or to you to send to Jamese Meyer. If the recommender sends the letter to you to mail, the letter must be in a sealed envelope with the recommender's signature across the envelope seal.

（1）简历；（2）一份解释并阐明自己对市场营销感兴趣的文书；（3）如果推荐老师/老板不能网上提交推荐信，则可以邮寄。

○ 截止日期

Completed applications should be submitted by February 15 for the summer (June) admission. There is no fall or spring admission. Admission decisions are communicated on a rolling basis and all decisions will be made by early April.

学校的申请截止以夏季入学日期为准，是每年的 2 月 15 日，这就给中国学生一个小小难题，即在学校大四毕业时就已经拿到签证并订好机票，相对于 9 月入学的学校来说，这个时间安排得太紧张了。

○ 就业情况

The Terry College MMR is recognized for its exceptional success in placement. Demand for experienced MMRs is high and salaries are competitive (average salary $70,000 since 2005). Both client and supplier firms conduct interviews for MMR students and placements are available nationwide.

Coca-Cola Center 是学校和可口可乐公司共同设置的一个项目研究中心。

The Center is funded by endowment grants from the Coca-Cola Company, The Coca-Cola Foundation, AC Nielsen, M/A/R/C/ Inc., Audits and Surveys, MRCA, and the membership donations of an extensive list of leading firms on the MMR Board of Advisors. These funds support assistantships for the MMR students, faculty research grants, teaching materials, and seminars by industrial leaders. The faculty of the Marketing Department appreciates this support by these firms and invites the participation of other firms.

佐治亚大学的市场营销硕士的就业率居全美相同项目的领先地位，由于和南部大企业有密切联系，学校的职业办公室与这些企业共同设立很多辅导课、修改简历环节与现场招聘会。毕业生平均年薪 7 万 ~7.5 万美元。从就业的便利角度来看，佐治亚大学一直都名列前茅。

2. Denver University: Master of Marketing Research 丹佛大学市场营销硕士

http://www.daniels.du.edu/schoolsdepartments/marketing/degreesprograms/graduate/graduate.html

○ 学校基本概况

丹佛大学是一所私立大学，建校于 1854 年，位于美国科罗拉多州 Denver 大学公园的中心，那里是丹佛市历史上非常有名的地区，同时也是一个安全的居住区。作为美国科罗拉多州的首府，丹佛也是该州最大的城市，有人口 230 多万。而且丹佛是整个洛基山地区 (Rocky Mountain) 企业、文化、金融和娱乐活动的聚集地。丹佛市全年有 300 天阳光明媚的日子，气候宜人，适合旅游。丹佛大学是洛基山区最老也最大的四年制私立大学。它作为二级国家级大学，入选《纽约时报大学指南》的"二百大"，并获得三颗星的学术评分。丹佛大学的学生来自全美和将近 100 个国家。学校拥有将近 9 000 名学生，包括 3 500 名本科生以及 5 500 名研究生。

丹佛大学学制为 4 年。学校的校历为 Quarter。学校颁授学位：学士、硕士、博士。图书馆：藏书 156 万册，缩微资料 77 万件，期刊 9 669 种。科研机构：高空实验室、丹佛研究所、学术研究中心、儿童研究中心、婚姻研究中心。研究生院、工商管理学院、人类服务学院 (含教育学院、职业心理学学院)、法学院、艺术和人文学院 (含音乐学院、艺术学院)、数学和计算机科学学院、自然科学学院、社会科学学院、国际问题研究学院、社会工作学院。该校的体育设施相当完备，学生可在先进的健身中心健身，在奥林匹克级的游泳池游泳，并享受滑冰与冰上竞技。丹佛市为不同生活方式的学生提供多种文化和娱乐。丹佛大学所在的社区也有不少美丽的公园、咖啡店及私人餐厅。

○ 院系介绍和专业优势

A healthy bottom line starts with top-notch marketing.

The Department of Marketing at the Daniels College of Business offers marketing degrees and programs that fully immerse you in the business of marketing. Graduate students delve even deeper by following one of four specialized marketing tracks including one of the only Integrated Marketing Communication programs housed in a business college.

丹佛大学的丹尼尔商学院在科罗拉多及美国西部均有盛名。学校的市场营销硕士项目最具实力的有三个方面：

（1）品牌战略与分析；（2）国际市场营销策略；（3）消费者心理分析与判断研究。这个学院不大，但学费及生活费较高，而且学时一般较长，要完成市场营销硕士项目，很多学生修完了要求的学分后，往往会增加到 42 个学分。

Whichever facet of marketing you want to pursue, the degrees and programs offered by the Department of Marketing prepare you to contribute to the bottom line with top-notch marketing.

Points of pride for the Department of Marketing at Daniels:

Marketing pioneers who teach from experience. Our faculty has far-reaching experience and influence in the industry as leading marketing researchers and practitioners. In the classroom, they're experts at bridging theory to application, and outside the classroom they'll help you make industry connections and identify opportunities.

Innovative and always relevant: Experiential learning and creative class formats are hallmarks of a Daniels education. We invite high-profile executives to the classroom for candid conversations and internships. Team projects give students field-tested experience.

　　学校市场营销课程的任课教师多为行业内有经验及有职务的兼职教授，因而学生对实际工作中遇到的市场营销思维与策略会有非常不同的理解，这也优于照本宣科式的纯理论学习。

Networking events that advance industry discourse: In addition to small classes that foster collaboration and networking between students and faculty, the department hosts two monthly roundtables for marketing professionals, supply chain professionals, students and faculty. They are a unique opportunity to engage and connect with top practitioners.

　　学校提供面试与交际平台，与行业人士更多接触。

Four tracks to a brilliant career: Graduate students can select from four concentrations to better position themselves for success in their chosen marketing specialty. Undergraduates can also pursue their interests and career goals through a diverse range of electives.

　　可以选择四个专业方向来做职业准备。

○ 申请必备条件和资料要求

　　（1）Completed application: While it is desirable to submit your application form after you have acquired and submitted the information listed below, doing so is NOT required. 申请表格

　　（2）$100 nonrefundable application fee: To be paid when the application is submitted. 申请费用

　　（3）Official transcript: Submit one official transcript from each higher-education institution you attended in officially sealed envelopes. Documents that arrive in opened envelopes will not be considered official. If transcripts are in a language other than English, you must submit original copies of the transcripts as well as translation in officially sealed envelopes, sent directly from the issuing institution. Documents that arrive in opened envelopes and/or marked "issued to student" will not be considered official. International students must provide documentation verifying that you've received the recognized equivalent of a U.S. bachelor's degree. Applicants with foreign credentials must also submit official proof of the degree earned (e.g., a copy of diploma or certificate) with an English translation. The Office of International Admission will evaluate the equivalency of degrees earned outside the United States. Please send official transcripts to the Graduate Admissions Office, Daniels College of Business, University of Denver, 2101 S University Blvd., Suite 255, Denver, CO 80208-8921. 成绩单上必须明确学位、学时、学分及学生本人的姓名、学号。大学成绩单要直接寄送到商学院研究生办公室，由他们对国际生的成绩单进行评估。

　　（4）GMAT or GRE scores: The GMAT or GRE is not required for the Executive MBA and graduate business certificates. The GMAT is required for all students who wish to be considered for merit-based scholarships or graduate assistantships. 标准考试成绩，推荐 GMAT 考试

　　（5）Two letters of recommendation: Submitted by individuals (nonrelatives) who can evaluate your academic and/or work performance, as well as your potential for success in graduate school. Provide the email addresses of your recommenders where requested in your program application. They will receive an e-mail from Daniels with instructions on how to submit the completed recommendation form online. If you prefer to contact your recommenders directly, you may download the letter of recommendation form for ALL graduate programs (MBA, IMBA, EMBA, PMBA and specialized master's degrees) and have them send the completed form to Daniels@du.edu. 至少两封推荐信

（6）Professional resume: Submit a resume that focuses on your unique strengths and accomplishments. 职业生涯和经历的简历

（7）TOEFL OR IELTS results, if required: An official score report for the TOEFL or IELTS must be submitted by any applicant whose native language is not English. 学校接受雅思成绩，TOEFL 的最低分数线为 90 分，雅思则为 6.5 分，不满足条件的申请人必须到大学的语言中心进一步学习。

（8）Verification of Financial Support and Visa Information Form (international students only): International students must apply for a student visa and provide a letter of financial verification. 财产表格的填写和递交。

（9）Admissions Interview: Interviews are required for Executive MBA and Professional MBA applicants and those who wish to be considered for merit-based scholarships and graduate assistantships. You will be contacted to schedule an interview after your complete application is received. 面试一般会由商学院老师邀请满足条件的申请人进行。

（10）Essays

Essays are assessed for clarity, organization, conciseness and grammar. Through the essays, you can communicate what you hope to achieve at Daniels and how you will contribute to the Daniels community. Take advantage of the optional essay question (#3) to let us know what sets you apart from others applying to the program. 三份小文书需要提交。

（11）Pre-Orientation Evaluation: All international students are required to attend the International Student Pre-Orientation. During pre-orientation, any international student who has not completed GPP and whose native language is not English will go through a comprehensive evaluation of English language skills in both writing and speaking. As a result of this evaluation, students may need to enroll in one or both of the GPP courses (Writing Workshop and Speaking Workshop), each of which consists of 10 hours of instruction per week.

丹佛大学商学院在考虑录取时，一般会从申请人的工作经历入手，但这并不是必须的，有良好的实习经历和感受，能在申请文书及简历中正确和恰当表现的学生，也能弥补这一方面的缺失。可以这么说，从工作经历及实习经验上来看，只要学生能恰如其分地展示自己在领导能力、团队协作精神、组织协调能力、管理技巧和沟通能力这几大方面的潜力与准备，就可以满足对于工作经历要求的基本条件。

根据丹佛大学的安排，商学院在入学前会对所有国际学生开设先导课程，所有满足语言要求的学生也最好能参加这个两周的暑期课程，以便更好地融入即将开始的研究生学习中去。

○ 截止日期

For Fall Entry (September) 秋季入学

November 15	Priority Admission（优先录取） Merit-based financial assistance consideration（奖学金申请时间）
January 15	Round Two Admission Merit-based financial assistance consideration（奖学金申请时间）
March 15	Round Three Admission Merit-based financial assistance consideration on a funds-available basis; final deadline for international students（奖学金申请时间）
May 15	Round Four Admission Final merit-based financial assistance consideration on a funds-available basis（奖学金申请时间）

Merit-based financial assistance includes scholarships and graduate assistantships (non-Executive programs only).

International applicants must apply by March 15 to allow time to obtain a student visa.

秋季：5 月 15 日为最后截止日期。

For Spring Entry (March) 春季入学

October 1	Priority admission（优先录取） Merit-based financial assistance consideration（奖学金申请时间）
December 1	Round Two Admission Merit-based financial assistance consideration; final deadline for international students.（奖学金申请时间）
February 1	Round Three Admission Final merit-based financial assistance consideration on a funds-available basis.（奖学金申请时间）

Merit-based financial assistance includes scholarships and graduate assistantships (non-executive programs only).

International applicants must apply by December 1 to allow time to obtain a student visa.

Applications received after February 1 will be considered on a space-available basis.

春季 2 月 1 日为最后截止日期。

○ 核心课程

Choose from four integrated courses of study:

（1）Integrated Marketing Communication（整合市场营销）: the strategic skills you need to implement consistent messaging across all touch points. Daniels is one of the few business colleges in the US to have an Integrated Marketing Communication track housed in a business college.

（2）Customer Experience Marketing（消费者经验营销）: the tools you need to understand how customers view business.

（3）Integrated Marketing Strategy（整合市场战略）: marketing from a big-picture perspective, including study of broad-based research, planning, and management.

（4）Supply Chain Management（供应链管理）: the mechanics and strategy behind providing products on time every time, with less cost and greater service.

从四大专业方向中选择自己喜欢和专注的方向进行学习。注意这里面包含了供应链管理的学习，这也是美国市场营销发展的趋势。

COURSE 具体课程

Daniels Compass Courses

BUS 4610	The Essence of Enterprise（企业基础知识）
BUS 4620	Ethics for the 21st Century Professional（职业道德理念）

Marketing Core Courses 市场营销核心课程

MKTG 4100	Marketing Concepts（市场概念）
MKTG 4510	Concepts of Buyer Behavior（买方行为理念）
MKTG 4520	Marketing Metrics（市场营销衡量）
MKTG 4530	Marketing Research（市场研究）
MKTG 4900	Advanced Marketing Strategy（高级市场战略）

Marketing Elective Courses 学校推荐的部分选修课

Strongly Recommended

MKTG 4540	Product & Service Innovation（产品及服务创新）
MKTG 4370	Marketing Channels & Logistics（市场渠道及物流）
MKTG 4220	Customer Experience Management（消费者经验管理）
MKTG 4810	Integrated Marketing Communication（整合市场营销）

Other Marketing Electives by Area 其余选修课

Integrated Marketing Communication (IMC) Courses (整合营销课程)

MKTG 4820	Brand Management（品牌管理）
MKTG 4850	Advanced IMC Campaign（高级市场战略）
MKTG 4705	Topics: Experience Design and Leadership（设计及领导力）
MKTG 4240	Advanced CEM Integration（高级消费者经验管理课程）

Customer Experience Management (CEM) Courses

MKTG 4705	Topics: Experience Design and Leadership（设计及领导力）
MKTG 4240	Advanced CEM Integration（高级消费者经验管理课程）

| MKTG 4820 | Brand Management（品牌管理） |
| MKTG 4850 | Advanced IMC Campaign（高级市场战略） |

Integrated Marketing Strategy (IMS) Courses 整合营销课程

| MKTG 4630 | International Marketing（国际市场） |
| MKTG 4670 | Competitive Marketing Strategies（市场竞争策略） |

Supply Chain Management (SCM) Courses

MKTG 4360	Transportation Systems（运输系统）
MKTG 4375	Strategic Sourcing（生产配置战略）
MKTG 4380	Global Supply Chain Management（全球供应链管理）
MKTG 4705	Topics: Improving Supply Chain Performance（改善供应链研究）
MKTG 4705	Topics: Supply Chain Technology（供应链科技）

○ 费用和奖学金

由于丹佛大学对奖学金及费用说明很详细，这里我抓住这个机会和大家说明一下奖学金与费用事宜。

1. Graduate Program Tuition

Tuition for Daniels College of Business graduate programs is based on a cost per credit hour set by the University of Denver. Tuition costs are the same for all students whether they are residents or nonresidents of Colorado.

Master's degrees:　　　　　　$1,026 per credit hour

商学院每个学分为 1 026 美元。

2. Daniels Program Fee

All students are assessed a $950 program fee that supports the preparatory and experiential learning components of required courses as well as costs associated with graduation and commencement activities. 商学院设施和图书馆等项目收费

3. Health Fee 健康管理费用

A health fee of approximately $144 per quarter is assessed for graduate students unless a Graduate Student Health Fee Waiver Form is completed (this form is accessible only after the first tuition deposit). Students not covered by this health fee may use the Student Health Center on a fee-for-service basis. 健康费用每个 quarter 144 美元，即完成一个学年需支付 420 美元。

4. Student Health Insurance 在校生医疗保险

All students attending the University of Denver are required to have health insurance.

Students may participate in the Student Health Insurance program or use their own carrier. The 2010—2011 annual premium is approximately $2,420. A waiver form is required if the student has his/her own insurance carrier.

健康保险费：如果参与学校的健康保险计划，则每年需支付 2 420 美元。当然丹佛当地也有很多便宜些的学生保险计划，学生们也可以选择支付那些当地的保险计划。

5. Laptop Computer 电脑费用

All students are required to bring or purchase a laptop computer. The average cost of a laptop computer is $2,000. Please plan your finances accordingly.

6. Additional Fees 其他费用

Additional fees may include the following:
University Technology Services Fee—$4 per credit hour.
Graduate Program and Activity Fee—$50 per quarter. This fee covers activities that enhance the educational experience of graduate students, including graduate student organizations, guest speakers, award events, graduation events and welcoming events.

额外费用包括计算机使用费，每个学分 4 美元，如果是 40 学分，则近 160 美元；另外研究生的项目费与活动费每年约 150 美元。

7. Living Expenses & Summer Quarter

In addition to the tuition and fees listed above, students relocating to Denver should budget approximately $3,600 in living expenses based on a moderate lifestyle in which students share living expenses with a roommate. Daniels tuition and fees do not include housing expenses, international or local travel, or textbook costs ($600~$1,749 yearly).

The academic year consists of three quarters or nine months. If you take classes in the summer, you will be responsible for tuition and fees during the summer quarter. Please prepare your finances accordingly.

这里一个 quarter（季度）3 个月的生活费约为 3 600 美元，如果加上房租和书本费，3 个月最少也会花费 1 500 美元 ~1 800 美元。

○ 关于奖学金

The GMAT is required of all those wishing to be considered for merit-based scholarships. An admission interview is required for merit-based scholarship consideration. Both U.S. and international students may apply for merit-based scholarships. Most merit-based scholarships range from $2,000~$15,000 total, disbursed equally over the duration of a student's program. A limited number of Dean's Scholarships, ranging from $15,000~$25,000 may also be awarded, depending on the availability of funds.

国际学生也可以申请奖学金，一般我辅导的学生获得的均为 10 000 美元左右的奖学金。至于系主任奖学金（Dean Scholarship），初次申请的学生必须成绩优异才能拿到，这个数目为 15 000 美元 ~25 000 美元。

（1）Need-based scholarships

Need-based scholarships, which range from $1,500~$6,000/year for a maximum of two years, may be awarded after the student has confirmed their attendance at Daniels. The amount is dependent on the level of need as determined by the Free Application for Federal Student Aid (FAFSA). Please contact the University of Denver, Office of Financial Aid for more information.

这里的 Need-based 即根据学生家庭收入较低或经济状况较差的情况给予，这个就不是我们说的 Merit-based 学习优异奖学金。注意，一般来说，在美国年收入在 3.5 万美元以下为贫困家庭，但家庭年收入 6 万美元以下的也在很多学校可以申请到助学金。

（2）Other scholarships

The Herbst-Dillon Scholarship provides scholarship support to undergraduate and graduate students who are single parents pursuing degrees at the Daniels College of Business. There is no GPA requirement for this scholarship, although students must be in good standing at the University. Eligible scholarship recipients must have financial need as demonstrated by their FAFSA.

特别奖学金，这些奖学金往往由基金会或个人捐赠，发放时学生必须满足特定条件才能申请到：如同性恋者，单亲家庭学生，中国在美移民第二代学生或残疾人。

Scholarships and grants for Executive MBA students.

We believe that cohort diversity improves the EMBA experience, therefore department scholarships or program grants may be offered to individuals who work in nonprofit organizations or are a part of an under-represented industry or category.

这个是给行政 MBA 学生的，不适用于我们申请市场营销的中国研究生。

（3）Loans

Many graduate students at Daniels College of Business help fund their education through loans. All federal loans require the submission of the Free Application for Federal Student Aid (FAFSA). Applicants must be U.S. citizens.

1）Federal Stafford Loans

Subsidized and unsubsidized Stafford loans are available to students enrolled at least half-time in a degree-seeking program. Commercial lenders who participate in the Federal Family Education Loan Program (FFELP) make these low-interest loans. Students with demonstrated need are eligible for a subsidized loan, and the government will pay the interest while the student is in school and during a six-month grace period. Unsubsidized loans are awarded to those without remaining need, and the interest accrues on the loan during school, the grace period and through repayment.

注意，Federal Stafford Loans（联邦助学金）中国学生不够条件申请，这个奖学金适合绿卡持有人或美国公民。

2）Federal Perkins Loans

The Perkins Loan is a federally guaranteed, fixed-rate, low-interest loan for undergraduate and graduate students enrolled at least half-time in an eligible program. Students with demonstrated financial need who meet the Office of Financial Aid application deadlines are considered for the loan up to $6,000 for graduates per academic year.

Federal Perkins Loans 是贷款，有低息、固定利息的特点，偿还期从毕业开始计算，但也是美国公民才能申请。

3）Graduate/Professional PLUS Loans

Graduate/Professional PLUS loans are available to credit-worthy graduate students who are enrolled at least half-time (4 credit hours or more per quarter/semester) regardless of need. Commercial lenders who participate in the Federal Family Education Loan Program (FFELP) make these loans.

这项贷款是丹佛大学联合参加联邦教育贷款项目的贷款组织或机构，给有需要的学生提供有偿资助。一般申请的条件是必须信用记录良好，而中国学生无信用记录，必须找在美国的亲戚朋友做担保人方可申请。

3. University of Florida: Master of Market Research 佛罗里达大学市场营销硕士

http://warrington.ufl.edu/mkt/programs/ms/

○ 学校基本概况

佛罗里达大学位于美国东南部的佛罗里达州甘斯威尔城，是全美十所最大的大学之一，多次被业内评为全美领先的研究性大学。它的历史可以回溯至 1853 年，学校最早建于佛罗里达州东部的奥卡拉镇，后来与佛罗里达农业学院合并，于 1905 年迁校至甘斯威尔城，并正式定名为佛罗里达大学。该大学共有九个图书馆，内藏有各种书籍、图纸、音乐、影像等，涵盖几乎所有领域，可谓包罗万象。20 世纪初，佛罗里达大学从美国国家航空航天局获得雄厚的研究经费，对一系列空间领域的科研项目展开研究。该校的竞争非常激烈，尤其是一些热门专业，炙手可热。对于留学生而言，该校所提供的课程、服务以及研究教学都颇有口碑，因此每年慕名申请的国际学生非常多。

佛罗里达大学在校学生约 48 800 人，其中本科生大概有 34 500 人，教职员工 4 534 人。该校共设有如下 16 个学院：农业和生命科学学院，工商管理学院，设计、建筑和规划学院，教育学院，工程学院，艺术学院，新闻与交流学院，法学院，文理学院，护理学院，医药学院等。

❍ 院系介绍和专业优势

The Master's of Science in Marketing program is an intensive research-oriented experience designed for students who wish to pursue research in an academic environment. The M.S. program is a 30-credit, non-thesis program designed exclusively for students whose eventual goal is to earn a Ph.D. and pursue an academic career. The M.S. program provides a strong foundation of research skills that enhance students' prospects for admission into Ph.D. programs at other universities. The program is not designed for students interested in managerial careers in business: that purpose is served by the MBA program.

佛罗里达大学的市场营销硕士项目比较特别，这个项目不是纯粹商科硕士的项目，在这里举这个学校做例子是很有意义的。首先，这个项目只有30学分，按照一门课一般3学分计算，10~11门课即可完成，因此，项目的时间不超过一年；其次，这个项目不是针对以找工作为目的同学设立的，而是针对那些想成为教授或学科研究人员的学生，即PhD（博士生）设置的；再次，学校对在申请文书中体现不同职业追求的学生会比较排斥，一般不予录取，而大部分项目中的学生，要继续申请本校的博士学位，都会得到帮助与青睐；最后，项目的研究方式也比较偏数量化，对申请人所具备和展现的数学与统计能力的要求较高。

❍ 核心课程

The M.S. program emphasizes the development of sophisticated academic research skills. As such, M.S. students are expected to adopt a scholarly mindset and pursue their studies more like Ph.D. students than master's students. Indeed, much of the required and constrained elective coursework is comprised of Ph.D. seminars.

这里明确提出，核心课程是偏理论研究方向的。

Required Courses (Consumer Behavior Emphasis) 消费行为学方向必修课程

Course	Title
MAR 7636	Research Methods in Marketing 市场研究方法
MAR 7507	Perspectives on Consumer Behavior 消费行为视角与观点
STA 4210	Regression Analysis 回归分析
STA 4211orSTA 4212	Regression Analysis / Experimental Design实证设计与回归分析 Categorical Data Analysis 分类数据处理
MAR 7576orMAR 7588	Consumer Preference Formation and Change 消费者偏好形成与改变 Consumer Information Processing and Decision Making 消费信息整合与决策
MAR 7666orMAR 7786	Marketing Decision Models 市场决策计算模型 Marketing Literature 市场理论

Constrained Elective Courses 选修课

Course	Title
MAR 5806	Problems and Methods in Marketing Management 市场营销管理的问题与方法 [required for non-marketing undergraduate majors]
MAR 7925	Workshop in Marketing Research 市场研究专题
MAR7626	Multivariate Statistical Methods 多元统计方法
MAR6930	Judgment and Decision Making 判断与决策
MAR7622	Experimental Design 实证设计
SOP 6509	Seminar: Interpersonal Relations and Group Processes 研讨会：人际关系与群体过程
SOP 6419	Seminar: Attitudes and Social Cognition 研讨会：态度与社会认知
EDF 6436	Theory of Measurement 计量理论
EDF 7412	Structural Equation Models 结构方程模型

Research Courses 研究专项课程

Course	Title
MAR 6905	Individual Work 独立研究
MAR 6910	Supervised Research （导师）指导研究

In some cases, due to student interests, course scheduling, and the presence of acceptable alternative courses, certain modifications may be acceptable. Each student is required to meet with his/her primary advisor either prior to or at the very beginning of his/her entry to the program to outline a program of study. Progress will be reviewed by the supervisory committee each semester, and adjustments to the program of study may be made as necessary.

Although twelve credits are considered a "full load" for graduate students, in practice many students take less. Given the intensive nature of the coursework in this program, students should carefully balance their course load with any outside employment or other demands on their time. It is anticipated that the M.S. program can be completed comfortably in one and a half years. For example, a student entering in Fall 2006 should complete 20~24 hours of coursework during the first academic year and graduate in December 2007.

这里学校对学生选课程给出了指导意见。由于课程内容比较艰难与深奥，学校不建议学生们在一年内完成项目，而是在一年半即三个学期内完成项目，并积极与导师沟通选课情况，这也是市场营销项目中不多的几个在硕士阶段设立导师辅导选课制度的学校。

○ 录取必备条件和材料

Students who believe their backgrounds, experience, or special qualifications are consistent with the goals of the M.S. program are encouraged to apply. In evaluating applicants for admission, the following are considered minimum requirements:

（1）combined verbal and quantitative score of 1250 on the Graduate Records Examination or a score of 600 on the Graduate Management Admissions Test; GRE 考试分数有最低要求，同时，根据经验 GMAT 考试要求 650 分以上。

（2）a TOEFL score of 250 (for international students only); TOEFL 机考分数需 100 分以上。

（3）a record of previous scholastic excellence in either business or closely related social science disciplines (e.g., psychology, sociology); 学校偏好社会科学专业背景的学生。

（4）evidence of oral communication skills. No industry experience is required. 并不需要专业或工作经历，但有相关研究生经历最佳。

In addition, it is essential that the student has clear educational and professional goals that are consistent with the requirements and objectives of the M.S. program. Evidence of such goals includes:

a statement articulating the applicant's professional goals with sufficient specificity to enable the admissions committee to judge the degree of congruence between these goals and the requirements and objectives of the program; and an indication that the applicant is familiar with and understands the requirements of the program.

学校对于申请人的学习计划和职业目标很关注，对于这个项目的研究方法、数量分析和理论基础准备不足的学生，不建议申请。因而对于文书的要求，是申请人必须以个人学习计划和写作样本为主来展现自己和这个项目的契合度。

注意，这个学校不提供硕士阶段的奖学金，只有进入博士阶段才会有奖学金。

第五章

物流管理、供应链管理专业硕士
Master of Science in Logistics and
Supply Chain Management

物流管理和供应链管理专业的简单介绍

物流管理专业和供应链研究是紧密相连的，从学科的演化上讲，这个专业是由工程管理和工业工程研究专业的分支细化而来的。工程管理专业研究由于结合了管理学的知识，逐渐向商学院的教学和研究靠拢。其中，商学院的市场开发和市场行销研究又必须关注仓储、运输、规划、上下游供应等环节，因此，本来完全由工学院的工程管理专业就可以涵盖的研究，现在必须由工学院和商学院共同联手完成。可以这么说，大多数的美国商学院的物流和供应链管理专业都是从工程学院嫁接过来的，颁发的学位也是以理学硕士学位为主。那么在工程学院下还有物流专业吗？有部分学校仍然有这样的设置。

总的来说，主要有三个方式可以在美国研究生院获得物流专业的教育。第一个途径是本书讨论的重点，即进入商学院攻读物流／供应链管理专业硕士，一般需要一年半到两年的时间；第二个途径是攻读高等学院的MBA专业，在第二年选择物流专业课程；第三个途径是进入工程学院学习工业工程或工程管理专业，在学习过程中研修物流方面的课程。

无论是哪一种途径，物流专业研究生学习在美国大学中主要涉及以下几个部分的内容。首先是物流中心的管理与流程，这个总体构架的学习将贯穿每一个阶段的物流及供应链专业研究，对于物流中心所包含的细分环节的学习，也是一个重要的组成部分：运输、仓储、配送和分销等。其次，对于物流优化和战略规划的学习，则需要研究生加强在统计、数量化分析及计算机模拟等基本能力方面的学习。可以这么说，一个本身学习社会科学专业的学生，如本科在中国人民大学学习经济学的学生，不适合到美国的商学院去学习物流专业的研究生。

原因很简单：在工程学、数学以及计算机能力等方面，学经济学的学生不具备与理工背景学生竞争的实力。

那么在评估众多申请者的背景时，美国商学院的物流专业研究生录取委员会多数情况下会关注什么方面呢？又有哪些方面是最为重要的？下面我简单地进行分析及讲解。主要的因素包括：专业知识背景、工作实践能力、数理分析能力、语言能力及面试表现。这几个因素都是录取与奖学金发放的直接因素，而从重要性上讲，则应该这么排列：最为重要的是工作实践能力，有相关的物流与供应链管理工作实践，会给申请极大地加分。这里我也提醒应届生，要合理和尽早地安排自己的专业实践与实习，尤其是大三那一年的暑假不能轻易浪费。第二重要的因素就是数理与分析能力，这个能力可以通过同学们的 GRE/GMAT、数理课程分数或工程/理工背景来体现，其次下面两个因素才轮到本科专业知识是否学过物流以及语言考试表现与面试。可以这么说，物流本专业的学生在申请录取及奖学金时比工程或相关理工专业的学生有优势，而有相关工程专业背景的学生，比学习社科专业的申请物流专业的学生更有优势。但注意，结合我以上的分析及申请特点，还是以中国人民大学一个学经济的学生为例，如果他的实践和学习经历较强，在一家大型的第三方物流公司实习了三个月，同时自己的数学背景过硬，那么他同样也具备强大的竞争力，与另一位来自南开大学的物流本专业的学生共同角逐物流专业的录取与奖学金。

随着物流行业在中国的逐渐兴盛以及我国物流市场急需规范化、信息化和系统化的呼声日益高涨，相关物流专业人才，尤其是在美国顶尖商学院物流专业毕业的学生，将成为市场上的佼佼者。下面我们来一起看看几个标准的物流/供应链的美国研究生项目，了解更多申请的细节和注意事项。

金融工程专业院校名录

以下是几个我们最常申请的物流和供应链管理学校，部分美国大学的物流专业已经和市场营销结合，另外，MBA 项目下的物流方向也提供物流专项研究的机会。

1. MIT 麻省理工学院
2. Michigan State University 密歇根州立大学
3. University of Pennsylvania 宾夕法尼亚大学
4. Carnegie Mellon University 卡内基梅隆大学
5. Penn State University 宾夕法尼亚州立大学
6. Arizona State University 亚利桑那州立大学
7. Ohio State University 俄亥俄州立大学
8. Michigan University-Ann Arbor 密西根大学安娜堡分校
9. Stanford University 斯坦福大学
10. Northwestern University 西北大学
11. University of Tennessee 田纳西大学
12. University of Maryland-College Park 马里兰大学帕克分校
13. Purdue University 普渡大学

张旭老师点评名校

1. University of Maryland: Master of Science in Logistics 马里兰大学帕克分校物流管理硕士

http://www.rhsmith.umd.edu/ms/supplychain/

○ 学校基本概况

马里兰大学帕克分校创建于 1862 年，位于马里兰州，是一所非常著名的州立大学。该校所处地理位置优越，校园环境优美，研究经费充足，学术声望较高，综合排名在全美大学前 50，是一所不可多得的理想学府。该校也是全美大学联盟（The Association of American University，简称 AAU）的 61 个盟校之一，与美国的伊利诺伊大学香槟分校、UC-Berkley、UCLA 等都有合作的教学计划。

马里兰大学帕克分校下设 13 个学院，分别为：教育学院、工程学院、农业与自然资源学院、建筑规划与保护学院、艺术与人文学院、行为与社会科学学院、化学与生命科学学院、计算机数学与物理学院、健康与人类表现学院、信息学院、商学院、新闻学院、公共政策学院。

○ 院系介绍和专业优势

The Supply Chain Management Center (SCMC), established in 1998, was one of the first SCM centers in academia, garnering clients such as the Department of Defense (DOD) and the Science Applications International Corporation (SAIC). The center builds on the university's half-century commitment to advancing supply chain practices and research, and is distinguished by state-of-the-art technology. It has built working prototypes of leading-edge supply chain portals, developed RFID demos to help hospitals lower costs and improve patient care by managing their inventories in real time, and, through its collaboration with Delft University in the Netherlands and with Interactive Learning Solutions (ILS), Inc., created the world's first real-time global supply chain game, helping students prepare for careers and compete for jobs by learning in a decision-rich environment that closely mimics today's complex global supply chain. A new version of this game has been designed to mirror volatility in a global environment. The center is currently working on a multidisciplinary collaboration with the University of Maryland to design a national test bed for Cyber Supply Chain Risk management.

We have one of the most technologically advanced facilities in the world for research in supply chain management—our Supply Chain Laboratory. The lab provides students with the opportunity to receive training in industry leading supply chain software, such as SAP enterprise resource planning (ERP) and i2 network design.

马里兰大学帕克分校的物流和供应链管理专业是美国东部地区历史最悠久、实力最雄厚的项目之一，众多美国公司及政府商业机构与大学合作，学校的科研能力一流，实时模拟方面的设备尤其优秀。

马里兰大学也和世界各国的学校有深入的合作，物流研究中心便与 ILS（互动学习科技公司）合作率先开设了美国物流实时模拟课堂。该中心还借助马里兰大学优异的计算机研究实力开发了"虚拟供应链风险管理"方案，供老师与学生们验证物流试验室或课堂上所学的知识。

马里兰大学的商学院另外两大优势也对物流研究项目有极大的促进与帮助，项目的课程内容也或多或少地带有浓郁的技术风格与色彩。这两大优势之一是马里兰大学医疗设备与医院信息管理方面是由专门研究的项目设置的；优势之二针对电子工程、信息科技与计算机硬件开发，商学院也设立了许多交叉课程和交流项目，对高科技管理与开发有着很好的理论与实践基础和研究。

○ 申请必备条件和申请材料

（1）The equivalent of a US bachelor's degree 四年本科学位

（2）The Graduate Record Examination (GRE) or the Graduate Management Admissions Test (GMAT). At least one official score must be submitted. 标准考试成绩，接受 GRE

（3）A completed online application form that includes a written essay articulating your qualifications and motivation for pursuing advanced education. 申请表格

（4）Application fee of $75 申请费用

（5）Two official transcripts from all undergraduate and graduate institutions that you have previously attended 两份官方大学成绩单

（6）Two letters of recommendation from supervisors within your organization or from professors familiar with your work 至少两封推荐信

（7）Admissions interview, if required. After initial screening, the Admissions Office may select candidates for interviews which may be done in person or by telephone. The Admissions Office will contact you to schedule an interview time. 录取过程中的面试

（8）Proof of English language proficiency (TOEFL or IELTS official scores). 语言成绩

对于 TOEFL 成绩的要求，大家要注意，如果一个学生在英语为主要语言或教学语言的国家学习超过两年的时间，TOEFL 成绩就不需要提供。所以经常出现的情况是，一个在英国、美国或加拿大读本科或高中的学生在申请时不需要提供外语成绩，同时，一个转学到美国或英国读大二、大三的学生，大部分学校也不需要提供语言成绩。

○ 国际学生要求

Academic Credentials

By the application deadline date, the Admissions Office must receive:

Complete official transcripts/ mark sheets (in the original language). We can also accept notarized copies of these documents if official copies are not available. An authorized transcript with literal English translations.

Copy of diploma/degree received if this information is not listed on transcript/mark sheets and English translation of diploma/degree received.

Translations should not be interpretive, and actual names of all degrees, diplomas, and certificates must appear in the translation. If you are in need of a translation service, a list of English translation companies can be found here.

对于大学成绩单和研究生成绩单，学校要求成绩单上必须出现学位和所获证书的具体名称和时间。在中国大学的成绩单和毕业证书上，有的学生获得的商科本科学位可以写成 Bachelor of Business Administration。如果学校成绩单没有写明所获学位，在读证明这个时候就可以派上用场。

English Test Scores (TOEFL, IELTS)

Applicants must achieve the following scores to qualify for full admission. Provisional admission is not an option for MS students. For the TOEFL, applicants must score at least 100. In addition, on the individual sections applicants must score at least:

Reading: 26

Listening: 24

Writing: 24

Speaking: 22

Applicants who take the IELTS must score a minimum of 7.0. In addition to the individual sections, applicant must score at least:

Reading: 7.0

Listening: 7.0

Writing: 7.0

Speaking: 6.5

这里学校对于 TOEFL 考试每个单项规定了最低要求。

Financial Resources

International applicants applying for an F-1 visa must submit the Certification of Finance Form and supporting financial documents at the time of application. Applicants to the supply chain management program must show $74,500 in available funds.

马里兰大学地处新英格兰地区的核心位置，临近首都华盛顿特区，商学院项目费用较为昂贵，在申请时学生必须出示相应数目的存款证明。这个存款证明的开具是很简单的，但必须把签证的时间也考虑进去，大家在申请时要和辅导老师仔细商量清楚。

Immigration

Immigrants need to copy both sides of their Alien Registration cards while non-immigrants need to provide copies of both sides of their I-94 form and a copy of the most recent visa stamp in their passports.

F-1 visa holders are also required to copy both sides of their I-20 form. J-1 visa holders are also required to copy both sides of the original and most recent IAP-66 form. To enter the United States most foreign students will need a passport from their government and a visa from the U.S. Consulate. To apply for a visa, the student must provide evidence of a minimum of 48 graduate unit hours, or the equivalent of a full course of study. The accompanying spouse or child of an F-1 student enters the U.S. on an F-2 visa, which does not permit employment of any kind. Another commonly granted visa is the Exchange Visitor visa (J-1), generally for students sponsored by agencies, foundations, or their home governments. It is granted only with the presentation of a Certificate of Eligibility Form (IAP-66). The accompanying spouse or child enters the U.S. on a J-2 visa, which may in some circumstances permit employment with approval from the U.S.

For further information, please refer to U.S. Citizenship and Immigration Services or U.S. Department of State. U.S. Immigration and Naturalization Service. It is important to note that, in many cases, an Exchange Visitor must leave the U.S. at the conclusion of the program, may not change visa status, and may not be eligible for any other visa until a two-year home country residency has been completed.

这里说明一下 F-1/2 与 J-1/2 签证的问题。首先我们中国学生去美国，大部分使用的是 F-1 学生签证，F-2 为学生的配偶到美国陪读的签证，而 J-1 签证是给予访问学者的，一般区别 F 与 J 类签证的标准有两个：（1）F 类学生会拿到学校授予的学位，而 J 类一般不会拿到学位；（2）F 类签证的学生要么自己付学费与生活费，要么拿学校的奖学金，而 J 类签证是基金会或国家出资负担该学生的生活费与学费。注意 F2 类签证是不能在美国工作的。

○ 班级构成

The admissions committee carefully considers every component of the application file. Previous academic performance, substantive letters of recommendation, clear career goals, and strong standardized test scores are among the criteria considered.

A competitive applicant will possess the following:

GMAT score in the mid 600's or higher

GRE scores in the mid 600's or higher on each section

Undergraduate grade point average of 3.3 and higher (of a 4.0 scale)

TOEFL score of at least 100 (must meet minimum requirements for unconditional admission as stated by the university)

这里学校提示具备基本竞争力的申请人应有的考试成绩。GMAT 成绩按照我们的经验，中国学生应达到 660 分以上才有竞争力，而托福成绩则必须在 100 分以上，否则很难进入录取委员会文书审理环节。

○ 核心课程

MS in Business: Supply Chain Management—Curriculum: Program Format

The Smith MS in Business: Supply Chain Management is designed for full-time students but is also available to those wishing to take fewer credit hours per semester on a part-time basis. Classes will have afternoon and evening options. This is a cohort-based, lock-step program requiring 30 credits for graduation. Full-time students may complete the program in one academic year; part-time students in 21 months. Classes are held at the University of Maryland's College Park campus, a short distance from Washington D.C., Baltimore, and northern Virginia—a great place to live, work and make lasting connections in industry.

项目课程为 30 学分左右，一个学年完成，即两到三个学期（包含暑期课程）。

Required Course descriptions

USI 672 Global Supply Chain Management (2 Credits) 全球供应链管理

Offers a practical blueprint for understanding, building, implementing, and sustaining supply chains in today's rapidly changing global supply chain environment. Provides a survey of the evolution of supply chain strategies, business models and technologies; current best practices in demand and supply management; and methodologies for conducting supply chain-wide diagnostic assessments and formulating process improvement plans.

BUSI 634 Operations Management (2 Credits) 运营管理

Concerned with efficient and effective design and operation of business processes for delivering products and/or services. Emphasis is given to process analysis and design, capacity management and bottlenecks, waiting lines and the impact of uncertainty in process performance, quality management, lean, six-sigma, and revenue management.

BULM 744 Global Supply Chain Risk Management (3 Credits) 全球供应链风险管理

Explores methods to build enterprise resilience from the perspectives of the supply chain planner and supply chain manager. Addresses concerns assessing strategic and operational risks, day to day uncertainties in demand and supply, and ensuring business continuity after low probability but high impact events such as a terrorist attack or earthquake.

BULM XXX Negotiations in Supply Chain Management (2 Credits) 供应链管理中的谈判问题

Develops strategies and tactics for negotiating with suppliers and customers. Course uses simulations, role playing, and game playing to outline strategies and tactics. Special emphasis is given to cross-cultural negotiations.

BULM 733 Global Trade Logistics (2 Credits) 国际贸易物流

Acquaints students with managerial issues in international logistics and transportation, and provides students with an understanding of issues related to import/export management and the global marketplace.

BULM 742 Global Supply Chain Resources Planning (3 Credits) 国际物流资源优化

Provides an understanding of how firms use an advanced supply chain planning (ASCP) application as an integral part of their materials management process which includes such activities as production planning, materials requirements planning, and distribution requirements planning.

BULM XXX Executives in Supply Chain Management (3 Credits) 国际物流的管理层

Designed to provide students intensive interaction with senior supply chain executives from a cross-section of industries. Executives share their insights on leading competitive supply chains in the global marketplace, while students research the competitive supply chain dynamics of each executive's industry.

BULM 730 Transportation Management (3 Credits) 交通管理

An overview of the transportation field with an emphasis on freight movements from the perspective of both providers of capacity and users of freight services. Examines the characteristics of the freight modes and the role of each mode as a major component of logistics and supply chain management.

BUSI 683 Global Economic Environment (2 Credits) 全球经贸环境

Relationship between national and international economic environments. Determinants of output, interest rates, prices and exchange rates. Analysis of effect of economic policies (fiscal, monetary, trade, tax) on the firm, on supply chains, and on the economy.

BULM XXX Purchasing Management (2 Credits) 采购环节管理

Examines purchasing strategies from both a tactical and strategic viewpoint. Special emphasis is placed on developing purchasing strategies from international suppliers and the trade-offs between outsourcing and insourcing.

BULM XXX The Green Supply Chain (2 Credits) 环保物流与供应链

Analyzes the environmental impacts across supply chains. Discussions will center around the costs and benefits from reducing environmental impacts through supply chain management.

<u>Choose from one of the following two options below</u>: 以下两门课程选择一门

BULM XXX Capstone Learning Projects 单独学习计划
Supply Chain Strategy (4 Credits) 供应链策略
Students are required to undertake an assessment of the supply chain strategy of a firm. The major requirement is a documented report analyzing the various aspects of the firm's supply chain strategy, strengths and weaknesses, and recommendation for improvement.

International Study Trip (4 Credits) 国际交流与学习旅行

Students will travel to an international destination in order to deepen their understanding of global supply chains. Destinations will vary from year to year. Major requirement will be a written report on the supply chain operations of the foreign country using specific examples from the field trip.

○ 截止日期

We are now accepting applications for the fall 2011 cohort. Please note that the acceptance process will begin with the first application deadline date and continue until the cohort reaches its maximum limit as determined by the Smith School of Business.

Application Deadline	Decision Mailing Date
December 1, 2010	March 1, 2011
February 15, 2011	April 15, 2011
April 1, 2011	June 1, 2011

马里兰大学只录取秋季入学的学生，截止日期分三轮。

2. Case Western Reserve University 凯斯西储大学 MSM-OR/SC

链接：http://weatherhead.case.edu/degrees/msm-operations-research-supply-chain/

○ 学校基本概况

凯斯西储大学是俄亥俄州第一学府，也是一所在美国居于领先地位的私立研究大学。它于 1967 年正式成立，由凯斯理工学院和西储两所学校合并而成。该大学的图书馆拥有藏书将近 190 万册并且可以通过网络查询。该校有十几位校友和教师获得过诺贝尔奖。在全美拥有良好声誉，吸引了来自世界各地的许多优秀学子。

凯斯西储大学拥有 3 700 名本科学生，其余为研究生和专科学生。教员职工 2 400 人。该大学本科院系设置如下：艺术与科学学院、大众传播学院、国际关系学院、商学院、工程与应用科学学院、公共健康和健康服务学院。研究生院系设置如下：牙科医药学院、凯斯工程学院、法学院、魏德海管理学院、药学院、波尔顿护士学院、孟德尔社会应用科学院、研究学院。

○ 院系介绍和专业优势

The Master of Science in Management-Operations Research and Supply Chain Management (MSM-OR/SC) degree is designed for individuals with quantitative training who seek to obtain a position in operations management or a management position in manufacturing, service, or consulting firms that are part of sophisticated national or global supply chains.

At Weatherhead, small class sizes mean one-on-one interaction with academic pioneers and industry leaders. Our faculty excel in teaching as well as research, and the opportunity to share their insights and excitement in the most up-to-date and creative areas of management studies is one that Weatherhead students prize. The diversity of our student body, too, enriches the graduate experience with points of view from countries and cultures around the world. Because students tend to learn from one another as much as from teachers, teamwork is a prominent feature of many classes; Weatherhead students form friendships within and outside of the classroom.

The MSM-OR/SC curriculum provides students with the fundamentals of business as well as depth and focus in the principles and concepts of operations and supply chain management. This unique program produces highly knowledgeable professionals well prepared to make organizations more efficient and competitive.

凯斯西储大学是一所理工科研究很强的大学，在了解学校和做专业调查时必须明确这方面的情况。这个项目虽然名称上叫管理科学硕士，但偏重的是以理工科能力为基础的运营管理与供应链研究。换句话说，成功的申请人或项目的毕业生，必须在数学与统计方面有较为扎实的基础与准备，因为项目的教学方式与内容和别的物流项目有很大不同，凯斯西储更注重与培养学生对物流过程和运营的数学解释与原理分析。至于商业管理方面的基础课程，项目中会有涉及，但不会非常深入地学习，因此不是一个特别有管理学色彩的项目。

这个项目对于申请者的数学课程作了要求，必须学过至少一学期的线性代数，最好有微积分方面的基本了解，包括微分方程等内容的学习。

○ 班级构成

The MSM-OR/SC degree attracts individuals with a quantitative undergraduate degree who have an interest in gaining expertise in the field of operations research or supply chain management. Typical undergraduate majors include:

Engineering 工程
Statistics 统计
Computer science 计算机
Economics 经济学
Mathematics 数学
Business 商科

Students beginning this program must have a working knowledge of undergraduate calculus, including differentiation and integration, and one semester of undergraduate linear algebra. Work experience is beneficial but not required for admission; many students pursue the MSM-OR/SC immediately following the completion of their undergraduate degree.

Upon completion of the MSM-OR/SC program, students will:

Be equipped with analytical and supply chain skills to become an agent of positive change at their organization within the first few years of work. Speak and understand the language of business. Have a working knowledge of all functional areas of an organization and the ability to communicate effectively with colleagues in these areas.

Have a network of regional, national, and international business contacts.

从班级构成上看，学校偏向于本科修过工程、计算机与统计课程或专业的学生，其中单纯学过经济学与商科的学生不占主力。

○ 申请必备条件和材料

Required Application Materials
（1）Transcripts 大学成绩单
（2）Standardized test scores GMAT(code WTJ-F1-10) or GRE(code 1105-02) 标准考试
（3）An English proficiency exam score for non-native English speakers 托福
（4）Two essays 两份申请文书
（5）Current resume 简历
（6）Two letters of recommendation 至少两封推荐信
（7）Application fee: $100 申请费用
（8）Prerequisites 条件

An undergraduate degree from an accredited institution
Undergraduate calculus that includes single and multivariate differentiation and integration. One semester of undergraduate linear algebra.

申请文书的要求没写明白，应该是两封推荐信、三份申请文书以及申请人自己学过多元微积分的证明与描述。

○ 截止日期

Applicants are considered in several application rounds throughout the year.（以 2011 年为例）

	Application	Notification
第一轮	November 1, 2010	March 1, 2011
第二轮	January 8, 2011	March 1, 2011
第三轮	March 1, 2011	April 22, 2011
第四轮	April 15, 2011	May 22, 2011
第五轮	July 1, 2011 (International:May 1)	Varies

○ 费用与奖学金

Enrollment in the MSM-OR/SC for Fall 2011 is $16,000 per semester.

For courses beyond those defined in the program, the cost is $1,771 per credit hour. Tuition rates are subject to change.

Scholarships 奖学金

Applicants to the MSM-OR/SC program may request that they be considered for merit-based scholarships. Materials beyond the standard application are not required for consideration. Scholarships are based on academic and professional qualifications and are not need-based. Scholarship recipients are informed of the award in their admission letter. Candidates are encouraged to apply early for maximum scholarship availability.

从费用上讲，这个项目共需 39 学分完成，一般的中国学生会在三个学期内完成，按照每个学期 16 000 美元计算，大致需要总共 45 000 美元的学费，超出 39 学分以外的选修课学分另外计算。

Financial Aid 助学金和其他

Application for need-based financial aid is a separate process from application for program admission. These funding opportunities are administered by Case Western Reserve University's Office of Financial Aid and are available for domestic applicants only. The 39-credit hour MSM-OR/SC is a three-semester, full-time program beginning in the Fall Semester of each year. The curriculum comprises the following three components:

学校一般比较慷慨，以往我辅导的学生大部分申请到不同数额的奖学金及助学金。

○ 核心课程

Business Core (9 credits) 商业管理基础（9 学分）

The Business Core introduces students to business fundamentals and includes a professional development course, a unique feature of the Weatherhead MSM-OR/SC not found in most of our competitors' programs.

- Financial Management for Supply Chain 供应链金融管理
- Market Space Management 市场份额与空间
- Professional Development A & B 职业发展

Operations Research Core (12 credits) 运营管理研究（12 学分）

The Operations Research Core provides the mathematical, statistical, and computational skills needed by analysts in research and development groups in manufacturing and services companies and consulting firms.

- Optimization Modeling 最优化模型
- Probability, Statistics, and Forecasting 概率、统计与预测

- Integrated Problem Solving in Supply Chain Management 供应链管理问题的整合解决方案
- Stochastic Models 离散模型

Computer Simulations 计算模拟
- Supply Chain Courses (18 credits) 供应链（18 学分）

Supply chain courses build upon the business and quantitative foundation to provide advanced knowledge in operations and supply chain management.
- Operations Management 运营管理
- Six Sigma and Quality Management 六大指标研究与质量管理

Four elective courses 选修课
- Sustainable Operations 可持续运营
- Project Management 项目管理
- Enterprise Resource Planning in the Supply Chain 企业资源规划与供应链
- Supply Management in Supply Chain 供应链中的供应管理
- Supply Chain Logistics 供应链物流
- Simulating Real-World Operations Dilemmas: "The Beer Game" 实际案例模拟：啤酒游戏

If there's one interest that most students have in common, it's probably beer! So it will come as no surprise that a favorite logistics demonstration among students in Weatherhead's MSM-OR/SC program is known, quite simply, as "the Beer Game." This classroom activity is a theory constraints problem that teaches students how to get through a bottleneck—no pun intended—in production.

This popular exercise illustrates a basic production line snag. Take a given product that goes through four different processes during manufacture, and imagine that each process takes a different amount of time. One process finishes 30 units a day, another, 22 units a day, still another, 40 units a day.

Operations professor Daniel Solow, PhD, uses beer as the sample product when his classes conduct this experiment. Unfortunately, however, none is consumed in the process!

这里是一位教授以啤酒作为产品案例的物流流程分析。

STEM OPT Degree 研修科学学位的外国学生在美国实习

The MSM-OR/SC program qualifies as a STEM OPT degree (science, technology, engineering, or math), which allows international students in a technical field to apply for a 17-month extension to their OPT (optional practical training) period. This extension means that students could be eligible for up to two and a half years of work in the United States.

根据美国国会通过的最新法规，凡是学习科技、工程、数学等专业的外国学生，可以将在美毕业后实习期（OPT）申请延长至30个月的期限。凯斯西储大学的这个项目满足这一要求。

○ 职业发展与就业情况

Weatherhead students are encouraged to connect with the Career Management Office early on in their academic program to gain the most from the resources and services available. In addition to planning a variety of networking events, our office offers coaching, resume reviewing, mock interviews, and dress-for-success workshops.

Graduates of our MSM-OR/SC program are in great demand in the logistics, consulting, manufacturing, health care, banking, and insurance industries. Historically, students receive offers of employment shortly after (or even before) graduation.

The following firms and organizations have invested in Weatherhead MSM-OR/SC graduates: Accenture, Alcoa, American Greetings, Booz Allen Hamilton, BP Amoco, Capital One, Deloitte & Touche, Federal Reserve Banks, FedEx, First National Bank, Flight Options, General Electric, Goodyear Tire and Rubber Company, Hewlett-Packard, KeyCorp, Intuit, Lincoln Electric, McKinsey & Company, Penske Logistics Progressive Insurance, Transtar Industries, Inc., TRW Inc. ,Yucatan Foods.

凯斯西储大学的就业指导办公室工作比较积极，在组织校园春秋两季的面试与指导学生联系企业方面卓有成效。学生毕业后工作的单位可参考一下列表，主要集中在物流、咨询、生产、健康管理以及保险行业。除了本地的企业外，也可以从上面列表中看到一些大型跨国公司。我辅导的两个学生，一个在健康行业，另一个在银行金融服务部门找到了不错的工作。

3. University of Michigan—Ann Arbor (Ross): 密歇根大学安娜堡分校供应链管理硕士

链接：http://www.bus.umich.edu/Admissions/MSCM/Whyross.htm

○ 学校基本概况

密歇根大学由3所独立的大学分校组成，安娜堡分校（University of Michigan, Ann Arbor）于1817年建立，是密歇根大学最好的分校，在美国乃至世界范围内享有盛名，也是美国10佳综合性大学之一，被誉为"公立常春藤院校"和"公立大学的典范"。密歇根大学历史悠久，师资优良，学风纯正，声名远扬，特别是拥有全美最高的研究预算以及顶尖的文理学院、法学院、商学院、医学院以及工学院。它开设有1 500多门本科课程，几乎涵盖了所有的学科领域，是美国课程设置最丰富的大学之一。在美国国家研究委员会

（NRC，National Research Council) 对美国各大学研究生院 41 个学科的评估中，密歇根大学总分排名第三。多项调查表明，密歇根大学超过 70% 的专业排在全美前 10 名，是当之无愧的美国"学术重地"。

密歇根大学安娜堡分校有本科生将近 26 000 人，研究生大约 12 000 多人，教职员工6 238 人。该大学设有 19 个学院，分别为：法学院、文理学院、医学院、商学院、牙医学院、教育学院、工程学院、建筑与城市规划学院、艺术设计学院、拉克哈姆研究生院、信息与图书馆研究学院、音乐戏剧学院、自然资源学院、护理学院、药学院、运动学院、公共卫生学院、福特公共政策学院和社会工作学院。

❍ 院系介绍和专业优势

Supply chain management touches every function of global commerce: marketing, sourcing, manufacturing, logistics, inventory management, information technology, and customer relations. It's not simply a tactical function; it's a business function. It's about the people, processes, and technology that propel products through the global economy. Now more than ever, companies need innovative leaders with the vision and skill to manage the entire life cycle of goods and services. Business leaders view the supply chain as the central nervous system of the world economy. Companies are seeking leaders with backgrounds in engineering, economics, information science, systems analysis, and other fields who have the specialized knowledge to hit the ground running and solidify the company's long-term competitive advantage.

Students in the Ross School's Master of Supply Chain Management Program (MSCM) learn from our world-renowned faculty in operations and management science, as well as top-ranked researchers in all business disciplines. MSCM students are admitted to the Tauber Institute for Global Operations, a partnership between the Ross School and U-M's College of Engineering. In addition, students develop ties to industry through the MSCM Corporate Advisory Council, a consortium of senior executives and decision-makers for Fortune 100 and 500 companies. Upon graduation Ross alumni join a network of more than 40,000 business school graduates and half a million University of Michigan alumni around the world.

从美国工业与市场发展的规律来看，一般来说，五大湖区及东部地区学校的物流专业都比较有名，大家可以看一下学校排名列表的情况。密歇根大学是比较早将物流与市场营销结合起来教授课程的学校，这个项目在国际商务、存货管理及国际生产规范等几个领域也与物流专业研究有着相当好的结合。

物流专业的发展，已经到了这么一个阶段：商业理论只是基础，一名高级物流职业人士应对交通运输、工程管理、市场营销、消费心理学和信息系统都有深入的了解，从这个意义上讲，密歇根大学的物流项目最大的特点就是整合系统的研究与能力培养。这个项目之所以要求所有学生均成为 Tanber（拓伯国际运营研究中心）成员以及设立行业指导委员会来指导学生的实习、竞赛与就业，就是要让学生从一开始就以全球化及全行业（全流程）的视觉来对物流专业知识进行学习。

Action-based learning takes many forms in the Ross MSCM Program.

Tauber Institute for Global Operations. The Tauber Institute integrates the strengths of Ross with U-M's College of Engineering, in active partnership with industry, to create a new standard of education for operations, supply chain management, and global manufacturing professionals. All MSCM students are members of the institute and complete an enhanced curriculum that integrates business and engineering courses with leadership and team-building seminars.

拓伯国际运营研究中心与我国的社科院也有合作，这个研究中心是罗斯商学院与工程学院共同管理的，物流专业的学生通过它完成部分工程学、管理学以及领导力培养课程。这个中心的特点也是整个项目的特点：高度实用化。因而，无相关工作经验的学生就要注意了。以下是这个学校的几个课程特色。

1. Paid Summer Projects 实习项目

A paid, team-based summer project through the Tauber Institute provides real-world, in-company experience with one of the school's corporate partners. Student teams work with peers and faculty to deliver a multidisciplinary solution to a real business challenge facing the organization. Projects last 14 weeks and range from strategic analysis and supply chain audits to supply chain design issues and distribution challenges.

学校提供有工资的暑假实习项目，这是在物流专业学校中不多见的，也是最有价值的一个附加项目。

2. Leadership Development 领导力项目

MSCM students learn to lead globally diverse teams and build organizational cultures that foster innovation. This training begins through LeadershipAdvantage, an integral and required element of the MSCM Program. As part of the Tauber Institute, LeadershipAdvantage presents 16 intensive modules led by industry experts. These modules provide methodical and comprehensive preparation to maximize one's performance on the summer project and, subsequently, on launching a supply chain career.

领导力发展计划，由 16 个实际操作模块构成，旨在培养学生处理管理过程中的一些实际问题解决能力。

Personal Leadership Assessment During the first semester, students complete a personal leadership assessment that addresses both team leadership interaction and individual leadership characteristics critical to succeeding in the industry. The assessment gives an accurate appraisal of strengths and weaknesses and helps define one's leadership style.

3. Team-building Courses 团队协作能力培养计划

Two half-day, active-learning seminars are designed to develop communication, planning, and cooperation skills. Students are presented with incomplete data, ambiguous or contradictory goals, and diverse styles of communication and leadership. The experience helps develop a unified group more capable of engaging in challenging endeavors through positive teamwork.

Team Dynamics Training Throughout the year, guest lecturers lead interactive discussions on topics such as recognizing and adapting to different communication styles, assigning team roles and goal setting, managing conflict, decision-making, and the role of power, influence, and leadership in business.

这也包括团队组织沟通与决策能力培养计划。

MSCM Boot Camp, a rigorous introduction to the basic business disciplines: economics, finance, strategy, accounting, marketing, communications, organizational behavior, and statistics. Boot Camp covers 78 hours of class time spread across 26 modules. It takes place throughout the first term and provides MSCM students with the fundamental grounding in all business disciplines.

Tauber LeadershipAdvantage, a series of leadership and teamwork modules offered by the Tauber Institute for Global Operations. Content covers value stream mapping, driving system change, personal interviewing skills, negotiation, diagnostic interviewing, and Six Sigma.

Tauber Summer Project, a 14-week, paid consulting project sponsored by a firm seeking to resolve an organizational challenge. Projects range from strategic analysis and supply chain audits to supply chain design issues and distribution challenges.

由于包含了带薪的暑假实习项目及众多商业领导力与团队协作培养计划，密歇根大学的物流项目从每年 1 月即春季入学，项目需要大约 30~32 学分才能毕业。Boot Camp 即训练营之意，不同于一般学校开学前的 Orientation(熟悉过程)，这个训练营会训练学生掌握基本的商业技巧，大约耗时 78 小时。拓伯领导力项目与暑期计划也是这个训练营发展而来的两大特色项目。

班级构成

Undergraduate Majors	Business	22.2%
	Economics	11.1%
	Engineering	44.4%
	Liberal Arts & Science	22.2%
Full-time Work Experience	Average 5 years	
	Range < 1.5~11 years	
Average Age	29 years	
Women	33.3%	

续前表

Undergraduate Majors	Business	22.2%
Citizenship Distribution	International	45.5%
	Domestic	55.5%
GPA: Average	3.24/4.0	
GMAT Score	Average	668
	80% Range	640~710
GRE Average	1294	
Class Size	18	

　　从班级构成上看，基本可以确定，没有工作经验或相关理工背景的学生会在申请罗斯商学院这个项目时遇到更仔细的审核。班级学生平均年龄指示了最佳的申请人背景应该是在工程或物流行业待上超过 3 年时间，或有相当长度（超过 6 个月）的实习经历。

　　对于中国学生来说，入学要求的 GMAT 成绩为 700 分左右，GRE 则为 1 300 分，每年接近 20 人的班级中，大约一半学生来自工程类专业，剩下一半为商科专业和经济类专业。这里，我们对 Liberal Arts 的解读不是一般的人类学或社会学等偏文科的专业。

○ 核心课程

Select a title below for a detailed course description of these required components of the MSCM curriculum.

1. Manufacturing and Supply Operations—OMS 605　生产与供应运营 3 credits

This course covers the basic concepts and techniques of operations and inventory management. The foundation of the course is a system of manufacturing laws collectively known as factory physics. These laws relate in a consistent manner various measures of operational performance such as throughput, cycle time, work-in-process, customer service, variability, and quality, and provide a framework for evaluating and improving operations.

2. Supply Chain Analytics—OMS 618　供应链分析 3 credits

This course introduces students to decision support models that are most frequently used in logistics and supply chain applications. Specific topics include: the role of decision support tools in dealing with a spectrum of logistical problems, effective communication of suggested solutions, specific models and techniques, including: DC location and network design, optimizing inventory levels in distribution network, computation of transfer prices, revenue management, yield management, estimation of product and customer costs, aggregate planning and resource allocation decisions, product changes/economies of scale, integrating supply chain and demand management (benefits and costs of delayed differentiation, mass customizations).

3. Logistics—OMS 621 物流学 2.25 credits

Logistics refers to the planning, implementation, and control of the efficient forward and reverse flow and storage of goods, services, and information between the point of origin and point of consumption in order to meet consumer demand. Primary topics include the management of facilities, warehousing, transportation, and management and design of integrated logistics networks. Other topics with ancillary coverage include technology in logistics, third-party logistics, international logistics, and revenue management.

Instruction will be by a combination of lectures, case studies, and numerical assignments. Students also will run computer simulations of a logistics system. The aim is to train students to perform and manage logistical functions within an organization, as well as assess and design the overall logistics strategy of the organization.

4. Strategic Sourcing and Procurement Management—OMS 624 战略生产配置与购买管理 2.25 credits

This course will focus on the important topic of strategic sourcing and purchasing management. Topics will include: make or buy (outsourcing), supplier selection, supplier relationships, supplier performance evaluation strategic cost management, product design and sourcing strategy, e-sourcing (auctions vs.relationships) negotiation, global sourcing, compliance issues

5. Project Management—OMS 616 项目管理学 1.5 credits

This course focuses on strategies and tools useful in management of nonrepetitive business activities. Examples of such activities include construction, new product development and market introduction, consulting engagements, and organization restructurings. Tools to be introduced include work breakdown structure, network representation, PERT/CPM models and analysis, Gantt charts, time and cost models, PM software, and probabilistic analysis. Strategy considerations covered will include dealing with uncertainty, resource constraints, dealing with shared and requested versus dedicated and commanded resources, milestone management, and project portfolio and knowledge management.

6. Supply Chain Management—OMS 620 供应链管理 3 credits

This is a comprehensive course covering a broad range of topics in the management of supply chains. Content emphasizes managerial issues and challenges as opposed to technical aspects. Topics include: strategy and role of supply chain, inventory management in efficient supply chains, challenges in managing responsive supply chains, management of transportation and distribution, role of network design, supply chain performance measurement supply chain coordination, incentive issues, role of technology, e-business models.

7. Information Technology in Supply Chain and Logistics—OMS 623 供应链与物流中的信息科技 1.5 credits

Information technology plays an increasingly important role in business. This course will explore IT's role in supply chain and logistics functions. Topics will include: supply chain digitization and business innovation, supply chain strategy and IT choice, MRP and ERP (evolution and implementation issues), supplier relationship management, customer relationship management, role of IT in transportation and warehousing/distribution decision support systems, emerging technologies and supply chain visibility.

8. Topics in Global Operations—OMS 701 国际运营相关研究 3 credits

This course is part of the Tauber Institute. Designed as a series of modules that present various aspects of global operations, this class is taught by a Tauber co-director and 12 College of Engineering and Ross faculty members. Topics range from such traditional operations issues as lean manufacturing and design for manufacturability, to such less-mainstream topics as ethical, legal, and environmental considerations in operations. Emphasis has been placed on engaging all Tauber students, from all participating programs and levels of experience, and drawing on their diversity to fuel discussion.

9. (Special) Topics in Supply Chain Management 供应链管理特别课题 1.5 credits

This course covers a wide range of topics of current interest in supply chain management. Each of six class units (two class meetings each) will focus on a particular industry, a particular issue in the industry, and a region that the industry/issue nexus highlights. Students explore supply chain challenges unique to an industry vertical, and focus on specific topical issues in that vertical, rooted in the context of a specific region of the world. Thus students learn how supply chain challenges are affected by industry vertical, topical issues, and geography. Class will be conducted as a seminar, with student groups preparing case studies, presenting to the class, and managing discussions in a portion of each class meeting. A required group project allows students to explore at greater depth an industry/issue/region of their own choosing.

10. Manufacturing Strategies—IOE 425 生产战略 2 credits

In this course, students review the philosophies, systems, and practices utilized by world-class manufacturers to meet current manufacturing challenges, focusing on lean production in the automotive industry, including material flow, plant-floor quality assurance, job design, and management practices. Students tour plants to analyze the extent and potential of the philosophies.

○ 申请必备条件和材料要求

1. Academic Experience 学术背景

（1）Admission to the Ross MSCM Program is open to graduates of accredited colleges and universities who have degrees in virtually any area of study. Previous coursework in engineering, science, and mathematics is important but not essential. Before enrolling, students must:Complete the equivalent of a four-year U.S. bachelor's degree. The Ross School reserves the right to review the academic records of international applicants and to determine whether the academic credentials presented from a non-U.S. institution qualify for consideration. 大学四年本科学位

（2）Take the Graduate Management Admission Test (GMAT) or the Graduate Record Examination (GRE). International students must also take the Test of English as a Foreign Language (TOEFL) or International English Language Testing System (IELTS) exam if their first language is not English.

学校接受雅思成绩，对 GRE 与 GMAT 成绩没有偏好。

（3）Work Experience

We do not require a minimum number of years work experience prior to entering the MSCM Program. However, we do expect that most of our admitted students will have at least some work experience. We evaluate work experience not in terms of quantity but in terms of quality, i.e., the impact the applicant has had on their organization and his or her natural leadership qualities. Those who join us at an earlier stage in their careers should have superb academic credentials and the maturity and self-confidence to handle the intensity of the program.

学校对工作经验不设最低年限，但期望有经验的申请人来就读这个专业。

To best assess each candidate's qualifications, we require the following materials with each application.

（4）Current resume 简历

（5）Two letters of recommendation 至少两封推荐信

（6）Essays 四份申请文书

Each element of the application plays an integral role in the overall admission evaluation; no single piece of the application is weighted more heavily than the other. The MSCM Program will contact qualified applicants to schedule an interview.

这里稍微总结一下罗斯商学院物流项目对标准考试分数的基本要求。从我辅导的学生的经历来看，如果是 GRE 考试的成绩，不可能低于 1 300 分的总分，而且数学部分有严格的分数要求，低于 730 分基本不可能进入下一轮。另外，GMAT 考试分数从班级构成来看，80% 的学生的分数在 650~750 分之间，也就意味着对中国内地学生的分数要求不会低于 700 分，原因很简单，中国学生的 GMAT 分数这两年越来越高。那么学校对托福考试的要求呢？一般我建议达到的分数也不是很高，因为托福不是起决定作用的考试，iBT 有 100 分即可，这里学校对 GPA（本科成绩均分）也有要求，大部分即超过 80% 的学生的本科专业 GPA 超过 3.3 分（4 分制计算），那么中国学生也必须满足这个条件。

○ 截止日期

MSCM is a one-year program that begins each January.

Early application deadline is April 1. 早申请截止日

Standard application deadline is August 1. 标准申请截止日

Specifically, August 1, 2011（最后截止日）, is the standard application deadline for the MSCM class that begins in January 2012. Applications received after August 1, 2011 will be reviewed on a space-available basis. Admission is open to graduates of accredited colleges and universities who have degrees in virtually any area of study. Previous coursework in engineering, science, and mathematics is important but not essential. Interviews are scheduled by the MSCM Program Office and are by invitation only.

注意申请的截止日，一般根据经验，面试会在每轮截止后的两到三周内发出邀请。

○ 就业情况

The Ross MSCM Program positions students to assume leadership positions in supply chain management and operations. Supply chain professionals are in high demand, and MSCM graduates are working in locations as diverse as Chicago; San Jose, Calif.; Houston; Singapore; the Philippines; and Venezuela. They are impacting such industries as telecommunications, consulting, oil and gas, computers and electronics, automotive, logistics, transportation, and manufacturing.

Students of the MSCM Class of 2009 boast 100% placement in full-time positions and internships. Graduates from the Class of 2009 are working for companies such as: Booz & Co., BorgWarner Inc., Cisco Systems Inc., CNH America LLC Dell Inc., Intel Corp., Oracle Corp., Pacific Drilling Services Inc., Rightaway Delivery LLC Ryder Systems Inc., SCG Paper Public Co. Ltd., Schlumberger Ltd., Steelcase Inc., United Technologies Corp. The positions held within these companies include supply chain analysts, senior consultants, supply chain managers, directors, and vice presidents, as well as positions in leadership development rotational programs.

密歇根大学的物流专业连续三年（2008、2009、2010）毕业生的就业率均接近100%。还有一点值得注意的是，这个项目在亚洲地区的名声也非常响亮，对于希望在香港地区、新加坡、东南亚地区工作的学生，这是比较好的一点。毕业生刚出校门时在行业内的工作职位包括：物流行业分析员、商业咨询公司顾问、物流经理、生产企业高级顾问和战略管理部门分析员等。一般来说，初出茅庐的毕业生在物流行业也必须先从分析员做起，然后才是经理及总监。而在特定的公司内部工作，则有可能开始的时候却以物流/供应管理顾问的职位开展工作。从行业的分布上看，电子、医疗、贸易、咨询、海运及仓储、跨国商业公司等均包含在物流毕业生的就职范围内。

Ross MSCM graduates enjoy such success in the full-time job market because our program's unique design packs numerous opportunities for students to build their network and gain hands-on experience that complements their studies. Students also enjoy access to the Ross School's highly regarded Office of Career Development (OCD). Due to the unique nature of the MSCM Program, we offer pre-arrival career counseling in order to help students clarify goals. OCD consists of two staff groups—career counseling and recruiter relations—that provide such critical resources as: Individual counseling and workshops, self-assessment, job search strategy, self-directed search, resume writing, networking, interviewing skills, negotiating skills. Online databases, Recruiting events and corporate presentations, On-campus interviewing.

A distinct advantage of the Ross MSCM Program is the connection between students and industry leaders via the MSCM Corporate Advisory Council. Council members are actively engaged in program development, summer projects, and other student initiatives. These relationships position Ross MSCM graduates to make an immediate impact in industry once they graduate. A key benefit of the Ross MSCM Program is access to industry leaders through the MSCM Corporate Advisory Council. Council members work with MSCM Program administrators to center the curriculum on the fundamental skills companies need to address their supply chain issues.

密歇根大学的职业办公室与企业指导委员会共同指导学生在毕业找工作及面试时的众多事宜，企业指导委员会也会组织企业与校友来学校与毕业生见面，带薪暑期项目的含金量当然就体现在毕业的这个关键时刻；任何实际工作经历都会给求职者的简历加分。

管理学和商业学硕士
Master of Management Science, Master of Commerce

管理学专业的简单介绍

美国的部分商学院设置了商科的管理学专业硕士项目。这样的项目往往不像金融或会计那样专注于某一领域的研究和学习，而是将几乎所有主要的商科科目结合起来统一进行讲授。在下面我们举的例子里大家可以看到，有的管理学项目提供组合式的课程，也就是说，一门现代金融市场课，有可能是一位金融教授讲前面三节课，接着一位国际传媒教授讲后面两节课，然后是管理学老师讲下一堂课等等。这个专业颁发的学位名称一般叫管理学硕士（Master of Management Science），有的项目的名称起得比较中性，如商业学硕士（Master of Commerce）。

当然，我们知道，这一类的项目不是很多见，在我的另一本书美国 TOP 60 名校逐一点评中涉及的 60 个学校中，设立管理学的研究生商科项目屈指可数。而且，这些项目往往有三个很显著的特点：第一，不欢迎本科学习工商管理专业的学生申请，明令禁止拿到工商管理学士的学生申请；第二，往往对本科的学习成绩单需要进行第三方认证，也就是申请人必须额外支付一笔费用给某个学校指定的评估机构，对该申请人所就读的本科院校出具的成绩单进行逐个科目或整体认证；第三，申请的截止日期很早，审理的过程也和大部分商学院项目有显著的差别。

有的学生认为管理学项目比较看重工作经验，但是事实上大部分的管理学学士都没有工作经验，而且本科就读专业也五花八门。那么申请递交后，学校主要会喜欢什么样的申请人呢？可以这么说，管理学研究生项目喜欢招收本科就是偏经济、贸易、会计或统计等专业的学生，注意，每一年也会有少部分背景完全是工科的学生被录取。其次，有志于在行业研究、商业报道评论、咨询和战略管理等方向进行职业发展的学生比较受到青睐。这本身就是一个比较宽泛的交叉面很大的专业方向，所以，在申请的文书写作中既要明确自己的职业方向，又要说清楚自己的职业规划和这个管理学的项目非常匹配，不至于空洞无物。

近年有些学习外语专业的学生也在申请这个专业，但是最后结果都不是特别理想，我认为主要是本身对经济方面知识的准备就偏少，而且职业目标规划也很难勾勒出来，这也是大家在申请时需要格外注意的。

下面我根据学校的类别，挑选几个比较有代表性的管理学相关硕士项目进行说明，大致把它们的特点讲清楚。

张旭老师点评名校

1. Columbia University 哥伦比亚大学 MIA 项目

链接：http://sipa.columbia.edu/academics/degree_programs/mia/index.html

○ 学校基本概况

学校的介绍前面已有，请大家参考。

○ 院系介绍和专业优势

Master of International Affairs 国际关系研究硕士

The MIA curriculum has been designed to develop international affairs professionals who understand the increasingly complex issues that transcend national boundaries and who have the managerial skills to apply their knowledge to real world situations. The curriculum has core requirements that are similar to the core of all SIPA degree programs and characteristics, which are unique to the MIA.

As is appropriate for a curriculum that prepares students for globally-oriented careers, the MIA core focuses more on international issues than other SIPA programs, and requires students to demonstrate proficiency in a foreign language other than English. Building on SIPA's commitment to the practical application of knowledge, the MIA requires an internship that is usually performed during the summer after the first year of course work provides hands-on experience. Similarly, MIA students who enter SIPA from the Fall 2010 semester onwards (and all MPA students) are required to take a capstone workshop that present real-life assignments for teams of SIPA students working for diverse organizations in the public, private and non-profit sectors.

哥伦比亚大学的国际关系学院设立了几个硕士项目，其中国际关系硕士比较受关注，这个项目隶属于哥伦比亚大学国际关系学院 SIPA。SIPA 大楼邻近法学院，坐落在阿姆斯特丹大街上，我刚到学校的时候，博士生的办公室就在 SIPA 大楼里，地下室也有一个社会科学的图书馆。在平时上课的时候，政治学、东亚系、社会学、历史系与国际关系专业的学生在 SIPA 大楼里一起上课。

MIA 这个专业并不是纯粹意义上的国际政治研究，而是融合了国际金融、经济与贸易政策、公共关系、传媒与及区域文化研究的综合学位。由于每年申请金融学与会计学的学生很多，大家在寻找学校时往往会看到这个项目，也被这个项目的管理与金融部分所吸引。

MIA 这个项目的要求比较特别，下文我们会看到，除文书比较难写以外，学校对申请人的外语、数学能力与及实际操作（工作经历）尤其是国际化经验特别看重，这些因素都是我们在申请 MIA 项目时必须时刻关注的。

○ 核心课程

The curriculum of the MIA degree program is designed to provide students with qualitative and quantitative analytical skills and with the hands-on management skills required by leaders in the major fields of international affairs, combined with substantive knowledge of a policy concentration and demonstrated foreign language ability. The program of study requires 54 graduate points and four semesters of full-time enrollment. Dual degree students and students with advanced standing from prior graduate degrees may be able to reduce their period of study. See below under advanced standing for details.

MIA 课程由 54 学分组成，一般需要 4 个学期才能完成。

Total Credits: Minimum of 54 Credits. The core curriculum provides students with the knowledge and skills that any fast-track policy expert or manager is expected to bring to the table, whether in the public, private or non-profit sector. These core competencies include economic and political analysis, quantitative techniques and critical management skills.

Core Requirements		
	MIA | Point requirements	MPA | Point requirements
Politics 政治学	Conceptual Foundations of International Affairs and one course from a menu of courses on interstate relations国际关系理论基础	Politics of Policymaking Ⅰ and Politics of Policymaking Ⅱ 政策和政治分析
Economics (select one sequence, corresponding to your concentration below) 计量经济学	Economic Analysis Ⅰ and Ⅱ or Economics Ⅰ and Ⅱ 经济分析	
Statistics 统计学	Quantitative Analysis 数量分析	
Management (choose one) 管理学	Public Management or Nonprofit Management 公共管理和非营利组织管理	
Financial Management (choose one) 金融管理	Budgeting, Accounting or Economics of Finance 预算、会计或金融经济学	
Internship 实习	Required	
Workshop 研讨会	Required	Required
Foreign Language Proficiency 第二外语	Required	Not required

○ 申请必备条件和材料

Please note that instructions on this page are meant for applicants to our two-year full-time MIA, MPA and MPA in Development Practice programs. For details on our other degree programs.

（1）Admission to the School of International and Public Affairs is competitive, based in large part on academic excellence and professional focus. The applicant must have a bachelor's degree or evidence of equivalent preparation, as determined by the Director of Admissions. 四年制本科学位

（2）The core curriculum at SIPA includes required coursework in economics, statistics and financial management. The Admissions Committee is therefore quite interested in the quantitative aptitude of applicants to our program. This most typically includes coursework and/or professional experience related to mathematics, statistics and economics.

由于项目课程涉及统计、经济学与金融管理，哥伦比亚大学表示比较偏向于有数学与计量经济学方面背景的学生。

Also of note this can be quantitative experience as it pertains to areas such as science or engineering. While there are no specific course requirements to apply, most successful candidates have a record of success in courses such as:

1）Microeconomics

2）Macroeconomics

3）Math courses such as Linear Algebra, Pre-Calculus or Calculus

4）Statistics

这里进一步将四门基础课程列出: 宏观经济学、微观经济学、大学高等数学课程与统计。

For the Master of International Affairs (MIA), MPA in Development Practice and for MPA students that choose Economic and Political Development, as a concentration, proficiency in a second language is a graduation requirement. Applicants to these programs should therefore have at least an elementary understanding of a second language when applying. Proficiency is defined as being able to achieve a grade of "B" or better in an intermediate level Ⅱ language course.

这个规定针对母语是英语的申请人，要求掌握除了英语之外的第二门外语，在学习与水平考试上不能低于B这个级别。对于我们中国学生来说，除了中文是我们的母语，如能展示第三门语言的基础能力，则更占优势。

The average age of incoming students is approximately 27, with most applicants having had several years of relevant professional experience before deciding to return to school. A small percentage of students—those who have significant fieldwork or internship experience—apply directly from undergraduate institutions and represent about 8-10% of each year's incoming class. Applicants are encouraged to gain applicable work or internship experience, even if it means delaying graduate study for one year or more.

　　这一点要求尤为重要，在每年 SIPA 录取的班级中，平均年龄为 27 岁，平均工作年限为 2~3 年，当然，适合应届生的申请录取名额每年为 10% 左右，这些应届生也必须具备相关的实习经历，如大三上学期开始比较固定地每周有一定小时数的时间在相关的企业、组织或国际性机构工作与实习。对于这个要求，大部分中国学生很难，但有相当一部分学生的确具备这个条件。从我辅导的学生申请 SIPA 收到的反馈看，学校会对缺乏实习经历但各方面条件优秀的学生建议申请材料保留一年，第二年继续申请入学资格，所以，对于本科应届生来说，要仔细考虑 MIA 的这个特殊要求，对比其余几个哥伦比亚大学 SIPA 的硕士学位与辅导老师商量后再决定最后申请方向。

　　We strongly encourage all applicants to submit all of the required documents through the SIPA application Web site. 100% of the application process can be completed on line. All documents, including transcripts and test scores can be uploaded to the application Web site for admission consideration. We will use unofficial copies of transcripts and test scores for admission consideration. Candidates offered admission will later be required to supply official transcripts and test scores prior to enrollment.

　　SIPA utilizes an online application system that helps expedite the receipt and tracking of information. Applicants are able to track the receipt of letters of recommendation once the names of these individuals have been entered into the application system. We therefore recommend that applicants start an application and enter the names of these three individuals as soon as possible.

　　Please do note that the Admissions Committee only accepts documents that are specifically asked for in our instructions. As much as we would like to be able to read writing samples and other information you might wish to submit, our tight timeline and desire to treat every applicant fairly means that we will only put required documents in the file—all other documents will be discarded.

　　SIPA 的申请全部在线完成，包括申请表格、推荐信与成绩单提交，只有学生在被录取后才需要提交正式的大学成绩单与标准考试官方成绩单。学校也不接受超出要求范围内的其余材料，如 CD、录音或别的图文材料，这个要求可以说是非常严格。

　　（3）Personal statement—broken into three parts 文书题目

　　由于项目申请难度较大，也有代表性，这里我把 SIPA 的几个主要申请文书举例说明一下。

First Question (500 Word Maximum)

　　What distinct impact do you hope to have on the world in the future? Please be as clear as possible about your future goals, the policy/public service issue(s) you are passionate about, and your personal motivation(s). Be sure to include details regarding the features of SIPA that you believe are integral to helping you in your pursuits and what skills you need to develop to achieve a lasting impact.

　　500 字文书，题目为你希望对我们生活的世界产生怎么样的影响？请描述清楚你的目标，并加入你所要阐述的细节与经历。

Second Question/Topic (300 Word Maximum)

Please CHOOSE ONE of these options to write about—do not address both, pick one or the other.

1）Describe a policy issue that has impacted your life, either in a negative or positive way. If given the opportunity to amend the policy, what action would you take and why?

2）Describe a conversation or experience that challenged your beliefs or caused you to reevaluate your perspective on life.

二选一的300字文书，题目为：①描述对你的生活产生影响的一项政策或一个事件，正面或负面影响均可，如果你有机会改变这项政策或这个事件，你会怎么做？②描述改变你看法或挑战你已有思维的一次经历或谈话。

Third Question/Response (200 Word Maximum)

Please share any additional information about yourself that you believe would be of interest to the Admissions Committee. Please focus on information that is not already reflected in the other parts of your application or might not be clear in the information submitted.

选择性文书，题目为写一写任何你认为值得评审委员会考虑的事实或经历。

（4）Standard Résumé/CV 简历，注意学校有特别要求的格式

（5）Quantitative/Language Résumé/CV 数量化背景列表

（6）Test Scores: GRE or GMAT for all applicants (results must have been achieved within five years of applying) 标准考试成绩

（7）Three letters of recommendation: The names of the individuals you chose can be submitted on the application 三封推荐信

（8）Academic Transcripts 非官方成绩单

（9）Application fee—$85 申请费用

（10）Candidates may choose to submit an essay to be considered for candidacy in the SIPA International Fellows Program. This is not a requirement, it is an optional part of the admission application. If applicants wish to be considered, a 300 word essay will need to be uploaded as part of the admission application. This essay is separate from the personal statement topics above. Applicants interested in IFP consideration are asked to respond to the following: In 300 words or less, please explain your interest in the International Fellows Program.

有意申请国际研究员项目奖学金的学生，还必须写一篇300字左右的文书，阐述自己对SIPA这个项目的兴趣。

◯ 截止日期

Master of International Affairs (MIA) and Master of Public Administration (MPA) programs
• Fall Application Deadline: January 5th.
（1）Program in Economic Policy Management (PEPM) 经济政策管理项目

（2）Program in Environmental Science Policy (PESP) 环境科学政策项目

（3）Executive MPA Program (EMPA) 行政公共管理硕士项目

（4）PhD in Sustainable Development 可持续发展博士项目

○ 职业发展和前景

Students graduating with a Master of International Affairs (MIA) degree pursue careers as varied as the global world in which we live. Our most recent alums went to work with the Turkish Government, the Congressional Research Service, U.S. Department of State, the United Nations, the World Bank, McKinsey and Company, Deutsche Bank, ABC, Proctor and Gamble, The Conservation Fund, Open Society Institute, Population Services International, Japan Society, Community Counseling Service and Horn Relief in Africa, in addition to many other organizations. For more detailed information regarding alumni employment, see employment statistics under "Career Services."

EMPLOYMENT OVERVIEW 就业回顾		
Total Graduating	336	Percentage of Total Reporting
Total Reporting	268	100.0%
Employed/Further Study	226	84.3%
Not Seeking Employment	0	0.0%
Seeking Employment	42	15.7%

ALUMNI EMPLOYMENT BY SECTOR 校友回顾			
	Total Reporting	Percentage of Total Employed	Median Salary
Public Sector	56	24.8%	$55,000
Private Sector	103	45.6%	$82,000
Nonprofit Sector	50	22.1%	$46,000
Further Study	15	6.6%	

从我辅导的几个学生的就业情况来看，哥伦比亚大学 SIPA 的名声与优秀的课程设置均带给他们很大的就业便利。在纽约地区，单是 SIPA 的校友会成员，比较活跃的就有3 000 多人。这些校友与 SIPA 紧密合作，对学生们的实习、指导、规划以及就业面试机会，都起到了无与伦比的作用。这几个学生也是依靠 SIPA 校友会的帮助，一个在香港的高盛公司代表处工作，一个在纽约中国银行代表处工作，另一个则在时代华纳实习三个月后到了德意志银行工作。这里学校也列举了一些相关的就业去向与就业数据，大家可以参考一下。

2. John Hopkins University: Real Estate Program 约翰·霍普金斯大学地产项目

http://carey.jhu.edu/our_programs/MS_Programs/full_time/FT_msre/

○ 学校基本概况

约翰·霍普金斯大学（简称霍普金斯大学）1876年创建，是一所著名的研究型私立大学。创办人是马里兰州的大银行家霍普金斯，学校因而得名。该大学的校区分为几块，主要校园在巴尔的摩市内。霍普金斯大学一直就强调卓越和优秀，是一所精英主义至上的学校。该校注重培养学生的分析能力，奖学金充裕，医学院科目设置齐全，历史上有33位校友和教研人员获得过诺贝尔奖。尽管是一所私立大学，但霍普金斯常年获得美国联邦政府的巨额科研拨款。根据美国自然科学基金会（NSF）的统计，霍普金斯大学在科学、医学和工程学的研究开支连续30年位列全球第一。其图书资料十分丰富，据统计，图书馆藏有图书300万册，订阅期刊2万多种。

霍普金斯大学现有在校生19 000人左右，其中本科生仅有4 744人，其余均为研究生。学校有涉及领域广泛的专业40个左右，主要的研究所和院系有医学院、公共卫生管理和公共保健学院、音乐学院、工程学院、物理及应用物理研究中心、卡内基文化研究中心、外国政策研究中心、人文研究中心、国际研究学院。绝大部分专业授予硕士和博士学位。

○ 院系介绍和专业优势

The Edward St. John Real Estate Program offers a full-time Accelerated Master of Science degree. Students acquire a comprehensive understanding of real estate investment, development, and management, with an emphasis on the necessity of smart, sustainable development. Students are trained both in theory and application as they are guided by a faculty composed of Johns Hopkins professors and of practitioners drawn from the region's leading investment, development, law, architectural, engineering, and planning firms. A supportive network of alumni and business professionals is available to students throughout their 12-month course of study.

霍普金斯大学不是传统意义上的商科学校，不像哥伦比亚大学或宾夕法尼亚大学。霍普金斯大学的地产与MBA项目均为近几年新开设的新项目。一经推出，这个项目就非常受欢迎。当然霍普金斯大学最牛气的是它的医学院与国际研究学院，尤其是国际研究学院，号称全美历史最悠久和最难攻读的学院，它的国际研究项目也包含了国际经济、金融与贸易政策的研究，与南京大学有合作项目。

地产项目时间为一年。注意，这包含暑假的实习时间，项目的侧重点在于培养有志于在地产行业发展的年轻职业人士，传授地产开发、地产管理与地产金融方面的最前沿知识与创新。地产项目在霍普金斯大学的主校区有班级，同时在巴尔的摩校区也开班。

During the summer, students participate in internships that provide hands-on experience.

暑期学生会参加实习项目。

The academic distinction of the university has made it a destination for students from across the globe since Johns Hopkins was established in 1876 as the first American research university. The University's faculty is as diverse in nationality as are our students, and includes hundreds of scholars from around the world. While more than 10 percent of all students enrolled at the University are citizens of nations other than the United States, the goal for enrollment of international students in the charter class of our Global MBA program is far higher.

这里讲明了学校的优势在于联合霍普金斯大学其余相关院系来对地产项目学生进行培养，当然由于这个项目的受欢迎程度，一般的班级只有 10% 是国际学生。

International perspectives permeate the course of study throughout the Real Estate program, starting with an orientation program that explores the mosaic of world cultures from a business perspective. Students examine how societies organize themselves, how they develop institutional structures, and how they define roles for such institutional bulwarks as government and the public sector, private enterprise, and the media.

这里说明的是项目的国际化视角与国际化培养角度。

○ 核心课程

The program is 36 credits. Students complete core courses in topics including: enterprise, analysis, law, building and design, finance, investments, and construction. An overview of the Johns Hopkins Carey Business School course schedule is available for viewing. Please note that the courses displayed are for planning purposes only, and information such as dates, times, locations, and instructors is subject to change.

	Title	Term	Location
BU.132.615 (81)	Land Use Regulation 地产法规	Fall 2010	巴尔的摩
BU.132.640 (51)	Legal Issues in Real Estate 地产相关法律问题	Fall 2010	华盛顿特区
BU.132.640 (I5)	Legal Issues in Real Estate 地产相关法律问题	Fall 2010	巴尔的摩
BU.132.640 (R0)	Legal Issues in Real Estate 地产相关法律问题	Fall 2010	巴尔的摩
BU.242.601 (51)	Real Estate Market Analysis 地产市场分析	Fall 2010	华盛顿特区
BU.242.601 (I5)	Real Estate Market Analysis 地产市场分析	Fall 2010	华盛顿特区
BU.242.701 (81)	Capital Markets & Real Estate 资本市场和地产业	Fall 2010	巴尔的摩

续前表

BU.242.701 (I8)	Capital Markets & Real Estate 资本市场和地产业	Fall 2010	未定
BU.242.720 (81)	Real Estate Risk & Opportunities 地产风险和机会	Fall 2010	巴尔的摩
BU.242.720 (I8)	Real Estate Risk & Opportunities 地产风险和机会	Fall 2010	华盛顿特区
BU.245.720 (R0)	Contemporary Topics in Real Estate: Development Modeling and Analysis 地产项目研究：发展模型和分析	Fall 2010	巴尔的摩
BU.767.715 (81)	Real Estate Law 地产法律	Fall 2010	巴尔的摩
BU.767.730 (51)	Market and Feasibility Analysis 市场和可行性分析	Fall 2010	华盛顿特区
BU.767.730 (81)	Market and Feasibility Analysis 市场和可行性分析	Fall 2010	巴尔的摩
BU.767.797 (51)	Real Estate Capital Markets 地产和资本市场	Fall 2010	华盛顿特区
BU.767.810 (52)	Practicum in Real Estate 地产实操项目	Fall 2010	华盛顿特区
BU.767.810 (81)	Practicum in Real Estate 地产实操项目	Fall 2010	巴尔的摩

　　地产项目总学分为 36 学分，大约需要两个学期完成，课程涵盖了法律、企业管理、金融分析、建筑与设计、投资管理等方面。

○ 申请必备条件和材料

　　When reviewing applications for admission:

　　（1）Official transcripts from all post-secondary institutions where 12 or more credits were earned. Applicants who hold degrees or who have earned credits from non-U.S. institutions must have their academic records evaluated course-by-course, by an authorized credential evaluation agency. If you have earned a degree from a non-U.S. institution, have your coursework evaluated by one of three authorized credential evaluation agencies. To evaluate your degree, receive an assessment of the overall grade point average and a course-by-course evaluation.

　　学校的这个要求比较麻烦，但也有可取之处，对于国际学生来说，申请霍普金斯大学的地产项目需要提交第三方机构认证过的成绩单。这个机构一般根据我的经验，就是 WES 公司。由于学校还要求逐门课程认证，这就很麻烦，当然，好处也很明显：经过 WES 评估的成绩单，GPA 往往会高一些。

（2）A resume, exhibiting:

Strong potential for success as a student, leader, and manager

Active community involvement

简历要求写明自己的学术、学生活动以及社区活动经历。

（3）An essay, demonstrating excellent communication skills and stating clear personal and professional goals. Specific requirements vary by program; details can be found on the online application. 申请文书

（4）Two letters of recommendation 两封推荐信

（5）GMAT scores—requirement varies by program. A waiver request form can be found on the online application. GMAT 成绩

（6）TOEFL or IELTS scores for non-native English speakers. A waiver request form can be found on the online application. Take the Test of English as a Foreign Language (TOEFL) or International English Language Testing System (IELTS). The preferred minimum TOEFL score is 600 (paper-based), 250 (computer-based), and 100 (Internet-based). The preferred minimum IELTS score is 7.0. Waivers from the TOEFL or IELTS may be granted if you have earned a degree from a college or university where English is the language of instruction. A waiver request form can be found at the online application. Individual programs may require additional evidence to demonstrate English language proficiency. The TOEFL code for the Johns Hopkins University Carey Business School is 0834, IELTS does not require a code.

学校接受雅思成绩，一般要求 7 分以上，托福分数为 100 分。

Please note: most documents can be uploaded through the online application.

All official documents that need to be mailed (including transcripts, credential evaluations, and official test scores) should be sent to:

这里要注意，容易混淆的是，虽然学校要求所有官方材料必须寄送到学校办公室，但由于国际学生的成绩单是经过 WES 或认证机构认证的，所以国际学生的大学成绩单由 WES 等认证机构直接寄送到学校。

（7）Application Essay

The Admissions Committee at the Carey Business School wants to understand if what students want out of a program coincides with what the curriculum has to offer. Applicants are encouraged to write a complete essay including information regarding the following:

1）What are my learning needs? What are the skills and competencies I want to develop?

2）What are my career goals? What does that look like short-term and long-term?

3）What outcomes am I expecting as a result of my graduate experience? What do I want this graduate program to enable me to do?

4）How will this graduate program enable me to meet the needs and goals I've identified?

学校对申请文书作了详尽的要求。

1）你的学习要求是什么？有什么技能与本领想在霍普金斯大学获得提升？

2）你的长期与短期的职业目标是什么？

3）在霍普金斯大学就读这个（地产）项目，你的目的是什么？想得到或学到什么？

4）这个项目为什么最适合我并最有利于实现我的目标？

○ 国际学生要求

We offer a wide range of flexible programs in business and management that allow you to attend classes full- or part-time. Classes are offered evenings and weekends and are scheduled at four locations throughout the Baltimore-Washington area.

学校提供全日制或非全日制的课程。

Due to the nature of our programs, you will need to register for classes at more than one campus if you are full-time student. We recommend that you have a car, since university transportation is not available between campuses, and public transportation is limited.

由于学生在巴尔的摩与华盛顿均要上课，学校建议学生能拥有一辆车，按照美国二手车市场价格，一辆普通的小汽车，大约 3 000 美元即可购得。注意看前面核心课程要求所开列的商科地址。

No financial aid is available at this time for international students. Please see the Loans and Scholarships section for information about scholarships available from private organizations to some international students.

学校不向国际学生发放奖学金。

As an international student, you are charged the same tuition rates as a US student. Costs for courses vary by program and location. Please see Tuition and Fees for specific information.

国际学生所交的学费与美加学生是一样的，根据学校信息，地产项目学费大约在 4.5 万~5 万美元/年。

As an F-1 student, you need to show proof that you can afford all tuition and living expenses for one academic year to receive an I-20. The current amounts are: In order to receive a student (F-1) visa, you must be fully admitted to a degree program well in advance of the start of the semester (read about our deadlines). Full-time status/full course of study is defined at the Carey Business School as enrolled in minimally 9 credits each fall and minimally 9 credits each spring semester for graduate study and minimally 12 credits each fall and minimally 12 credits each spring semester for undergraduate study.

这里是移民/签证的基本要求。根据美国移民规划局的规定，F-1 学生签证必须是在美国全日制学习或学位项目的学生才能获得。因而，非全日制学生拿不到 F-1 签证，即使学校录取了，也不太可能通过签证。那么什么样的学生才算是霍普金斯大学的全日制学生？必须是春季学期与秋季学期都修习超过或等于 9 个学分的学生。

We do not issue certificates of eligibility (Form I-20) for provisional acceptance to a degree program nor do we issue an I-20 for any of the certificate programs.

学校对于非全日制与证书项目的国际学生不予发放 I-20 表格，I-20 表即为 F-1 学生签证所必需的签证表格。

As an F-1 student enrolled in a full-course of study, you will complete your degree program within 2-3 years depending upon the program and other factors.

这里需要说明一下，一般学生在拿到录取通知书后，学校会发放 I-20 表格用于获得签证。如果一个硕士项目需要 36 学分，一年完成，则学校会在 I-20 上写明，允许学生在两年内完成。这个时间按惯例是需要完成学位时间的两倍。

○ 截止日期

Master of Science in Real Estate

(Accelerated Full-Time Program) 地产项目截止时间

Application rounds

Round 1	November 21, 2010
Round 2	January 16, 2011
Round 3	March 13, 2011
Round 4	May 15, 2011
Round 5	June 15, 2011

○ 就业情况和职业发展

We can assist you in securing candidates for internships and full-time positions, and help you achieve visibility at our campus locations throughout Maryland and Washington DC. To help you begin building your recruitment strategy with the Carey Business School, we have compiled quick links to help you get started.

由于这是一个较新的项目，这里学校没有给出具体的毕业生就业数据。根据我与学校项目办公室老师联系的情况来看，超过一半的学生在毕业时已经获得工作机会，基本的工作行业去向均与地产开发、设计、地产金融有紧密联系。

2. Tulane University: Master of Risk Management 杜兰大学风险管理硕士项目

http://www.freeman.tulane.edu/programs/mrisk/admission.php

○ 学校基本概况

杜兰大学建于 1834 年，是一所享誉全球的综合性私立大学，在美国享有"南部的哈佛"（Harvard of the South）之美誉。该大学位于美国南部路易斯安那州新奥尔良市的圣查尔斯大街，临近密西西比河，风景优美，离商业区只有15分钟的路程，到历史悠久的著名法国区，也只需要搭乘一小段市内电车。该大学规模不是很大，但是教学严谨，对学生要求严格，拥有包括诺贝尔奖得主及众多国际知名学者在内的1 000余名教研人员。99%的教研人员拥有各自从事的研究领域里的最高学位。该大学在US News 2006美国大学综合排名中居于第43名，US News 2007美国大学综合排名居于第44名。

杜兰大学的研究生专业设置如下：会计、西班牙语言文学、社会科学、心理学、物理学、自然科学、哲学、音乐、多学科研究、法律、拉丁美洲研究、EMBA、机械工程、数学、材料工程、管理科学、历史、临床医疗、有机化学、神经科学、经济学、英语语言文学、电子、电器、通讯、生态学、戏剧学、计算机、比较文学、土木工程、古典语言文学、细胞生物学、工商管理、生物医学工程、生物科学、艺术、艺术品鉴赏、动物遗传学、动物生理学、解剖学等。

○ 院系介绍和专业优势

Are you ready for the quantitative side of finance? Are you ready to help financial institutions, companies, and governments projects? Freeman's Master of Risk Management (MRISK) is a specialized program designed for those who are ready to focus and advance in this challenging area of finance. MRISK is an intensive full-time program with enrollment starting in December. The program includes coursework in finance, risk management, econometrics, and energy finance. The MRISK is an 11 month, 34 credit hour graduate program.

MRISK graduates are prepared to meet the demand of today's financial arena. They have mastered the analytical and practical tools necessary to manage financial risk in a modern, global environment. An important aspect of the program is that every graduate will have the opportunity to sit for Level 1 of the Financial Risk Management examination (FRM) offered by Global Association of Risk Professionals (GARP).

The Freeman Career Management Center works with you throughout the MRISK program to develop professional opportunities. Unique Freeman events like Freeman Days in New York, Houston, and New Orleans help you build networks within the larger financial markets.

弗里曼商学院是美国南部较为著名的商学院，学院的特色是创新与改革，商学院的很多项目都独领潮头，别具一格。这个风险管理硕士项目亦是如此，专门培养立志在企业风险管理行业工作的年轻人。风险管理是金融学中的一个分支，涉及数学分析、统计推测与数量模型等方面，不是一个定性研究的领域，确切说应该是定量研究与金融服务的结合。由于风险管理行业需要分析员或风险顾问参加三级的金融风险管理资格考试，弗里曼的这个项目可以帮助学生们通过课程的学习直接完成资格考试第一级的准备。

完成这个项目需要34学分，大约11个月完成，而且项目开课时间为12月份，与很多在9月份商学院硕士项目有很大差别，这也需要学生在申请这个学校的项目时格外注意。

○ 核心课程

MRISK Curriculum

Winter on-line session: 在线冬季课程

- Financial Management 金融管理

Foundation MRISK courses: 风险基础课程

- Financial Modeling 金融建模
- Fixed Income Analysis 固定收益分析
- Econometrics 计量经济学
- Investments 投资学

MRISK courses (18 credit hours):

- Risk Management Ⅰ 风险管理Ⅰ
- Risk Management Ⅱ 风险管理Ⅱ
- Options and other Derivative Securities 期权与其他金融衍生品
- Energy Fundamentals and Trading 石油交易及能源产品交易
- Energy Markets, Institutions, and Policy 能源市场、机构及政策
- Advanced Energy Trading and Finance 高级能源交易与金融

○ 申请必备条件和材料

We complete and review applications with unofficial transcript/s and self reported score reports; however, if admitted, official credentials must be submitted prior to enrollment. Please do not submit paper credentials to our office, all required application credentials can be uploaded or self reported in the online application. Score reports can be submitted to us directly, but all other credentials should be submitted via the online application system. A complete application is sent to the Admissions Committee for review after the below credentials have been received by our office.

与所有比较自信的商学院项目一样，弗里曼商学院的风险管理项目的申请流程很简单明了。对于所有的大学成绩单、研究生成绩单、GMAT 成绩与托福成绩这些很多学校需要原件寄送的材料，这个项目明确要求全部用扫描件上传，直到录取后学生才有必要提交官方正式文件。

- Online Application Form ($125 application fee) 在线申请表及申请费
- Resume (uploaded online) 简历
- Two Essays (uploaded online) 两份文书
- Two Letters of Recommendation (submitted online) 两封推荐信
- Undergraduate Transcript/s from Accredited University (uploaded online) 本科成绩单
- GMAT Report GMAT 成绩报告

- TOEFL/IELTS Report (international students) 托福或雅思
- Affidavit of Support (uploaded online, international students) 财产证明

The Freeman School looks for the following base line TOEFL scores: 600 (paper based); 250 (computer based); 100 (Internet based). We require a minimum of 7 on the IELTS. In order to be successful in this program your English language skills should be fluent.

Since international applicants are not eligible for financial aid or fellowships in this program, the Affidavit of Support must also be provided along with copies of supporting financial documentation.

对于国际学生，按照我辅导的学生的经验，一般需要提交不低于 7 分的雅思和至少 105 分的托福成绩。至于 GMAT 成绩，大部分申请的中国学生分数在 680~700 分上下。这里学校也要求在申请时即提交财产证明，以表明申请人有能力支付在校期间生活费与学费，学校一般不给予国际学生奖学金。

○ 截止日期

Please note, the Master of Risk Management program starts with an intensive on-line course in December. Classes start in January.

Submission Date	Decision Notification	Commitment Deadline	
Domestic 美国申请人	November 1	November 15	December 1
International 国际生	October 1	November 1	November 15

After November 1, domestic applications will be accepted on a space available basis. International applicants should apply no later than October 1 to ensure visa processing.

○ 就业情况

对我来说，弗里曼商学院的这个风险管理项目比较陌生，因为直到两年前才有我辅导的一个学生进入这个项目学习。根据这个学生反映的就业情况来看，首先，学校的职业辅导办公室工作不是很得力，很多活动没能组织好，但校友以及学校在南部各州尤其是邻近的得克萨斯州的名气都对找工作帮了很大的忙；其次，班上毕业的学生，有相当一部分学生找到了能源行业的工作，如美孚石油公司。也有一部分学生在专注于石油交易、能源产品市场研究、石油商品期货的金融公司工作。

在美国，有实力进行能源期货产品交易的公司多数和基金和私募合作，因此，最后这个学生找到的职位是一家基金公司的助理分析员。从风险管理的发展来看，这个行业不会涉及太多固定收益投资方面，而会向金融衍生品特别是房地产金融产品分析方面发展。现在，美国已经有几个商学院正在尝试开办房地产金融产品的风险评估课程与研讨会，也恰恰证明了这个专业将来的发展趋势。

会计硕士
Master of Science in Accounting,
Master of Accountancy (MAcc)

会计专业的简单介绍

关于会计专业的申请和文书，我们在"手把手"的第一本书里有过介绍。这里，我重点讲讲会计专业的几个核心问题。作为中国学生，我们到美国去学习会计，首先要了解清楚三大问题：美国会计专业学习什么，我们已经学习了什么或还需要学习什么和做什么来加强自己的申请背景，会计专业毕业后我们做什么性质的工作。注意，这些问题也是申请时学校文书要涉及的问题，所以必须在申请前就明确答案，并且和辅导老师确定方向和答案。

美国的会计专业分成两种：一种项目颁发理学的会计硕士学位即 Master of Science in Accounting，另一种直接颁发会计硕士学位（MAcc）。这两个学位的学习差别不大，关键在于，根据美国法律（具体到每个州都有不同），会计师获得从业资格考试认证以及开始执业，都必须首先具备一定数目的会计学分，这些学分又必须是经过美国会计师协会统一认证的。所以我们可以这么说，任何人都可以参加北美注册会计师考试并成为获得其认证的职业人士，只要这个申请人满足了所在州关于会计课程学习的要求。目前，大多数州对北美精算师考试没有这个学分的要求，同样，注册金融分析师考试也没有这个要求。我们在选择学校的时候，对颁发的学位可以不计较，但是所学的课程是否满足你要参加会计考试所在州的法律要求，如纽约州需要 200 小时，马萨诸塞州需要 250 小时等，就是你需要格外关注的。无论是 MSA 和 MAcc，学习的主要内容还是审计、报表和企业财务等课程。

在会计专业的录取时，很多学校对申请人之前的背景提出了要求，如必须上过某些核心课程。根据我的经验，其实归根结底就是主要的几门课，如管理会计、中级会计和审计、公司财务等。大部分国内院校的会计和财务专业都开设这样的课程，因此一位北京化工大学会计专业的学生，如何能在众多会计和经济类学生的申请材料中显得与众不同？我觉得首先还是专业课的学习，设计的会计基础课程是否齐全，分数表现是否优秀；其次就是作为一名准职业人士，这名申请人有没有积极参与别的会计相关的资格考试或认证，从而加强自己的背景，同理，这个申请人的实践和实习经历如何；再次，就是看申请人是否对不同的会计准则和会计理念有自己的看法和思考，这个可以通过论文、文章以及不同的文书来表现。

在美国，会计师工作是非常紧张和辛苦的，虽然四大会计师事务所和很多中型的本地事务所每年都会大量招收新人，但这些新人的薪酬水平只能处于职业人群中的中上地位，年薪平均 6 万~7 万美元。由于几个大的事务所招收的外国学生数量众多，在经济不景气的情况下，这些事务所往往会拒绝为中国学生提供 H1B 工作签证的担保。可以毫不夸张地说，一位会计毕业生的第一份工作往往都是和艰苦的费时费力的审计工作联系在一起的，大量的时间要花在处理报表和数字上，到客户处出差和蹲点也是很正常的事情。一个刚入行的会计师，在经过炼狱般的几年时间的锻炼之后，才能逐渐往市场、管理以及咨询这方面转移，或者出来自立门户，挂牌经营。

下面我们来看看几个样本学校，顺便讲讲申请时的一些重要注意事项。

金融工程专业院校名录

会计专业的硕士项目申请一般参考总体的会计排名，以下列出的项目有部分是只提供博士和 MBA 方向的课程，并没有 MAcc 或 MSA 项目。关于更加细化的 MAcc 列表，大家可以在哥伦比亚大学商学院和密歇根大学商学院的网页上找到连接，也请大家关注博创留学的网页更新。

1. University of Texas at Austin 得克萨斯大学奥斯汀分校
2. University of Pennsylvania 宾夕法尼亚大学
3. University of Chicago 芝加哥大学
4. University of Illinois Urbana Champaign 伊利诺伊大学香槟分校
5. University of Michigan Ann Arbor 密歇根大学安娜堡分校
6. Stanford University 斯坦福大学
7. Brigham Young University 杨百翰大学
8. University of Southern California 南加州大学
9. New York University 纽约大学
10. University of North Carolina at Chapel Hill 北卡罗来纳大学教堂山分校
11. Indiana University, Bloomington 印第安纳大学伯明顿分校
12. Columbia University 哥伦比亚大学
13. Northwestern University 西北大学
14. University of Notre Dame 圣母大学
15. Harvard University 哈佛大学
16. University of California Berkeley 加州大学伯克利分校
17. Duke University 杜克大学
18. Ohio State University 俄亥俄州立大学
19. University of Washington Seattle 华盛顿大学西雅图分校
20. Michigan State University 密歇根州立大学

21. University of Rochester 罗切斯特大学
22. Massachusetts Institute of Technology 麻省理工学院
23. University of Florida 佛罗里达大学
24. Cornell University 康奈尔大学
25. Arizona State University 亚利桑那州立大学
26. University of California Los Angeles 加州大学洛杉矶分校
27. The University of Iowa 爱荷华大学
28. Texas A&M University 得州农工大学
29. University of Georgia 佐治亚大学
30. University of Virginia 弗吉尼亚大学

张旭老师点评名校

1. George Washington University: Master of Accountancy 乔治·华盛顿大学会计硕士项目

http://www.gwu.edu/learn/graduateprofessional/findagraduateprogram/fulllistofprograms/
accountancy

○ 学校基本概况

乔治·华盛顿大学创建于 1821 年，主校区位于美国首都华盛顿特区市中心，是一所著名的私立综合性大学。该大学因为教育水平和其独特的教学特点而备受国内外学生青睐，成为全美最受欢迎的大学之一。乔治·华盛顿大学享有"最受欢迎的政治大学"的称号，它比邻国际货币基金组织、世界银行、国务院，距白宫只有几个街区。因为地理位置上的优越性，教授们常为政府出谋划策，使课堂教育不乏实际意义。学校还鼓励学生到政府机关、智囊团和咨询机构实习。

乔治·华盛顿大学有超过 10 000 名本科学生和 4 501 名教职员工。该大学设有 9 个学院：职业教育学院、哥伦比亚文理学院、Elliott 国际关系学院、法学院、教育与人类发展研究生院、商学院、工程与应用科学学院、医学院、公共卫生与健康服务学院。

○ 院系介绍和专业优势

GW's program, which may be pursued on a full-time or part-time basis, is tailored to individual interests and career objectives in accounting, financial management and tax practice. No business background is necessary prior to joining the program.

对于会计专业的学习，GWU 对原来的背景没有要求。但注意，中国学生不能申请非全日制学位。

In addition to required courses in accounting, finance, economics and statistics, students can choose from a wide range of specialized accounting subjects within the School of Business, as well as other business topics that help them prepare for their professional certification. Day and evening classes are available to accommodate working professionals, although prior work experience is not required.

The Master of Accountancy is a 30 ~ 37.5 credit program designed to prepare students for high-level professional careers in the public and private sectors. It is a flexible program tailored to individual interests and career objectives in accounting, financial management and tax practice. Students with a Bachelor of Science degree in Accounting from a US accredited university can complete the requirements in one year.

这个项目需要 30~37.5 学分，具备会计背景的学生一般可以在一年内完成。其余无专业课准备的学生，大约需要一年半完成。

○ 班级构成和录取历史记录

Average Age	25
Average GMAT	647
Countries Represented	USA, China, Korea, Turkey, Canada, Iran, South Africa, Netherland, Ghana
Male/Female	34/37
Domestic/International	42/29

从班级构成上看出，乔治·华盛顿大学对 GMAT 成绩的要求是比较高的。我辅导的学生在近两年都有被 GWU 录取的，GMAT 分数也是一路升高。从原先的 650 分一直到 740 分。这个班级大约有 80 人，据项目内我的学生反映，其中的国际学生占了大约一半。

○ 截止日期

Admission Deadlines:	Fall—May 15 Spring—November 15 Summer—March 15

一般来说，申请夏季项目的学生都无法安排合理的签证时间。

○ 录取必备条件和所需材料

Standardized test scores 标准考试	Either the Graduate Admissions Management Test (GMAT– institution code QK4-4F-04) or the Graduate Records Exam (GRE – institution code 5246) is required.
Recommendations required 推荐信	Two (2) recommendations
Prior academic records 成绩单	Transcripts required from all colleges and universities attended, whether or not credit was earned, the program was completed, or the credit appears as transfer credit on another transcript. Transcripts must be forwarded in their original sealed envelopes. If academic records are in a language other than English, a certified English language translation must be provided; translations alone will not be accepted.
Statement of purpose 个人陈述（两份文书）	In an essay limited to 500 words, discuss your long-term and short-term professional objectives and how your past experiences have contributed to and defined these objectives. Include in your statement why you want to pursue a graduate business degree at this point in time. You may also include your related qualifications, including collegiate, professional, and community activities, and any other substantial accomplishments not already mentioned in the application. You may explain any academic inconsistencies as part of your statement or as an addendum.
Additional requirements 简历	A current résumé is required.
International applicants only 国际学生要求	Please look carefully for details on required documents, earlier deadlines for applicants requiring an I-20 or DS-2019 from GW, and English language requirements. PLEASE NOTE that the minimum English language test scores required by this program are: Academic IETLS: an overall band score of 7.0 with no individual band score below 6.0; or TOEFL: 600 on paper-based, or 100 on Internet-based 学校接受雅思成绩，TOEFL分数100分以下就免谈了。 Prospective candidates for fellowships/assistantships must submit a completed application packet (including test scores) by January 15. Later applications will be considered if funds are still available. 奖学金申请在1月15日之前必须单独递交另一份申请，包括essay论文与表格。

○ 核心课程

The Master of Accountancy Program offers five paths as follows: A regular program consisting of 34.5~37.5 credits, a short program consisting of 30 credits available to students who have obtained a Bachelor of Science in Accounting from a US accredited university, or who have already passed the CPA examination, a short program consisting of 30 credits available to students who have obtained a Bachelor of Business Administration from an accredited US university, a five-year program for GW students who earn a bachelor of science in accounting in their fourth year and a five-year program for GW students who earn a bachelor of business administration in their fourth year.

对于已在美国大学念书、专业是会计的学生或通过 CPA 考试的学生，可以用 30 学分的课程获得这个会计硕士的学位。

The above paths require courses in accounting (minimum 15 credits), finance, economics and statistics. All the required courses can be waived out with or without substitution depending on previous academic performance. In addition to the required courses, students take between 6 and 10.5 of graduate elective credits from the school of business offerings which may include additional accounting courses.

Students who intend to take the CPA examination should be aware that the coursework required for admission to the examination varies from state to state. Students are advised to consult the Board of Accountancy for the state in which they plan to take the examination and choose electives that meet that state's requirements。

这个我们在前面讲过，各个州对参加 CPA 考试所需的会计学习时间要求不一样。

课程	学分	学期
Accy 6101 Financial Accounting Ⅰ 金融会计Ⅰ	1.5	F, S, Su
Accy 6102 Financial Accounting Ⅱ金融会计Ⅱ	1.5	F, S, Su
Accy 6103 Financial Reporting Standards 财务报表标准	3	F, S
Accy 6106 Financial Statement Analysis 财务报表分析	3	F, S, Su
Accy 6107 Financial and Tax Accounting for Corporate Combinations 金融与税务会计（企业整改合并）	3	S
Accy 6201 Managerial Accounting 管理会计	1.5	F, S
Accy 6202 Accounting and Control 会计学与内控	1.5	F, S
Accy 6301 Contemporary Auditing Theory 当代审计理论	3	F, S

续前表

课程	学分	学期
Accy 6302 Fraud Examination and Forensic Accounting 欺诈检验与实证会计	3	S
Accy 6401 Federal Income Taxation 联邦收入的课税	3	F, S
Accy 6402 Federal Income Taxation of Partnerships 合伙企业的联邦所得税	3	S
Accy 6403 Federal Income Taxation of Corporations 对公司企业收入的课税	3	F, S
Accy 6501 Accounting Information Systems & EDP 会计信息系统	3	F
Accy 6601 Business Law: Contracts, Torts and Property 商法：合同、侵权与财产	3	F, Su
Accy 6602 Business Law: Enterprise Organization 商法：企业组织	3	F, Su
Accy 6701 Government Accounting and Auditing 政府会计与审计	3	F, Su
Accy 6900 International Accounting 国际会计	1.5	S
Accy 6900 International Reporting and Control 国际会计报表与控制	1.5	S
Accy 6900 International Financial Reporting Standards 国际金融报表标准	1.5	S
Accy 6900 Controls, Alignment and the Organization 内控、统一与组织	1.5	F
Accy 6900 Management Accy: Gov and Not for Profit 管理会计：政府与非盈利组织	1.5	F, S
Accy 6900 Corporate Governance and Ethics 企业控制与道德	3	F
Accy 6900 Tax Accounting 税务会计	1.5	F
Accy 6900 Tax Research 税务研究	1.5	F
Accy 6900 International Taxation 国际税收	1.5	S
Accy 6900 Effective Business Presentations 商业演讲与表达方法	1.5	F, S
Accy 6900 Taxation of financial instruments 金融工具与税收	3	S

F = fall 秋

S = spring 春

Su = summer 夏

❏ 学校花费和奖学金

Master of Accountancy students are charged $1,175 per credit hour for tuition for the 2010-2011 academic year. The Student Association fee is $1 per credit hour, to a maximum of $15 per semester. The program is comprised of 36-37 credit hours.

会计专业每个学分的学费大约是 1 175 美元，36 学分大家可以估算一下。

$19,980.00	housing, meals, transportation, and personal expenses (full year)
$500.00	books and supplies (academic year)
$1,977.00	health insurance (full year)

2. University of North Carolina – Chapel Hill: Master of Accountancy 北卡罗来纳大学教堂山分校会计硕士

http://www.kenan-flagler.unc.edu/Programs/MAC/Oneyeardegree.cfm

❏ 学校基本概况

北卡罗来纳大学教堂山分校（University of North Carolina at Chapel Hill，简称 UNC）创办于 1789 年，是美国最早创立的公立大学之一。该大学是北卡罗来纳州大学系统最古老的教育机构，也是被列入公立常春藤的最初几所大学之一，还是北卡罗来纳州大学系统的旗舰机构。其国际名声、研究成就和教育水平都处于领先地位，被《美国新闻与世界报道》评为一级国家级大学，学术排名为全美第 16，被《纽约时报大学指南》给予五颗星最高的学术评分。除此之外，该大学的生源和师资都相当不错。校园有设施齐全的现代教学大楼、现代化器材的研究室、藏书丰富的图书馆、配套设施齐全的校舍、多样化的各色餐厅、标准的停车场、免费开放的体育馆及医院等。

UNC 在校学生约为 28 500 人，其中研究生有 10 500 多人。学校开设的学院有：文理学院、研究生院、Kenan-Flagler 商学院、牙医学院、教育学院、政府学院、法学院、药学院、公共健康学院、医学院、信息与图书馆科学学院、新闻与大众传媒学院、护理学院及社工学院。

❏ 院系介绍和专业优势

In only 1 year, May to May, the Program prepares you with the skills and credentials that make you highly marketable in the business world.

Both business and liberal arts graduates benefit from our program. You will develop your business, accounting, communication and leadership skills. The integrated setting prepares you to make an immediate contribution to the employer that hires you.

MAC students that graduate from UNC are recruited by prestigious employers. The 12-month program attracts top-notch students.

北卡罗来纳大学教堂山分校的会计研究生项目以严谨、全面与务实著称，也是比较难申请的一个项目。学校在录取时不考虑学生先前的工作经验。如果有 CPA 或会计经验为佳，但不强求。而且从班级构成上看，商科与社科专业为本科的学生占了 2/3 以上。

○ 班级构成和学校录取的历史记录

Averages for	
GMAT:	635
GPA:	3.38
Age:	24

A sampling of undergraduate majors in past years: Biology, Business & Management, Chemistry, Communications, Computer Science, Economics, Education, Engineering, English, Finance, History, Mathematics, Music, Political Science, Psychology, Public Health, Romance Languages, Social Science.

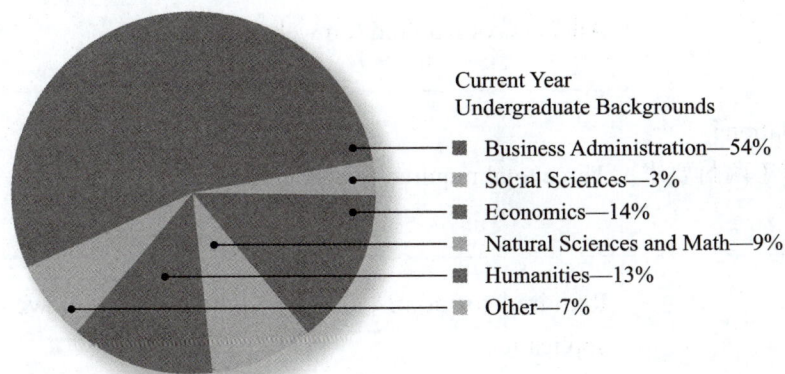

Current Year
Undergraduate Backgrounds
- Business Administration—54%
- Social Sciences—3%
- Economics—14%
- Natural Sciences and Math—9%
- Humanities—13%
- Other—7%

从班级的本科专业构成来看，商科背景的学生占了大多数，社会科学专业、经济和贸易类专业、人文类专业等占了其余的主要部分。同时，学校也对 GMAT 的最低分数提出了要求，我们中国学生在申请时，面临同一个战壕里的学生竞争要激烈些，所以分数要求要更高。

○ 申请必备条件和申请材料

Personal Data Sheet 个人信息申请表格	Name, address, contact information, education and professional history. Include education history and employment history with titles and dates—in reverse chronological order.
Application Fee 申请费	$100 non-refundable fee (paid by check, money order or credit card).
Transcripts 大学成绩单	U.S. bachelor's degree or equivalent. Upload copies of scanned official transcripts with your application. Upon enrollment, you must submit official sealed final transcripts. Admitted international applicants must submit WES reviewed transcripts. 注意：在申请时国际生不需要经过第三方机构的学分认证，一旦录取后，学校会要求国际生向WES递交成绩单认证。
Test Scores 考试成绩	Any non-native English speaking applicants who did not earn a degree at a US college or university must submit IELTS or TOEFL score reports to UNC—Chapel Hill (Institution code 5816, Department code 02). 学校接受雅思成绩，但偏好TOEFL。
Essays 申请文书	All 7 essays required (on web application).
Recommendations 三封推荐信（两封要求是学校教授）	Three total required (2 academic).
Interviews 面试	Required for admission. We contact you after we receive your application. Business attire expected for the interview.
Financial Certificate (International applicants only) 财产证明	The Financial Certificate must be completed by all international applicants. Please read carefully for complete instructions. 财产证明表格证明你的资金足以负担学习与生活费用，这个应在老师的指导下完成，在申请时寄出。

○ 截止日期

September 10 Deadline 9 月 10 日截止日

Open to all international applicants. International applicants are strongly encouraged to apply for this deadline to ensure sufficient processing time for visa applications.

December 1 Deadline 12 月 1 日截止日

Open to all applicants. Decisions are mailed by February 1.

March 1 Deadline 3 月 1 日截止日

Final deadline for all applicants. Decisions are mailed by May 1 and the program begins in late May.

○ 面试（Interviews）

UNC Kenan-Flagler is committed to interviewing each applicant to whom admission is offered. Applicants are contacted via email to schedule an interview after their application is complete. Business attire is expected for the interview.

北卡罗来纳大学教堂山分校的会计项目要求对每一位有希望被录取的申请人进行面试。

○ 核心课程

MAC 710 and 711 (6.0 credit hours) Financial Reporting A and B（金融报表 A 和 B）examine the theoretical foundations of financial reporting, the environmental factors that affect accounting standard setting and decision making, and the mechanics of accounting for events and transactions that have an economic effect on the firm. Course participants will gain an understanding of the preparation of financial statements, as well as the skills necessary to interpret financial accounting information. Prerequisites: 700 for 710, 710 for 711.

学生们要注意这是个必须修习的课程，否则不能毕业，同时这是要在第一学期完成的课程。

MAC 714 (1.5 credit hours) Financial Statement Analysis（金融报表分析）is the capstone course of the Financial Accounting sequence. It provides an applied perspective on analyzing firms' financial statements using lectures and Harvard case studies. Key topics include earnings management, profitability analysis, credit analysis, predicting financial distress, pro-forma business modeling, and industry analysis. Prerequisite: 712.

这是一门高级课程，内容涉及报表分析与制作，运用案例教学。

MAC 725 (1.5 credit hours) Cost Accounting（成本会计课程）examines the application of cost accounting techniques and practices for manufacturing, and service organizations. Special focus is given to the strategic context of cost system design and the application of cost accounting techniques to decision making. The course uses cases to help student contextualize cost accounting topics and to understand the impact of cost accounting information on firm decision making. Topics include cost accounting systems, strategic costing, activity-based costing, cost management systems, responsibility accounting, and transfer pricing. Prerequisite: 701.

MAC 730 (3.0 credit hours) Auditing and Assurance Services（审计与检查服务）offers a foundation in the external audit function and stresses the role and value of auditing in business. Students consider the effect of environmental factors and standards on auditors' judgments of client acceptance, risk assessment, planning, evidence gathering, and reporting. Prerequisite: 711.

MAC 740 (1.5 credit hours) Individual Income Taxation（个人所得税）covers major tax compliance and policy issues inherent to individual taxation, including filing status, income, deductions, gains and losses, and credits. Prerequisite: 700 (recommended).

MAC 741 (1.5 credit hours) Introduction to Business Taxation（商业税务入门）covers the major tax issues inherent in business taxation, including measurement of income, cost recovery deductions, property dispositions, nontaxable exchanges, and forms of organization. Prerequisite: 740.

MAC 742 (1.5 credit hours) Tax and Business Strategy（税务与商业策略）develops a conceptual framework for analyzing taxes that course participants apply to contemporary decision contexts including investments, compensation, organizational form, regulation, financial instruments, shelters, and family wealth planning. Prerequisite: 741.

MAC 743 (1.5 credit hours) Deloitte Corporate Taxation（德勤公司会计）analyzes tax laws with respect to corporate formation, shareholder distributions, liquidations, divestitures, mergers, and acquisitions. Prerequisite: 742.

这个项目与四大会计师事务所中的德勤有合作。在两个研究项目中会计理论研究中心的研究课程上，北卡会计学与德勤有深入的合作。

MAC 881 (1.0 credit hours) Ethical Aspects of Management（管理道德）addresses ethical theories coupled with critical thinking approaches to analyzing ethical issues. The course helps students understand when they confront ethical issues and provides a mechanism for helping students think their way through to making ethical decisions. Provides a useful way to identify and understand the values they bring to bear in making important decisions with ethical components.

○ 学费和奖学金

Estimated Financial Aid Budgets for Summer School 2011 and Academic Year 2011—2012

Academic year	NC residents	Non NC residents
Tuition and mandatory fees	$22,222	$41,354
Academic year total(with living expenses)	$43,916	$63,048

Living Expenses

	Per month	Per summer	Per academic year
Books	N/A	$1,150	$1,600
Food	$439	$1,298	$3,950
Health insurance	$103	$0	$926
Housing	$1,227	$3,606	$11,040
Miscellaneous	$308	$904	$2,774
Travel	$156	$430	$1,404
Total	$2,223	$7,388	$21,694

这个表格列举的是按照每学分 600 美元的学费来计算的，如果是州内居民，学费可降至 400 美元一学分。同时由于每个人生活习惯不一样，一般中国学生不会疯狂花钱，大家在看本书列出的生活费报表时要注意，除了学校必须交的杂费与服务费（含计算机使用和设施使用费）外，书费与住宿费等都是可以减免或省下的。

另外，从经验上看，北卡罗来纳大学教堂山分校一向比较吝啬给予商科学生奖学金。在以往我辅导的学生里，被录取的学生很少有拿到超过 1 万美元的奖学金，因而必须要准备好自己解决生活费。

○ 就业情况

MAC Career Services gives students a strong start to their accounting career. The chance to network with professionals in the accounting field allows students to thoroughly explore their employment options. View employment statistics to see where recent graduates are now. The MAC career services director has more than twenty years of experience. She helps each student explore job prospects and develop job search strategies. The MAC Office of Career Services offers a full range of services including: Job search workshops and career panels; Resume preparation and mock interviews; On-campus interviewing; Vacancy listings for off-campus contacts; Alumni career network service.

北卡罗来纳大学的职业指导办公室对国际学生在美国实习和找工作方面的指导有着丰富的经验。

Most of the on-campus MAC employers who interview F-1 visa holders with Optional Practical Training (OPT) have indicated that they will also interview visa holders who do not have OPT. Please note that if you are not eligible for OPT, your new employer will need to sponsor you immediately with the H1B visa in order for you to begin your first year of employment. If you are not granted the H1B, you will not be able to begin work with that employer. Students with OPT who are not granted the H1B for their first year of employment may be able to work under their OPT authorization and re-petition the following year for the H1B. However, it is at the discretion of each employer as to whether or not it will permit the candidate to work the first year under OPT if the candidate does not receive the H1B visa on the first try.

OPT 就是在美实习许可，由于会计专业不是科学项目，因而不能享受最新通过的 OPT 时间延长的福利。注意，OPT 虽然是实习许可，但所获得的工资、劳动保险、社会福利和必须缴纳的税收都是和正常员工一模一样的。只要在实习期间及时地和雇主沟通，并在每年工作签证申请截止日前及时向移民局递交申请，按时拿到 H1B 应该没有问题。

国际学生学完北卡罗来纳大学教堂山分校这个项目后，一般都能找到比较好的工作。学校也对以往找工作比较顺利的学生做了总结：英文好；适应美国工作环境；成绩优秀等。该校的这个项目在当地及国内几个州也享有盛誉。由于当地并不是很多学校提供 MAcc 教育，因此北卡罗来纳大学毕业生在各大会计师事务所均有众多的校友和支持者。

3. University of South California: Master of Accountancy 南加州大学会计硕士项目

http://www.marshall.usc.edu

○ 学校基本概况

南加州大学简称南加大，创建于 1880 年，是西部地区较早建立的高等学校之一，坐落于美国的洛杉矶市。南加大是一所充满生机与活力的综合性大学，现今已成为美国最具竞争力的大学之一，在全美大学评比中排名第 27。虽然只有 100 多年的历史，南加大的课程水平颇受学术界的认可。其商学院、电影、传播、建筑、医学及理工学院等在美国大学中特别出色，享有很高的知名度，而其电影学院更是全美同类院系中的佼佼者。根据卡内基教育基金会 2005 年公布的大学分类，南加大被归类为特高研究型大学 (very high research activity)。而在美国的高等学府中，只有 96 所获此殊荣。同时南加大还是获得联邦政府"研究与发展"经费最多的十所美国私立大学之一。

南加州大学拥有 16 800 名全日制本科生和 16 000 多名研究生。该大学拥有文理学院、研究院和 17 个专业学院。具体如下：文理学校、美中学院、研究院、会计学院、建筑学院、法学院、商学院、影视艺术学院、动画与数位艺术系、互动媒体系、传播学院、牙医学院、教育学院、工程学院、艺术学院、老人学研究所、药学院、医学院、音乐学院、公共管理学院、社工学院、戏剧学院等。

○ 院系介绍和专业优势

The Leventhal Master of Accounting (MAcc) program is a full-time, one-year program that begins in June for non-accounting undergraduate majors, and August for undergraduate accounting majors. Consistently ranked among the top graduate accounting programs in the country, the MAcc program at the University of Southern California prepares graduates for careers in:

Public Accounting 公共会计

Financial Services and Investment Banking 金融服务和投资银行

Government and non-profit 政府和非营利组织

Corporate Finance 公司金融

南加大的会计项目有 2 个开学时间，一个在 6 月针对本科非会计专业的学生，这些学生需要学习一些先期的课程。而 8 月则是针对本科为会计专业的学生。两个开学时间的毕业时间一致，为期均为一年。

Students study accounting in greater depth than is typically provided in an undergraduate accounting program or MBA program with a concentration in accounting. The objectives of the program include developing the sound conceptual, technical, analytical and communication skills that are required to succeed in the accounting profession.

项目学习的内容要远深于 MBA 会计方向，主要培养的是为政府、金融服务公司与投资银行、企业会计服务、公共企业业务等方面的会计人才。

To accomplish these objectives, the program takes an intensive approach with extensive use of the case study method and teamwork in all courses. The program employs a rigorous case analysis approach which requires students to exercise their analytical abilities and develop effective verbal and written communication skills. The case study method puts the student in the role of management, making decisions about issues now facing the business world. This enables the student to apply accounting and business concepts in various settings to give a broad perspective to the role of accounting rather than a narrow technical viewpoint. Students typically graduate the MAcc program having fullfilled the educational requirements to sit for the Uniform Certified Public Accountant (CPA) examination and have had exceptional success in passing the exam.

借助马歇尔商学院的优势，南加大的 MAcc 项目从一开始设立就严格地遵循会计实务、技巧必须与管理科学理论紧密结合的原则，在学习过程中也应用了小组实验与案例分析的教学方法。同时，值得庆幸的是，南加大的会计教育完全满足统一会计考试在加州及邻近 3 个州的考试准入资格。

○ 班级构成

Enrollment 176

MAcc 110

International Students 23%

Countries represented 13

Average Age 24

GMAT average 650

GMAT Range 550~770

TOEFL Average (iBT): 107

在大约 120 人的班级中，从平均年龄可以看出班级学生基本上以本科毕业生为主，而且对 GMAT 的要求较高。对于国际生来说，TOEFL 分数的门槛也是逐年提高，已经接近 110 分的水平。

Undergraduate Major：

Accounting 51%

Business Administration / Finance 17%

Social Sciences / Humanities 12%

Economics 10%

Natural Sciences / Engineering / Math 3%

Other 7%

南加大的录取班级构成表明，学校并不偏向于理工科专业学生，而是将更多名额给予了本科即有扎实会计学背景的学生。

○ 申请条必备件和申请材料

1. 语言要求

A minimum TOEFL score of 100 (iBT) / 250 (CBT) / 600 (PBT) is required to apply. On the iBT exam, you must score no less than 20 on each of the four test components. All applicants to the MAcc and MBT Full-time programs must submit official Graduate Management Admissions Test (GMAT) scores.

这个考试我前面已提到过。递交多次考试的分数，学校一般会考虑最高的分数。

2. 申请材料

（1）Personal Statement：Part of your application requires you to prepare a statement on your professional aspirations and how the program will help you to achieve them. The essay questions will be available in the online application. 除此之外还有两个选择性的文书题目。

（2）Letters of Recommendation：Two letters of recommendation are required for your application. References should address your personal qualities, potential to succeed in the profession, and your ability to perform well in the classroom. Choose references who know you in an academic or professional context and who are familiar with your academic achievements, credentials, career aspirations and work history (if applicable). It is preferred (though not required) that one of these letters be from an academic source (professor) that can attest to your ability to successfully complete a rigorous graduate degree program. The other letter may be from a non-academic source (employer) that is familiar with your work history and/or career goals. All letters of recommendation must be submitted using the online recommendation form found in the online application system. You will find instructions on setting up online recommendations when you start the application process.

对于推荐信，南加大要求至少两封推荐信分别是从学术背景与职业技能方面进行描述。虽然是学校建议这么安排，但从我辅导学生申请的经验看，这样的推荐信最能反映申请人的特点以及优势。如果 2~3 封推荐信均由教授撰写，则显得非常单薄。

（3）Resume：Please upload a business resume that includes your educational and professional information. Professional information should consist of employment history starting with your most recent experience. Your resume should not be more than one page in length.

简历上传并且写明职业 / 实习 / 工作经历。

（4）Interview：Interviews are by invitation only. Interviews are conducted by the admissions office staff and applicants will be contacted once all materials have been received. An invitation to interview indicates that your application has reached an advanced stage of consideration. Depending on where you are located, you will be asked to complete either an on-campus or a telephone interview. All admitted students will have received an interview.

注意，这里表明的意思是，如果申请人没有接到面试通知，八成是被拒了。从我辅导的学生的经历看，的确如此。

（5）Application Fee：The application fee is $85.

（6）International Education Requirements：Applicants must have obtained an equivalent to a 4-year U.S. bachelor's degree from an accedited college or university. A list of minimum education requirements by country can be found here.

本科学位是必需的，专科生与自考生不能申请。

（7）Transcripts：Transcripts from international universities must be submitted in the original language as well as in English. They must be sealed and sent directly from the university.

（8）Proof of Financial Support (I-20 Form)：International applicants must submit documented evidence of financial support. The U.S. government requires that all international applicants provide proof of ability to pay tuition and living expenses for themselves and their dependents (if applicable) before a formal letter of admission and an I-20 form can be issued. This document, stating your ability to pay for our one-year program, must be verified by a bank and dated within the last nine months. Applicants who are relying on support from their home government or other official agency must send USC a financial guarantee letter—preferably a bank letter—with the sponsor's name and address. Your sponsor's name (e.g. parents, relatives) on the financial document must be in English.

财产证明，这是向学校证明申请人拥有足够的资金支付学习费用，这个表格与证明的开具，必须与出国辅导老师商量清楚后填写。

○ 截止日期

January 10, 2010 is the deadline for priority scholarship consideration.

1 月 10 日为奖学金申请优先考虑日期，申请截止时间每年更新。

○ 核心课程

The MAcc is a one-year program and students typically take five courses each semester (Fall and Spring). Fall semester begins in late-August and commencement will be held in mid-May.

The Summer Intensive Program runs from mid-June to mid-August.

夏季课程是给部分无会计背景的学生准备的，毕业时间是来年的 5 月份。

(1) Required Courses 必修课程

    4 Required Accounting Courses 4 门必修会计课

    1 Communication Course 1 门交流课程

(2) Elective Courses 选修课程

    3 Accounting Elective Courses 3 门会计选修课程

    2 Floating Elective Courses 2 门浮动选修课程

(3) 1 Communication Course 1 门交流课程

    Additional Courses 加选课：Corporate Finance Course 公司金融

    总共是 10 门课, 30 units

会计主修课程

ACCT 585   Professional Accounting Concepts & Cases (Required Course) 职业会计理念和案例

ACCT 537   Management Control Systems 管理内部控制

ACCT 546   Auditing/Assurance Services 审计 / 检查服务

ACCT 557   Advanced Auditing Topics 高级审计

ACCT 574   Accounting in Global Environment (International) 国际会计

ACCT 581   Financial Statement Analysis 金融报表分析

ACCT 547   Enterprise Information Systems 企业信息系统

ACCT 548   Enterprise Systems: Design, Implementation, Security 企业系统：设计、应用与安全

ACCT 549   Advanced Enterprise Systems and Technologies 高级企业系统与技术

交流课程 <u>Communication Course (1)</u>

BUCO 533　Managing Communication in Organizations — or GSBA523T Communication for Accounting Professionals 组织内部管理交流

GSBA 523T Communication for Accounting Professionals— or BUCO 533 Managing Communication in Organizations 职业会计交流

选修课程 <u>Accounting Electives (Choose at least 3 courses)</u>

ACCT 537　Management Control Systems 管理内部控制

ACCT 546　Auditing/Assurance Services 审计 / 检查服务

ACCT 548　Enterprise Systems: Design, Implementation 企业系统：设计与应用

ACCT 549　Advanced Enterprise Systems and Technologies 高级企业系统与技术

ACCT 557　Advanced Auditing Topics 高级审计课题

ACCT 550T Tax Research and Practice 税务研究与实践

ACCT 560T Tax Theory 税务理论

ACCT 574　Accounting in Global Environment (International) 国际会计

ACCT 581　Financial Statement Analysis 金融报表分析

ACCT 582　Mergers and Acquisitions (Acct and Tax Views) 企业兼并与收购

ACCT 583　Accounting for Income Taxes 所得税会计

ACCT 584　Family Wealth Preservation 家庭理财

ACCT 587　Forensic Accounting 实证会计

ACCT 588　SEC Registration and Reporting 证监会注册与报表

○ 花费和学费

International Students must show proof of $61,966 in order to receive an I-20 Form.

Please note that international students attending the Summer Intensive Program should also budget an additional $13,067. The University does not provide application fee waivers to international students nor are they eligible for federal or university need-based financial aid from the USC Financial Aid Office. As a result, all international students should be prepared to meet all expenses from their own resources. Financial aid for international students is extremely limited and therefore should not be relied upon.

南加大费用惊人，同时不向国际生提供减免。

○ 就业情况

The Leventhal School of Accounting is committed to providing our Masters students with several opportunities to interact with accounting professionals and to explore employment options. The Director and Associate Director of the Masters programs, with more than twenty years of combined experience in a university setting, help each student to explore job prospects and develop job search strategies. A full range of services are provided to each graduate student including: job search workshops and career panels; resume preparation and mock interviews; a widely distributed resume book; recruiters breakfast and employer sponsored events; career fair; on-campus recruiting; comprehensive career information; alumni placement service.

南加大的会计毕业生在加州（湾区）地区的就业是相当不错的。我们中国学生面临的问题是毕业后的身份问题。近期美国国会一再延长国外学生在美毕业后的实习期限（Optional Practical Training）。同时，工作签证 H1B 也在逐渐放开。凭借南加大在加州及美国西部的盛名以及优秀的学生就业服务辅导，毕业生就业率一直较高。我辅导的两个学生曾在此校就读，均比较顺利地找到了工作。当然，这也和他们自身的拼搏与努力是分不开的。学校提供了较好的机会与平台。学生毕业后都要参加会计资格考试，还要经历面试的艰辛和试用期的残酷考验。可以毫不夸张地说，任何一份优厚的工作都来之不易，必须从申请学校的第一阶段开始就做好充分准备，从而迈向成功。

媒体管理、信息工程管理、健康管理等非主流商科专业硕士
Master of Media Management，Master of Information System Management and Master of Health Management

三个商科专业的简单介绍

　　这里我介绍几个商科专业中的少数派或者说非主流专业。一般来说，金融、会计、人力管理学这些大的方向，每个商学院都会有一个专门的系来作为这个专业方向老师的研究和教学平台，例如麻省理工学院斯隆商学院的金融系。这里我们要谈的几个偏门专业，在商学院内不一定有专门的系，而是某些别的专业方向的老师也做这方面的研究，或者 MBA 课程中有这么一项研究，因而才设立了这个方向的硕士学位。

　　大家可以看到，在排名靠前的学校项目内，有一个专业叫媒体管理（Media Management）。这个专业在前 60 名的学校里有好几个项目设置在商学院内，也有几个学校的传媒学院开设这个专业，例如雪城大学的 Newhouse 新闻传媒学院就设有这个专业方向的硕士。由于是管理学方向的研究，因此，在学习这个专业方向的课程时，会涉及相当多的工商管理课程，例如企业组织、媒体经济学、金融和国际传媒等。需要格外关注的是，这个专业有两个最主要的特点，是一般学生很难在申请过程中发现的，这里必须提一提。首先，关于媒体管理和娱乐行业的关系，我要说的是，在美国研究生院也有一个专业叫娱乐管理（Entertainment Management）和另一个专业叫运动经济学（Sports Industry Management）。这两个专业和媒体管理是脱不开关系的，有很大的交叉，只不过媒体管理更加关注的是娱乐业和体育界的上层建筑，即融资、并购、战略、公关、发展规划等。当然，许多媒体管理专业的毕业生离开学校后，都会进入娱乐圈工作，这也是再正常不过的。其次，这个专业的申请需要 GMAT 成绩。另外，本科读新闻、传媒或管理学相关专业的学生，均具备申请条件。传媒管理没有专门的排名，大家可以参考一般的传媒排名或南加州大学安南堡传媒学院在这方面的排名信息。

另一个小众的专业是信息工程管理专业（Management of Information System, MIS）。这个专业多设置在理工科较强的院校内，如弗吉尼亚理工学院和佐治亚理工学院等。这个专业属于交叉学科，也是工程学院或信息学院和商学院合作的产物。以数据库和系统优化为主项的信息系统学、管理学和计算机科学是 MIS 专业的最大特点。大家需要注意的是，这个专业的内容已经慢慢被金融、会计和物流等专业借鉴或吸收，这也是为什么只有少数的美国商学院单独开设这样的专门学科，更多的是采取课程设置的方法。这个专业的毕业生可以在咨询、市场销售、金融客户管理、物流系统等各个行业内就职，我认为就业前景在这 10 年内仍然是非常乐观的。

第三个小众的商科专业是健康管理（Health Management）。这个专业是从公共卫生管理专业演化而来的，所以带有很强的政策分析烙印，有的学校把这个项目叫做 Health Policy and Administration。至于这个项目是否设置在商学院下，需要看具体的学校。由于这个专业授予的是理学硕士学位，所以课程的核心不仅包括健康系统管理、服务质量监督、财务、会计、人力资源管理和决策分析、法律等偏商的课程，还有生物学、生理学基础、病理学、心理学等有关专业的课程，学习的内容可以说相当的广泛。一般来说，最好是具备一定的工作经验再来申请这个专业。在录取和发放奖学金时，学校也会考虑到申请人是否有相关的医疗管理和公共卫生经验，大多数院校要求的相关经历时间是 1 到 3 年。当然，本科就学习健康管理专业的学生，由于课程设置本身就有实践这一部分，因而可以免除工作经验的这一要求直接申请。在美国的健康、营养和医疗行业，这个专业的硕士毕业生还是很受欢迎的。

信息工程管理（MIS）专业院校名录

1. Massachusetts Institute of Technology 麻省理工学院
2. Carnegie Mellon University 卡内基梅隆大学
3. The University of Arizona 亚利桑那大学
4. The University of Texas at Austin 得克萨斯大学奥斯汀分校
5. University of Minnesota Twin Cities 明尼苏达大学双城分校
6. University of Maryland College Park 马里兰大学帕克分校
7. Georgia State University 佐治亚州立大学
8. University of Pennsylvania 宾夕法尼亚大学
9. University of Michigan Ann Arbor 密歇根大学安娜堡分校
10. Georgia Institute of Technology 佐治亚理工学院
11. University of California Berkeley 加州大学伯克利分校
12. Indiana University, Bloomington 印第安纳大学伯明顿分校
13. Purdue University,West Lafayette 普渡大学西拉法叶校区
14. The University of Georgia 佐治亚大学
15. New York University 纽约大学
16. University of Virginia 弗吉尼亚大学

17. Bentley University 本特利大学
18. University of Pittsburgh 匹兹堡大学
19. Arizona State University 亚利桑那州立大学
20. University of Illinois Urbana Champaign 伊利诺伊大学香槟分校

健康管理（HEALTH MANAGEMENT）专业院校名录

1. New York University 纽约大学
2. Harvard University 哈佛大学
3. Johns Hopkins University 约翰·霍普金斯大学
4. University of Michigan—Ann Arbor 密歇根大学安娜堡分校
5. University of California—Berkeley 加州大学伯克利分校
6. George Washington University 乔治·华盛顿大学
7. Carnegie Mellon University 卡内基梅隆大学
8. University of Southern California 南加州大学
9. Duke University 杜克大学
10. Syracuse University 雪城大学
11. University of North Carolina—Chapel Hill 北卡罗来纳大学教堂山分校
12. Georgetown University 乔治城大学
13. Indiana Uni-Purdue Uni—Indianapolis 印第安纳普渡大学
14. Brandeis University 布兰迪斯大学
15. Princeton University 普林斯顿大学
16. University of California—Los Angeles (UCLA) 加州大学洛杉矶分校
18. University of Minnesota—Twin Cities 明尼苏达大学双城分校
19. University of Chicago 芝加哥大学

张旭老师点评名校

1. Northwestern University: Master of Integrated Marketing 西北大学整合市场营销硕士项目

http://www.medill.northwestern.edu/admissions/graduate.aspx

○ 学校基本概况

西北大学创建于 1851 年，是一所美国著名的私立研究型大学。它的主校区位于伊利诺伊州的小镇艾文斯坦。校园面积不大，仅有 240 公顷，但环境优美，坐落在密歇根湖畔。该大学拥有 11 间图书馆，其中以 Deering 图书馆最具规模，总藏书达 390 多万册；学校拥有 611 台电脑可供学生使用，学生可以在校内外轻松登录国际网络；另外该大学的师资水准和学术水平都非常优秀，吸引了无数的本国和国际学生。该校历史上人才辈出，在1998 年的诺贝尔奖金获得者中就有两位来自西北大学。

西北大学拥有教职员工 2 563 名，学生总数超过 15 000 人，其中本科生有 7 826 名。该大学 9 个学院提供本科课程，10 个学院提供研究生课程。主要学院包括麦迪尔新闻学院、音乐学院、文理学院、语言学院、迈科密克工程及应用科学学院、教育及社会政策学院。

○ 院系介绍和专业优势

At Medill, some of the greatest minds in the industry will be among your professors. Here, you'll learn to create marketing strategies that engage customers. As a student, you'll gain a global perspective—by working in client-sponsored team projects or becoming a member of IMC's geographically diverse student population. You'll experience the challenges of real-world marketing environments and have the opportunity to solve problems using measurable strategies and tactics.

西北大学最著名的是其凯洛格商学院与麦迪尔新闻传播学院。麦迪尔学院的 IMC（整合营销项目）为全美领先的研究生项目，大胆创新、严谨治学是学院为人称道的特点。在过去的 5 年里，虽然 IMC 整合营销理念由西北大学几位教授率先倡导之后经历了较大的发展，但是除了西北大学、佛罗里达大学和密歇根州立大学等几所大学敢于鼎力坚持，许多一开始接受了 IMC 的学校如南加大和雪城大学相关项目正在悄然发生变化，逐渐偏离了 IMC 的轨道。

西北大学的整合营销并不依赖于对传媒与新闻的单纯研究，而是引入了大量的商业元素与商学研究方法论。例如，新闻报道的数字化、纸质媒体广告的数量化效果评估、广告策略与市场准入、新媒体方式与传媒行业兼并组合等，均是 IMC 的研究课题。如果说新闻在传统意义上是讲故事，那么本质上大众传媒就是在编故事，而 IMC 更进一步，去创造对故事的商业需求与市场偏好。在过去两年，我都很荣幸地辅导了两位学生成功拿到西北大学 IMC 的录取通知，心里面可以说有些嫉妒，因为这个项目确实很好，当然申请入学的竞争也是异常的激烈。

西北大学整合营销的研究亮点

Combining theory and practice 理论和实践结合

We combine real-world expertise and rigorous research to create powerful knowledge and innovation in marketing communications.

Creating significant brand interactions 创造品牌沟通和有效交流

The IMC process starts with understanding customers and stakeholders in order to identify insights that inform the creation of powerful communications that engage, entertain and connect with audiences.

Drawing meaning and insight from complex data 从市场数据到策略安排

Marketers are challenged to turn the growing avalanche of user information and data into strategies for significant and successful marketing communications.

Understanding that communications have shifted from push-to-pull and pass-along 有效连接消费者、传播和品牌

There is huge growth in consumer-initiated interactions with brands developing through networks, user-created content, advertising, reviews, word-of-mouth and search. The new curricula will equip graduates with the tools to leverage these powerful technologies and networks to connect consumers with brands.

Knowing that brands are open for business 24/7 不间断的品牌推广和市场传播技术手段

The consumer now expects the digital world to present all brands directly to them, consequently, all brands now must manage these consumer experiences and contacts—whether or not they result in an online transaction. The IMC curriculum will train graduates to connect with consumers and stakeholders through multiple technologies and mediums amidst this exciting landscape.

○ 班级构成和已录取学生情况

Graduate journalism students come to Medill from all over the world, and from different academic and professional backgrounds. Here's a snapshot (based on recent entering and admitted classes) to give you an idea of the company you'd keep if you are admitted to and choose to enroll at Medill:

Average Age: 25

12 different countries (in addition to the U.S.)

26 different states

学生平均年龄 25 岁，以本科毕业生居多，来自除美国外 12 个不同国家。

Undergraduate majors represented include, among others:（班级学生的专业背景）

American Studies 美国研究	Government 政府学
Anthropology 人类学	History 历史学
Arabic Language 阿拉伯语	International Studies 国际研究
Art History 艺术史	Journalism 新闻学
Biological Sciences 生物学	Law 法律
Business Administration 工商管理	Management 管理学
Classics 古典研究	Marketing 市场研究
Communication 传媒	Neuroscience 神经学
Computer Science 计算机科学	Philosophy 哲学
Economics 经济学	Political Science 政治学
English 英语	Psychology 心理学
Film/Video 电影	Sociology/Media and Society 社会学/媒体与社会
French 法语	Spanish 西班牙语
German 德语	Theater 戏剧研究

○ 核心课程

In addition to core classes such as consumer insight, marketing finance, and statistics and market research, you'll choose electives from one of five concentrations: brand and advertising strategy, corporate communications and public relations, direct and interactive marketing, marketing analytics, and media management.

在消费者选择、市场金融、统计和市场研究等核心课程基础上，有 5 个主要的选修研究方向是 IMC 项目特别设计的：品牌和广告策略、企业沟通和公关、互动营销和市场、市场分析、媒体管理等。

During the fourth quarter, students are divided into teams to tackle real marketing and communications challenges for global brands in the U.S. and abroad. Draftfcb, Best Buy, SC Johnson, Leap Wireless and Condé Nast are just a few examples of recent companies that have partnered with Medill IMC. You'll also have the option of enrolling in a summer immersion course that includes travel to countries such as India, China and South Korea. There, you will meet with leaders from top-tier companies, broadening your perspective of business practices worldwide.

课程设置中，大家可以注意到有很多实践相关的真实案例分析课程，这些课程会和 Best Buy 这样的公司合作进行营销和公关策略分析，这也显示了市场营销专业和传播专业日益接近的趋势。下面列出一些主要的核心课程，部分必修课和选修课暂不列出。

FALL 1st Quarter 秋季半学期

IMC 450-0 Marketing Finance 市场金融学

IMC 455-0 Consumer Insight 消费者选择

IMC 452-0 Marketing Management/Integrated Marketing 营销管理和整合营销

IMC 451-0 Statistics & Marketing Research 1 统计和市场分析 1

WINTER 2nd Quarter 冬季半学期

IMC 461-0 Media Economics & Technology 媒体经济和科技

IMC 460-0 IMC Strategic Process 整合营销战略过程

IMC 454-0 Communication Skills & Persuasive Messages 传播技巧和说服策略

IMC 451-1 Statistics and Market Research 2 统计和市场分析 2

SPRING 3rd Quarter 春季半学期

IMC 464-0 Intuitive Marketer 直观性营销

IMC 459-0 IMC Law, Policy & Ethics 整合营销相关法律、政策和道德

IMC 457-0 IMC Implementation: Managing Integration/Managing the Integration Process 整合营销实施过程

SUMMER 4th Quarter 夏季半学期

IMC 466 Global Perspectives 全球视野实践环节

IMC Team Projects 团队实践项目

FALL 5th Qquarter 秋季半学期

IMC 459-1 IMC Law, Policy & Ethics 整合营销法律、政策和道德

IMC 457-1 IMC Implementation: Managing Integration/Managing the Integration Process 整合营销实施过程

○ 申请必备条件和申请材料

Graduate IMC Application Requirements

（1）All applicants to the graduate Integrated Marketing Communications program at Medill must have, or expect to receive prior to enrollment, a bachelor's degree from an accredited college or university. All applicants must submit: application form.

申请人必须首先具备四年本科学士学位。

（2）$50 application fee (except Northwestern undergraduates).

（3）Official academic transcripts from each college, university or professional school attended after graduating from high school, whether or not a degree was earned. (Transcripts must be received by Medill in envelopes sealed by the issuing colleges or universities, or they won't be considered official.) If you have transfer credit, we need the transcript from the original grade-granting institution, even if the credit appears on your degree transcript. 两份官方成绩单

（4）Three letters of recommendation, from persons who are familiar with your academic or professional work and can comment meaningfully on your potential as a graduate student. These can be submitted via our online application system. Hard copy letters must be sealed in an envelope and signed across the seal by the recommender. Emailed recommendations are not considered official and won't be accepted.

三封推荐信，学校不接受电子邮件提交的推荐信，但可以从学校指定的申请网络系统提交。

（5）Professional statement addressing the questions posed in the application (for IMC applicants, 1,200 words combined total for four specific questions; for MSJ applicatnts, 500 words for the Professional Statement and 800 words for the News Essay.)

申请文书。IMC 申请人不用完成新闻学申请人所必须提交的新闻稿件题目。

（6）Official GRE or GMAT scores 官方标准考试成绩

（7）TOEFL (Test of English as a Foreign Language) score; the TOEFL must be taken within one year of the application deadline, and scores must be sent to Medill using institution code 1699-18. The preferred score is at least 106 on the Internet based test, 263 on the computer-based test and 650 on the paper-based test.

一般托福考试成绩。学校不推荐雅思，而且分数要求很高，根据经验，录取的学生托福一般均在 108 分左右。

（8）Résumé 简历

（9）A formal evaluative admissions interview is required. Interviews should be complete prior to the priority application deadline. Interviews are held in person at Medill or off campus when our admissions officers are traveling. For those unable to travel to Medill or a city we will visit, interviews may be held via Internet phone service with a webcam. Applicants should schedule their interview by signing on to their online application account, clicking on "search events," and following the instructions. Please make every effort to complete your interview prior to the priority application date.

面试是必须的，申请人应主动和学校联系，争取递交材料后在合适时间内进行面试，否则学校将有可能把你的面试排在最后。

（10）IMC applicants are also encouraged to submit links to online samples of their work.

根据我的经验，虽然 IMC 不是严格意义上的传媒和新闻项目，但是最好递交一份写作样本。这对于录取和奖学金有很大的好处。学生们在申请时要和辅导老师仔细商量定好题目。

Please note that international students are not eligible for federal financial aid or for most Medill scholarships. International students may find more information on outside scholarships for international students here.

国际学生不具备申请联邦奖学金的资格，这个问题我们前面讲过。

○ 截止日期

Medill uses a system of "priority" application deadlines. This means that files completed by the priority date go immediately into review, and a decision will be posted in the applicant's secure online account by midnight on the corresponding notification date. Medill reviews late completed applications from outstanding candidates on a space-available basis.

学院的申请截止日分为正常递交截止日和优先递交截止日。对于 IMC 项目来说，优先截止日为 1 月 15 日，正常截止日为 3 月 1 日。注意学校只接受秋季入学。

The graduate IMC program starts in the Fall quarter (September) only. Priority deadlines and their corresponding notification dates are: Full-Time Program Priority Deadline: January 15; Notification Date: On or before March 15.

○ 花费和学费

Currently, about 80% of all graduate students enrolled at Medill receive some form of financial aid assistance in the form of need-based loans, grants, and work-study. Merit-based scholarships are awarded to admitted students based on their admission application.

Tuition for the Master of Science in Journalism program is $12,204 per quarter.

大部分被麦迪尔学院录取的学生获得各种形式的奖学金、助学金、贷款、校贷款和半工半读机会。按照每半个学期 12 000 美元计算，全年的学费应为 36 000 美元左右，此数目不含其余学杂费与生活费用。

○ 就业情况

IMC graduates are consistently in demand at leading enterprises both large and small because they know how to successfully execute marketing strategies. And, unlike an MBA program, Medill IMC's curriculum dives deep into integrated marketing using data-driven insight along with new and traditional media formats. Finally, by enrolling in IMC's full-time or part-time curriculum, you become part of the Northwestern University community, known worldwide for its tradition of excellence.

Employers look to Medill as the pre-eminent source of young journalists who are well-educated in fundamentals, skilled in new techniques and willing and able to take on tough challenges. Every Spring, dozens of recruiters from media companies participate in Medill's Career Fair, and many more make individual recruiting visits. Throughout the year, staff in Medill's Career Services office provide specialized expertise and resources, including individual career counseling sessions, workshops and access to a robust jobs database. Each quarter, guest lecturers and school-wide speakers generously share their advice on how to take advantage of existing opportunities and how to create your own.

麦迪尔学院的 IMC 毕业生多在毕业后六个月内找到工作，除了得益于这个项目强大和前沿的研究和课程设置，还有学校颇费苦心为学生提供的各种就业和职业规划服务。

（1）Individual career advising（单独职业规划）—Our advising covers search strategy, offer negotiation strategy, self-assessment support, resume and cover letter review and other issues related to your career.

（2）Career-related workshops（职业生涯演讲和研讨会）—Session topics include resume development and cover letter writing, interview preparation, search strategies, internships, and many others.

（3）Career resource library（就业信息数据库）—Hard copy reference materials, computer workstations, scanner, fax and copier are available to you.

（4）Recruiting updates（就业信息）—Emails are sent to current student listservs highlighting career information, scheduled employer visits and job leads.

（5）"Hot Jobs" emails（工作机会邮件提醒）—Announcements are sent to current student listservs that contain job leads for which employers specifically request Medill applicants.

（6）On-Campus Recruiting（校园面试）—MCS coordinates IMC recruiting for full-time jobs and summer residencies.

2. Fordham University: Master of Media Management 福特汉姆大学媒体管理硕士项目

○ 学校基本概况

福特汉姆大学（Fordham University）是一所私立天主教色彩的大学，中等规模，知名度在纽约仅次于哥伦比亚大学和纽约大学。校园建筑古典庄重，学术气氛浓厚。福特汉姆大学的教育宗旨是国际性的。在纽约这个国际性的大都市，这所大学充分利用了身处国际商务、外交、信息、艺术、科技中心的优势，让学生在这个特殊的教室里获益匪浅。福特汉姆大学有三个校区，分别是 Rose Hill 校区（玫瑰山校区）、Lincoln Center 校区（林肯中心校区）和 Marymount 校区（玛丽山校区）。福特汉姆大学的 11 个学院招收大约 15 000 名本科生和硕士生。现在的学生来自 50 个州和 50 多个国家。福特汉姆大学教师共有 865 人（专职 497 人，兼职 368 人），90% 的专职教师有博士学位。

商学院、法学院及部分研究生院系所在地为布朗克斯和林肯中心。学校的校历为 Semester，颁授学士、硕士和博士学位。学生人数 12 256 人，其中研究生 5 351 人，学生来自 23 个国家。图书馆藏书 150 万册，缩微资料 130 万件，期刊 8 284 种。学校所设科研机构和实验室包括考尔德遗迹保护和生态学中心，家庭和儿童服务机构中心，第三老年中心，西班牙研究中心，社会研究所。研究生院有文理研究生院，商业管理研究生院，教育研究生院（管理、监督和城市政策学部，课程和教学学部，心理学和教育机构学部），宗教和宗教教育研究生院，社会服务研究生院，法学院。

○ 院系介绍和专业优势

MS in Communication and Media Management

While many such individuals do not wish to pursue a traditional MBA degree, they do need additional knowledge and skills that are acquired through graduate business studies. The Media Management program at Fordham Graduate School of Business is one of the first of its kind at a business school and is designed to meet the professional needs of:

（1）Individuals currently working in the media and entertainment industries, especially those in creative and content areas who need additional high-level professional training in business administration as well as in media management.

（2）Persons in business and other professions interested in specialized work in the media and entertainment industries.

Elite Master's Programs in US Business Schools: Critiques, Analysis and Samples

第八章 媒体管理、信息工程管理、健康管理等非主流商科专业硕士 Master of Media Management, Master of Information System Management and Master of Health Management

（3）Managers working in the diverse financial service sector interested in obtaining an extensive understanding of the media and entertainment industries.

（4）College graduates interested in securing comprehensive professional training prior to embarking on a career in the media and entertainment industries.

福特汉姆大学是为数不多的三所坐落于曼哈顿核心区的综合性大学，虽然本科学院与理学院在纽约上城的布朗克特区。商学院位于曼哈顿中城的 63 街附近，位置与哥伦比亚大学与纽约大学相媲美。该校的媒体管理专业是美国商学院中不多的几个项目之一。相对于两年制的工商管理硕士（MBA）来说，这个项目适合几类人群：（1）在媒体娱乐行业的创意部门工作的职业人士，他们需要商业管理知识培训；（2）对商业领域中特定的媒体行业感兴趣的职业人士；（3）服务于媒体与娱乐业的金融人士；（4）有志于进入媒体、娱乐及相关管理岗位的大学毕业生。

由于学校得天独厚的环境，这个项目针对电影、音乐、运动与戏剧等娱乐与创意行业设置的课程极为实用。大部分毕业生都能在这些领域或服务于这些领域的金融、咨询与中介行业获得待遇优厚的工作机会。以下是学校的几个研究方向。

Tracks Within the MS in Media Management

The Master of Science in Media Management is a 30-credit graduate program. Additional course prerequisites of up to nine credits in economics and quantitative methods may be required. Individuals with prior academic training in business administration may have some or all of the prerequisites waived.

（1）Electronic and Digital Media Industry 电子和媒体行业
（2）Entertainment Industry 娱乐业
（3）Publishing Industry 出版行业

媒体管理的三大路径方向：电子与数字媒体行业、娱乐行业及出版行业。项目的学分要求为 30 学分，根据路径不同，这个项目一般要求 9 学分的经济学与数量分析课程。只有满足这个要求才能顺利毕业。

Download the Academic Bulletin for more information and MS in Media Management course details.

MBA TRACK: The Communications and Media Management concentration, one of the first of its kind in a business school, is designed for students pursuing management careers in broadcasting, public relations, newspaper or magazine publishing, and new media. It also provides the financial and marketing expertise needed to attain top management positions in the communications industry.

学校也设置媒体管理方向的 MBA，针对有志于在广播、公关、报纸和出版等行业担当管理人的学生。注意申请 MBA 需要不低于 2 年的工作经验。

The Communications and Media Management faculty includes leading scholars and executives who bring cutting-edge information and experiences to the classroom. Programs sponsored by the Fordham Center for Communications invite prominent media figures to the campus for special lectures and presentations. Students concentrating in this area can organize their course work along three different tracks:

（1）Media and Entertainment Industries 媒体与娱乐行业

（2）Media Management 媒体管理

（3）Management Communication 管理者的沟通技巧

○ 班级构成和学校录取历史记录

2010 Class Profile

GMAT Score

Average: 709 Median: 700 Range: 620~770

GRE Quantitative score

Average: 791 Median: 785 Range: 720~800

Total GRE Score

Average: 1,278 Median: 1,280 Range: 1,170~1,390

Male/Female: 15 / 15

2010 年 GMAT 平均分为 700 分，范围为 620~770 分，GRE 总分平均分为 1 280 分，范围为 1 180~1 400 分。

2009 Class Profile

GMAT Score

Average: 680 Median: 690

GRE Quantitative Score

Average: 780 Median: 785 Range: 720~800

Male/Female: 13 / 9

2009 年 GMAT 平均分为 690 分，GRE 总分平均为 1 200~1 400 分。

2008 Class Profile

GMAT score:

Average: 690 Median: 700

GRE Quantitative Score

Average: 760 Median: 780

Male/Female: 11 / 10

2008 年 GMAT 平均分为 700 分。GRE 总分平均分为 1 180~1 380 分。

Undergraduate Programs Represented - Engineering, Math/Statistics, Economics/Finance and Business Administration

从班级构成上看，被录取的学生本科专业为商科、数学、统计、经济、金融与工商管理。有趣的是，本科学新闻与传媒的学生倒不是特别多。去年我辅导的一位学生，本科专业即为新闻，被录取时学校老师对她所学的专业表示极大的欢迎。

○ 核心课程

The Master of Science in Communications and Media Management is a 39-credit graduate program. This program is designed specifically to meet the professional needs of:

下面是两个大的方向，学位的总体要求是39学分，对于中国学生来说，大约需要三个学期才能完成。

Media Management

CM 7500 Media and Communication Industries 媒体与传播行业

Plus four of the following:

CM 7504 The Book Publishing Industry 图书出版业

CM 7510 Broadcast Management 广播行业管理

CM 7511 The Television Industry 电视行业

CM 7514 Broadcast and Cable Marketing and Advertising Sales 广播与有线电视 / 网络市场营销与广告

CM 7543 Newspapers, Magazines and their Electronic Ventures 报纸、杂志及其电子

CM 7556 New Media and Communication Law 新媒体与传播法

CM 7599 Special Topics in Media Management and Entertainment Industries 媒体管理与娱乐行业专题研究

(Business and the Media, The Business of Sports Television, Sports Media & Promotional Communication, Managing Across Media and The Music Industry)

Management Communication

CM 7500 Media and Communication Industries 媒体与传播行业

Plus four of the following:

CM 7525 Cross-Cultural Communication and Negotiation 跨文化交流与谈判

CM 7531 Communicating Corporate Image and Responsibility 企业形象与企业责任

CM 7533 Persuasion in Public Relations 公关说服技巧

CM 7537 Coping With Global Corporate Crisis 国际企业危机处理

CM 7550 Management Communication 管理传播

CM 7599 Special Topics in Communications and Media Management 传播与媒体管理专题研究

○ 入学必备条件和申请材料要求

Program Prerequisites (3 courses, 9 credits)

Students are not required to take all three courses concurrently. These courses may be combined with core courses, as long as the core course prerequisites have been met.

（1）Mathematical Methods for Business 商业数学方法

（2）Statistics 统计学

（3）Managerial Economics 管理经济学

（4）Fundamentals of Accounting 会计基础

（5）Business Law Ⅰ 商业法律Ⅰ

（6）Information Systems 信息系统

（7）Fundamentals of Management (BE6220, DG6820) 管理基础

（8）Financial Environment (AC6111) 金融环境

（9）Marketing Management (BE6220) 市场管理

（10）Operations Management (MG6613) 运营管理

（11）Business Policy (all Core Courses, taken near the end of program) 商业政策分析

在申请时，学生必须在以上课程内修满 9 学分的课程，这些课程不必是单独学习的，可以与核心课程一起完成。所以，递交的成绩单和申请文书必须反映这一点。

Application Requirements

(1) Application—online 申请表格

(2) All undergraduate- and graduate-level transcripts 大学成绩单

(3) Official GMAT score 官方 GMAT 成绩，学校接受但不建议考 GRE

(4) Two letters of recommendation 至少两封推荐信

(5) Personal statement 个人陈述和学习计划

(6) Professional resume 职业生涯简历

(7) TOEFL (If English is not your first language and you attended an undergraduate program where English was not the language in which course work was taught, you are required to submit an official TOEFL score.) 外语成绩

(8) Interviews 面试

(9) $130 application fee

Transcripts 大学成绩单

Applicants are required to submit transcripts for all course work that counted towards undergraduate-and graduate-level degrees. The transcripts must be forwarded to the Fordham Graduate School of Business Admissions Office in their official and original format with either the signature or seal of the university's registrar across the seal of the envelope. Any transcripts not received in this format will be considered void. Applicants submitting transcripts that are in a foreign language must have the transcripts translated into English by an official translating service. All international applicants whose undergraduate studies were taught in a country outside of the United States are required to submit a World Education Services (WES) evaluation of their undergraduate transcripts. Both the original and translated versions must be submitted in their official formats. While transcripts from Continuing Education Programs are not required, applicants may submit such transcripts as supplemental information.

对于大学成绩单的要求，学校提出国际生在申请时必须提交由第三方认证机构 (WES) 认证的成绩单。注意，如果时间紧迫，学生可以和学校商量免除 WES 认证程序。但这个免除申请是录取委员会根据个案来判断并决定的。在过去 2 年的申请中，福特汉姆商学院曾免除过个别学生的 WES 认证成绩单要求。具体如何申请 WES 认证，请大家注意 WES 官方网站上的说明，并和自己的辅导老师商量清楚，因为耗时大约需要一个月时间。

另外，关于这个成绩单索取表格，有很多学生不清楚，认为必须填写。其实这个表格是方便学生向学校教务处索要正式成绩单的，在申请时不用填写。

Letters of Recommendation

Letters of Recommendation are used to provide an insight to the applicant's managerial ability and motivation. Therefore, the Admissions Committee requires that applicants procure recommendations from individuals who can best attest to these attributes. Current supervisors, managers, clients and co-workers often prove to be the best source. However, the Admissions Committee understands that informing these individuals of future plans can be impossible for a variety of reasons. In such cases, letters from previous employers will be accepted. Applicants may also submit a supplemental recommendation if they wish to provide an academic or personal reference.

首先要注意的是，推荐信表格不必填写，因为大部分学校现在都开通了推荐信网上递交平台。推荐老师通过网络即可递交推荐信。这个表格里的大部分内容如学生活动、学习水平、排名及优缺点均可在推荐信网上递交平台填写。当然，如果推荐老师执意要用纸张信件推荐，那么这个表格必须填写并随文字信件一起递交到学校，这就非常麻烦了。

在这里，学校允许申请人递交超过 3 封推荐信，也允许前一个雇主作为推荐人，这是在众多商学院申请要求中不多见的。

Personal Statement

Personal Statements are an opportunity for applicants to express themselves in areas that may not have been reflected in other portions of the application. The topics outlined in the application are purposely vague to allow for such expression. The Admissions Committee asks that applicants limit their statements to the word counts of 500 to 750 words ascribed to each question. MSQF students should include information on why they are well trained and positioned to enter the quantitative field. This can be demonstrated through previous coursework and relevant experience (if any).

个人陈述即学习计划，大家可以参考一下后一章节附录的申请文书样本。有学生问字数超出要求有没有风险，我觉得最好按照要求来写，否则无法从网上提交。

Professional Resume

Resumes should be submitted in a professional format and include contact information (name, address, phone, fax, email), educational background, work experience, and skills.

职业简历要着重说明自己的工作和实习经历。

TOEFL

If English is not an applicant's first language and he or she did not attend an English-speaking undergraduate university, then the TOEFL is required. A minimum score of 600 on the paper version, 250 on the computer version, and 100 on the Internet-based version are required. If the applicant does not achieve this minimum score the admissions committee may ask an applicant to take the English as a Second Language (ESL) proficiency exam. Applicants whose undergraduate studies were taught in a language other than English can submit an IELTS score (minimum=7).

这个项目的托福考试成绩门槛是 100 分，但根据我辅导申请的学生情况来看，获得录取与奖学金的学生 TOEFL 一般在 105 分左右，预计这个分数近年仍会上扬。雅思分数也明确表示不能低于 7 分。

Interviews

Interviews are not a required component of the application. Applicants may, however, request an interview. An interview will not be granted until the individual's application has been deemed complete. As interview availability is limited, it is requested that an applicant submit his or her application at least 30 days before the application deadline to ensure an interview. The Admissions Committee may also request an applicant to come in for an interview. In this case the interview is a required component of the application process. An application will not be reviewed until the interview is completed. The Admissions Office will schedule a time that is most convenient for the applicant.

福特汉姆商学院重视面试。经过每一轮筛选出来的学生，都会收到学校的电话面试通知，这将是决定录取与奖学金多少的重要环节，申请的学生必须和辅导老师做好沟通和模拟，方能获得较为丰厚的奖学金。

○ 国际学生要求

Full-time students who will require an F-1 Student Visa or J-1 Visa must submit a notarized Affidavit of Support accompanied by original documentation that supports the information on the affidavit. (Supporting documentation includes personal bank statements, bank letters, sponsorships, or financial awards.)

All international applicants whose undergraduate studies were taught in a country outside of the United States are required to submit a World Education Services (WES) evaluation of their undergraduate transcripts.

这里所说的 Affidavit of Support 即与财产证明一起提交的一封承诺书。承诺书的格式无固定的样本，只要说明担保人承诺为受益人负担多少学费与生活费，以便受益人顺利完成在美国的学习即可。注意承诺人需签名，且姓名与财产证明表和银行证明上所示一致。

截止时间

Program	FALL TRIMESTER		SPRING TRIMERSTER		SUMMER TRIMESTER (Part-time only)
	Domestic Applicants	International Applicants	Domestk Applicants	International Applicants	Domestic Applicants Only
Traditional MBA	1-Jun	1-May	1-Nov	1-Oct	1-Mar
MBA in Accounting(CPA)	1-Jun	1-May	1-Nov	1-Oct	1-Mar
MTA Program (MBA in Acc+MSin Tax	1-Jun	1-May	N/A	N/A	N/A
Global Professional MBA(GPMBA)	1-Jun	1-May	1-Nov	1-Oct	N/A
JD/MBA	1-Jun	1-May	1-Nov	1-Oct	1-Mar
MS in Media Management	1-Jun	1-May	1-Nov	1-Oct	1-Mar
Ms in Accounting	1-Jun	1-May	1-Nov	1-Oct	1-Mar
Ms in Taxation	1-Jun	1-May	1-Nov	1-Oct	1-Mar
Ms in Quantiative Finance	1-Apr	1-May	N/A	N/A	N/A
Certificate Programs	1-Aug	1-May	1-Dec	1-Oct	1-Apr
Pre-MBA	1-Aug	N/A	1-Dec	N/A	1-Apr

花费和学费

2011—2012 Tuition and Related Fees (in US dollars):

Tuition per Credit	$1,158
Application Fee	$130
International Student Service (per term)	$26
University, General	$90
Technology Access	$66
Maintenance of Matriculation	$40
Graduate Business Orientation	$150

每学分大约 1 160 美元，这在纽约地区属于偏贵的一个项目。按照 39 学分来计算，学费大致需要 40 000 美元，加上纽约市昂贵的生活费，一年项目读下来的花费不是小数目。这还不包括消费额较大的书本费与学生保险费。

职业发展和就业

We recognize that making the commitment to earn a graduate business degree represents a choice to take your career to a higher level. The Office of Career Management is dedicated to preparing our students to compete effectively and successfully for a wider range and higher caliber of career opportunities.

Our students are strongly encouraged to start preparing for the job search from the time they start their studies. At the Orientation Career Workshop, new students will become familiar with the range of career services available, the skills that they will want to master, and how to plan their job search efforts for internships and full-time employment after graduation. We believe that students should not only learn about the self-marketing skills needed to be successful in the job market, but they should also take advantage of the opportunities provided here to practice and gain mastery of these skills while they are students. The career management skills mastered while at Fordham are designed to serve our graduates throughout their career.

福特汉姆商学院提供职业发展指导服务，主要内容包括：1）就业指导入门课程；2）简历修改服务；3）面试技巧讲授与模拟；4）就业数据库；5）校友联合会活动。作为商学院的传统，大部分在秋季入学的硕士生只要向职业指导办公室申请，即可与上一年或当年寻找工作的学生一样，参加当年底举行的校园招聘大会，这对刚到美国开始学习即面临一系列面试、简历、沟通与交际问题的中国学生来说也是很大的挑战。

3. University of Washington—at Seattle: Master of Information System Management
华盛顿大学西雅图分校信息工程管理项目

http://www.foster.washington.edu/academic/msis/Pages/MSIS.aspx

○ 学校基本概况

华盛顿大学（University of Washington）为美国顶尖著名公立学府之一，位于美国华盛顿州西雅图市，是一所建于1861年的公立研究型大学。这所大学有时又被称为"The U"或是"UW"（念成U-Dub）。这是美国太平洋西北区最大的一所大学，也是美国西岸历史最悠久的公立大学。华盛顿大学自建校以来，在各学科领域中成就卓著并拥有巨大影响，被誉为"公立常春藤校"之一。华盛顿大学同时也是美国重要的学术联盟美国大学联合会（Association of American Universities）的成员。建校时为私立学校，到1889年被收归华盛顿州所有。该大学主校区位于华盛顿湖（Washington Lake）和波蒂奇湾（Portage Bay）及联合湾（Union Bay）之间，占地超过700英亩。由于华盛顿大学坐落在西雅图市区内，所以交通十分便利。

华盛顿大学由三个校区组成，主校区在西雅图市东北角。除了西雅图校区提供博士学位的课程以外，华盛顿大学还有Bothell与Tacoma（华盛顿州）两个校区提供学士和硕士学位课程。该校是一所全方位发展的大型研究型高等学府，西雅图主校区包括17个学院，为一年级新生到博士在读生提供课程和专业研究机会。

自1974年以来，华盛顿大学是全美国接受最多联邦研发经费的公立大学。丰厚的研究经费使得该校取得了众多举世瞩目的研究成果。除了政府资助外，华盛顿大学亦有雄厚的私人及企业捐赠，比如总部在西雅图的微软和波音公司就长期资助华盛顿大学在计算机、资讯及工程方面的研究。微软总裁比尔·盖茨及保罗·艾伦（微软创办人之一）大力资助华盛顿大学，法学院大楼就是以盖茨之父的名义捐助的，玛丽·盖茨大楼以盖茨之母的名义所捐助，计算机工程大楼以保罗·艾伦的名义捐助。总研发经费与约翰·霍普金斯大学和密歇根大学长年维持全美前三名。

　　华盛顿大学的体育运动十分强劲，与斯坦福大学、加州大学伯克利分校和加州大学洛杉矶分校同属太平洋十所大学联合会，位居美国最高水平之列。

○ 院系介绍和专业优势

In modern organizations, there are growing demands for professionals and leaders who can harness the power of information technology in a way that can solve problems and create new opportunities. The Master of Science in Information Systems Program at the Foster School of Business, University of Washington, responds to these demands with a rigorous, yet practical, curriculum that provides professionals with the tools they need to bridge the gap between business and technology. Expand your knowledge and update your expertise here.

The four-quarter standardized program trains IS students to understand the role of information technology within an organizational context and to identify the appropriate technology solution to either solve an existing business problem or create a new business opportunity. Building on the Foster School's strong emphasis on strategic thinking and leadership, this program teaches students how to critically analyze business situations and use innovative approaches that suit those situations in a manner consistent with the overall organizational strategy.

　　商学院设置的信息工程管理专业都不是特别偏重技术流派，但必须有技术基础，重点是要培养信息系统管理有关的领导力、决策力以及组织管理、公司管理工具和知识等方面的技能。注意这个项目可以在一年内完成。

○ 核心课程

Summer Quarter 夏季半学期课程

（1）MSIS 501 (4): Information Technology and Organizational Strategy 信息科技和组织策略

Discusses the role of information technology (IT) in the development and execution of business strategy that takes into account competitors, customers, and firm competencies (including IT capabilities). Examines the impact of IT on two sets of strategic issues for a company——where to compete and how to compete. Helps students develop tools to use IT in aiding strategy implementation.

（2）MSIS 502 (2): Business Data Analysis and Decision Making 商业数据分析和决策

Statistical and modeling techniques for managerial decision making. Hypotheses testing, regression, analysis of variance, simulation, linear programming, and extensions.

（3）MSIS 503 (4): Operations and Business Process Management 运营和商业流程管理

Presents a framework to understand organizational processes, offers tools to improve these processes. Covers process improvement methodologies such as reengineering, TQM, six-sigma, simulation, and collaboration. Focuses on discussing applications and implementations of improvement programs in a wide variety of settings, including operational processes related to inventory and scheduling, service, and quality assurance.

Autumn Quarter 秋季半学期课程

（4）MSIS 511 (3): Digital Transformation of Organizations 数据转换和管理数字化

Impact of digital technologies within an organization, an industry, and an economy. Discusses system architecture that enables business processes and provides foundation for management and use of information systems within organizations. Covers issues related to workflow process changes, efficiency and effectiveness, innovation, convergence, competitive advantage, and sustainability. Uses case studies to illustrate concepts.

（5）MSIS 512 (4): Information Security and Assurance in a Networked World 信息安全和网络平台的保全

Introduces the various technical and administrative aspects of information security and assurance within a networked environment and provides the foundation for understanding the key issues related to them. Inspection and protection of information assets, detection of and reaction to internal and external threats, determining the levels of protection needed, and design of a consistent, reasonable information security architecture along with an implementable process.

（6）MSIS 521 (3): Information Technology and Marketing in the New Economy 信息科技、市场营销和新经济模式

Explores issues related to marketing models based on social networking/computing, such as concepts and applications of search engine optimization (SEO), viral marketing, web analytics, user generated content, the wisdom of crowds, and prediction markets.

Winter Quarter 冬季半学期课程

（7）MSIS 522 (4): Business Data Mining 商业数据处理

Decision support systems for managerial decision-making and business intelligence mining. Topics include naïve Bayesian classifier, decision trees, rule covering, association rule mining, and regression, as well as issues related to data cleaning, design, testing, and validation.

（8）MSIS 523 (2): Compliance and Legal Issues in Information Technology 信息科技产业法律和合规问题

The overall framework of information technology (IT) compliance, both generic and industry-specific. Intellectual property rights, privacy, and other legal issues relevant for IT.

（9）MSIS 524 (4): Managing Information Technology Projects 信息科技项目管理

Explores issues related to analyzing and managing complex information technology (IT) projects in a globalized and networked world. Covers topics such as life-cycle models, use case point estimation, function point analysis, COCOMO, scheduling and budgeting, project risk analysis, monitoring and control, contract design, outsourcing, and capability maturity model (CMM). Students manage a real-world information technology project in a simulated environment.

Spring Quarter 春季半学期课程

MSIS 526 (4): Enterprise Systems and Integration 企业信息系统和整合

Provides students with an overall understanding of the complex role of information systems in transforming organizational processes and integrating them as a part of an enterprise system. Topics include the concept of process-enabling information technologies and enterprise resource planning systems that support organizational manufacturing, customer service, and human resource management.

Elective Courses (Choose Any Three) 选择三门选修课

MSIS 541 (2): Advanced and Unstructured Data Mining 高级非结构化数据开发

MSIS 542 (2): Advanced Development Frameworks 高级发展框架策略

MSIS 543 (2): Advanced Database Systems and Data Warehouses 高级数据库和数据仓库

MSIS 544 (2): Managing Information Technology Resources 信息资源整合

MSIS 545 (2): Technology Entrepreneurship 信息行业创业学

MSIS 546 (2): Information Systems Economics 信息经济学

MSIS 547 (2): Contemporary Topics in Information Systems 信息工程课题

MSIS 561 (4): Modeling Techniques for Managerial Decision Making 管理层决策和模型化工具

All Quarters 毕业课程

MSIS 550 (4): MSIS Leadership Series 信息工程管理硕士项目领导力培养

Capstone learning experience consisting of 8 seminars and a final quarter student report. Seminars will be given by information technology (IT) leaders; each seminar will be followed by a session of questions and informal gathering. Seminar topics and speakers chosen based on the progression of other courses in the program. Each quarter, students have the opportunity to complement their in-class learning experience with related practical experience from two IT leaders. In the last quarter of studies, students must submit a written report summarizing these seminars, relating them to their coursework, and highlighting their practical relevance.

这里，大家要注意一些特别侧重于管理决策和信息科技与公司运营结合的课程，例如信息科技、市场营销和新经济模式这门课就很具备前瞻性。另外，信息工程管理硕士项目领导力培养这门课程是所有小学期都可以参加的，也是必须完成的一个规定项目。

○ 录取条件和必备材料

Each April, the Michael G. Foster School of Business enrolls up to 35 MSIS students. Our objective is to select students who demonstrate a strong aptitude for business, demonstrated leadership capacity, and a strong commitment to completing program requirements. Applicants are selected not only for their potential to benefit from the program, but also for the experience and knowledge they can contribute to the class. All applicants are evaluated using the following criteria:

每年项目招收大约 35 名学生，录取标准主要考虑以下几个方面：

(1) Past academic performance. We review each prospective student's undergraduate history, taking note of the difficulty of the curriculum and the scholastic quality of the school attended. We also consider the applicant's post baccalaureate academic experience, if any. Special attention is given to performance in courses taken in the Information Systems Area.

本科学术背景和研究经历。这里的研究经历指的是和信息工程相关的课程和课题，学自动化控制、计算机和电子工程的学生要列出课程和项目题目。

(2) General intellectual ability. We evaluate each individual's performance on the Graduate Management Admission Test (GMAT), which provides a measure of the applicant's general verbal and quantitative abilities. These attributes, which develop over a long period of time, are related to success in graduate management curricula. The GMAT requirement is waived for applicants who have graduated with an IS option from the Foster School in the last 3 years.

标准考试成绩展现基本的研究潜力，根据经验，这个学校要求的 GMAT 分数最少要 680 分。

(3) Managerial potential. We assess each prospective student's level of managerial responsibility by examining his or her accomplishments in school, community activities, internships, and work experience.

管理潜力和才能，这个在文书和简历内可以着重体现，文书按照商学院申请标准进行写作。

(4) Ability to communicate clearly, succinctly, and persuasively. The required essay demonstrates each applicant's level of writing competence, as well as his or her ability to think through issues. For international applicants, scores on TOEFL and/or TSE may be required if English is not the primary language of communication.

这是基本的沟通能力。对于国际学生来说，托福的口语和听力单项部分最好在 20 分以上。

○ 国际生需要递交的文件

（1）Applicant Profile 申请表格
（2）A Personal Statement Essay 申请文书和学习计划
（3）Résumé 简历
（4）2 Letters of Recommendation 至少两封推荐信
（5）Official GMAT Score Report (*waived for Foster IS option graduates within the last 3 years*) 官方 GMAT 成绩
（6）2 Copies of Official Transcripts 两份官方大学成绩单
（7）Foster School Statement of Integrity 诚实守信承诺书

Elite Master's Programs in US Business Schools: Critiques, Analysis and Samples

第八章 媒体管理、信息工程管理、健康管理等非主流商科专业硕士 Master of Media Management, Master of Information System Management and Master of Health Management

（8）$75 Non-refundable Application Fee 申请费用

（9）Proof of English Language Proficiency 英语成绩

（10）Interview (*by invitation only*) 面试

（11）Proof of Financial Ability Form 财产证明表格

注意，这里所说的诚实守信承诺书是这个学校特别要求的，是一个声明一样的表格，申请人在上面签字和承诺即可。

○ 截止日期

January 15 (early deadline) 1 月 15 日

Applicants requesting a student visa must apply by January 15.

○ 花费和学费

The total program fee for the 12-month program beginning each year in June is $30,000. The program fee is typically paid in quarterly installments over 4 quarters. Applicants completing their applications before January 15 will receive a $3,000 tuition credit, bringing their effective tuition to just $27,000. Program fee includes a $1,500 non-refundable and non-transferable acceptance fee, access to career services, hosted social functions and events, and registration service. Students in all fee-based programs, including this degree, are not eligible for the tuition exemption program, institutional tuition waivers or the Undergraduate/Graduate University Grant programs, including the Husky Promise program.

在 1 月 15 日前递交申请的录取学生，就会得到 3 000 美元的免学费奖励，这个一年的项目的整体收费是大约 3 万美元，其中包含其他入学费用、设施使用费和学籍注册费等。交纳这个项目费用的学生不能享受全免学费的奖学金或贷款优惠。

4. New York University: Master of Health Management 纽约大学健康管理硕士项目

http://wagner.nyu.edu/health/

○ 学校基本概况

纽约大学（NYU）成立于 1831 年，是全美最大的私立大学之一，也是美国唯一一座号称没有校园而把整个纽约城视为校园的学校。纽约大学的特色是注重理论与实务相结合，培养学生将所学知识灵活运用到实际挑战中的能力。该大学拥有先进的研究设备及图书数据，总图书馆拥有超过 200 万册的藏书、当代期刊、各式文献手稿和一个现代化的视听中心。因为地处纽约市中心，来自世界各地的作家、学者和金融家等在这里齐聚一堂，形成了国际化的人文艺术特色。该大学人才辈出，到 2008 年春为止，共有 31 名诺贝尔奖得主、16 名普利策奖得主、9 名国家科学奖章得主和 19 名奥斯卡金像奖得主等。它曾连续四年被 *Princeton Review* 评为美国学生最向往的名校。

纽约大学目前共有 14 个学院：文理学院、文理研究所、法律学院、医学院、牙医学院、商学院、教育学院、艺术学院、公共行政学院、公共服务学院、护理学院、个人学习学院、社工学院和理工学院。

○ 院系介绍和专业优势

MPA in Health Policy and Management in NYU Wagner's Health Policy and Management program has been recognized as one of the best in the country. Located in a school of public service rather than in a medical or public health school, our program crosses traditional boundaries, linking management, finance, and policy, and provides students with the cutting-edge concepts and skills needed to shape the future of health policy and management. Students graduate with a set of tools and experiences that allow them to understand both the delivery of health care services and the broader social, cultural, and economic factors that influence health outcomes. They work in every sector of the health care system, and experience firsthand the importance of health care delivery and health promotion in one of the most interesting, diverse, and complex cities in the world.

注意 NYU 的这个项目是商学院、文理学院、研究生院和公共管理学院共同创立的，设在公共管理学院内。项目的主要目的是培养学生对健康行业的管理、政策、服务流程的了解和技能，课程从工商管理、社会服务、经济和文化等各个角度进行授课和培养。

○ 核心课程

CORE-GP 1011 (4 credits) Statistics 统计学

CORE-GP 1018 (4 credits) Microeconomics 微观经济学

CORE-GP 1020 (4 credits) Managing Public Service Organizations 公共行业的组织和管理

CORE-GP 1021 (4 credits) Financial Management 金融管理学

Computer Proficiency (required if CORE-GP 1011 waived—SPSS—0 credits) 计算机和信息能力

Professional Experience Requirement (if required—0 credits) 实习和时间要求

选修课程还包括：

Economics 经济学

Sociology 社会学

Public Service and Public Management 公共服务和管理

Cultural Studies 文化研究

Policy Management and Budgeting 政策和预算管理

○ 申请必备条件和材料

When you "submit" your application online, we get all the components that you were able to provide us electronically, such as the general application, your resume, professional bio, personal statement, optional essay and maybe unofficial scanned academic transcripts. However, your application is not deemed "complete" until we receive all parts of your application. In order for us to deem your application as complete and begin the review process, we must receive the completed application by the appropriate deadlines:

（1）General application (online) 在线申请表格

（2）Resume (online) 简历

（3）Professional bio (online) 职业生涯（可以和简历一起）

（4）Personal statement (online) 个人陈述和学习计划

（5）Optional essay 自选文书

（6）Transcripts from all academic institutions that you've attended (official preferred, online unofficial sufficient for review) 大学成绩单

（7）Two official recommendation letters (two required—with a preference for one academic reference) 两封推荐信（其中一封必须是从学术角度）

（8）Standardized test scores 标准考生成绩

（9）TOEFL and TWE or IELTS scores are required 语言考试成绩

The admissions process is designed to review the overall potential of applicants to determine which students will succeed in their studies and their careers. Our review process is holistic, and decisions are not based on one single indicator. An admission decision will include the following criteria: 1) Academic history and aptitude, including previous grades received and/or relevant course work completed; 2) Professional experience and development, including internships, volunteer work, full-time and part-time positions.

根据经验来看，NYU 的这个项目也招收没有相关健康行业背景的学生。我辅导的学生里有本科专业是学生物医药和临床医学的。由于在美国学习临床几乎是不可能的事情，部分学习医药专业的学生也会选择这样偏管理而不是纯粹学习医疗科技的专业，为将来进入美国的医药和健康行业做管理工作打下基础。

○ 截止日期

Domestic and International students to apply for Merit based Scholarship should submit their applications no later than January 15th. The notification of scholarship and admission decision should be around March 15th.

申请截至每年的 1 月 15 日。

○ 学费和花费

NYU Wagner Tuition and Fees, 2011—2012 Academic Year

Financial planning for your graduate education is a key component of the enrollment process. Please see below for a schedule of fees for academic year 2011—2012.

	Fall 2011	Spring 2012
2011—2012 tuition per credit	$992	$992
Registration fee for 1st credit	$417	$431
Registration fee for each add'l credit	$61	$61
Academic Support Fee (per credit)	$12	$12

　　每学分的费用接近 1 000 美元，包含了学校登记和注册费用、学生活动费用及部分职业指导和设施使用费。

Fall 2011

Credits	Tuition	Fees	Total
4	$3,968	$648	$4,616
8	$7,936	$940	$8,876
12	$11,904	$1,232	$13,138
16	$15,872	$1,524	$17,396

Spring 2012

Credits	Tuition	Fee	Total
4	$3,968	$662	$4,630
8	$7,936	$954	$8,890
12	$11,904	$1,246	$13,150
16	$15,872	$1,538	$17,410

　　这是根据选取学分数目不一样而核定的学费。

生活费

Room and board (off campus) 校外住宿	$21,840
Basic health insurance 健康保险	$1,360
Books and supplies 书本和用具	$950
Transportation 交通	$800
Personal expenses 个人花销	$4,316

　　由于 NYU 在曼哈顿没有固定的学生宿舍，除了本科生和商学院学生，大部分研究生都住在校外，20 000 多美元的住宿费用是按照美国学生标准来定的，太高了。一般来说，中国学生在皇后区和布鲁克林区居住，可以将住宿费用控制在每年 8 000 美元以内。

○ 就业情况分析

Our graduates work in public and nonprofit management, health care management, urban planning, policy analysis, public finance, financial management, and managing international programs. In local, national, and international arenas, Wagner graduates can be found playing significant roles in the redevelopment of communities, advocacy for social justice and the provision of vital health and human services. See below for a sample of where our graduates are working:

这个专业的就业率还是很高的，大家可以参考一下下面学校提供的列表，相当部分的毕业生进入的是私营行业的医药企业、医疗保险行业及健康和营养行业公司，也有部分学生进入政府的公共卫生部门。注意大部分是非营利组织的管理岗位。

Employment By Sector

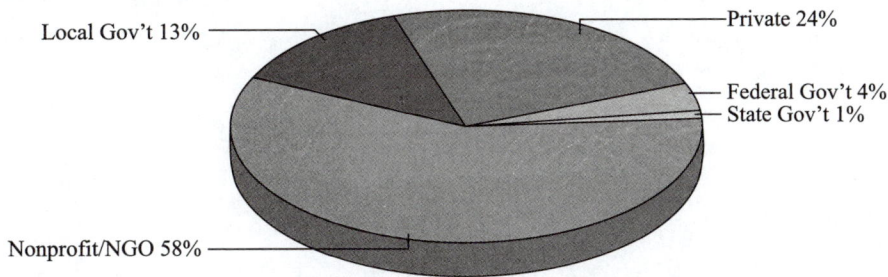

Local Gov't 13%
Private 24%
Federal Gov't 4%
State Gov't 1%
Nonprofit/NGO 58%

NYU Wagner's Office of Career Services (OCS) offers resources for students and alumni to build successful careers in public service and provides employers with access to qualified, well-prepared candidates to meet their staffing needs.

OCS is committed to assisting NYU Wagner students and alumni in developing, evaluating and implementing career decisions and plans. From the day they start classes, students are encouraged to take advantage of the many services offered through OCS, including the Career Directory, one-on-one Advisement, and a variety of career-related Events. Wagner students also have access to an assortment of services offered through the Wasserman Center for Career Development.

Students may apply for a $5,000 award to support their pursuit of a meaningful unpaid internship opportunity in the field of public service. Visit the Wagner Experience Fund page to learn more.

学校对就业的关注也体现在就业指导办公室的活动上，每年春秋两次的校园招聘会和商学院联合举办。平时，大纽约和三州（纽约、宾夕法尼亚和新泽西）地区的校友和企业人力部门也会定期到学校举行见面酒会和活动。更值得注意的是，学校提供 5 000 美元的奖学金给予有志于在公共管理和非盈利行业实习和工作的学生。

商科专业有关的主要文书范例

商科专业的申请文书各不相同，要求也不一样。在上面的学校论述和点评中，我们看到一些学校的文书题目样本，基本上围绕的主题有这么几个：

1. 你为什么选择我们这个专业？你凭什么认为你能学好？

2. 你的职业规划如何？现在这个时候来学习我们这个项目，是否适合你自己的理想和目标？

3. 为什么不选别的项目而单单挑中我们学校这个项目？对你的职业发展、学习兴趣和个人目标有什么帮助？

4. 你的到来，对我们这个项目有什么贡献或补充，换句话说，你怎么知道你本人最适合我们这个项目？

商科的申请文书很复杂，有以个人陈述的形式出现，也有以小而短的问答式短文形式出现，还有学生自己选择的文书题目形式，最后，很多学校要求一份专业简历（Professional Résumé），在格式、内容和时间节点上都有严格的规定，如哥伦比亚大学、密歇根大学和罗切斯特大学等。总的来说，我自己写了这么多商科的申请文书，也看了很多学生写的草稿，觉得上面列举的四个问题是申请的核心诉求，也是学校在处理上千份从中国寄送过去的申请文书时所看重的几个地方。下面，我分专业列举一些申请文书，作为案例给大家参考。

注意，和前一本书《手把手教你写作美国名校申请文书》一样，这本书的案例仅作为参考。大家不能照抄和照搬这里的文书，否则后果严重。任何一份申请文书，都必须在学生和辅导老师的紧密配合下完成，无论是自己蒙着头乱写或者一股脑扔到老师那里的行为，还是无良中介套用去年模板胡乱应付不知情学生的的情况，都会直接导致申请的失败。

金融专业的申请文书样本

1. <u>Explain your short-term and long-term career plans as specifically as possible. When combined with your studies at ABC, how will your background, previous experiences, interests and personal attributes enable you to pursue these goals successfully?</u> (500 words)

I plan to study in ABC's Master of Science in Finance program building upon my strength in finance fundamentals and learning of college level economics, statistics and computer languages. What attracts me particularly to ABC is its signature curriculum that targets the real time market practice and brings the vibrancy of financial operations, market changes and investment patterns to the classroom. This exciting and realistic learning design matches not only my undergraduate subjects but also my short-term and long-term career objectives.

An Economics student in R University of China, a school dubbed as China's London School of Economics for its rigorous economics course contents and stringent course requirements, I have got hands on two important subjects, *Management* and *Economics*. For the past several years, I have gone through both vigorous and rigorous trainings in various aspects of economics, including Macro/Micro-economics, Econometrics, Agricultural Economics, Development Economics, Calculus, Statistics, and Accounting, achieving an outstanding GPA of 3.75/4.0. These courses and several research projects on the capital market and macro aspects of economic development have armed me better to see things with a pair of "glasses of economist."

The innovative courses of ABC will definitely transform me into a totally different student of business, where I can readily draw on my economics background. I will also share with the class of my work experiences in the *C Securities Company Limited (C)* and *AZ Bank (AZ),* in small groups with professors team-teaching us. Such work experiences gave me practical hands-on in real business world that I can further question, test and absorb in my learning in classrooms of ABC. I have also been a keen student in various seminars, lectures and discussions in campus for international finance and economics subjects such as European welfare reform and US currency policy changes. Here, my insights of China and developing & new market will benefit me to learn courses in Financial Accounting, Financial Management and Global Strategy & Systems. Mathematics and quantitative methods are my fortes, which I will use them well in learning of Marketing & Quantitative Analysis. The Management and Leadership seminar will definitely resonate with my previous courses in business management and administration.

And finally, ABC will train me to form a truly globalized perspective toward future business world. I have been an excellent student in both management and economics in college, and now, I need more urgently than anytime a well-informed and truly enterprise-wide view of international business. ABC, with its internationalized and diversified student body and inter-disciplinary learning incentives, suits my needs perfectly.

I want to become what an ABC graduate becomes, a business professional with trained eyes and practiced hands. My career plan is to work successfully as a financial analyst, earning credentials for financial practice and focusing in my interested areas such as Financial

Management, Analysis of Public Companies and Private Investment strategies. I trust a Master's degree with ABC will be rewarding and invaluable to both my career and life.

2. In what ways would you impact ABC as a student and as an alumnus/alumna? How would you create change within the ABC community? (Not required for MMHC and EMBA applicants.)

What I can bring to ABC is definitely in concrete terms of both an international knowledge-based understanding, and a technique-based skill-set in finance. With a firm grasp of economics, finance and accounting in R University, I am more than just a student of economics. Instead, I see myself better fit for an integrated perspective toward a great varieties of issues in academics and the changing world of global business.

My education is an international and comprehensive one, as I am exposed to a mixed learning of international economics, international finance and international trade. I am interested in European welfare system reforms, US changing currency policy and the evolving East Asian capital market. In ABC, I would like to share with all my experience of winning the Prize in the University Securities Contest and my understanding that every financial deal or case is fundamentally different from one another: frameworks are more vital than solutions. My research experiences contributed to my understanding of the international economics: Project of Rural Economic Transformations and Market Capitalization Analysis for a clean and white producer: HA (600690.SH). I would like to share my experiences of doing research and analysis in China, and I believe it will be exciting to bring all these international understanding and specialized know-how to the classrooms of ABC.

For the past several years, I have set my mind to study and practice Finance as a career. Trying hard and reaching high, I adapt myself to applying the three step approach in every deal of international features: establish the structure of analysis, reasoning and communicating. I hope these experiences can be discussed with our classmates in ABC. I also want to take to classrooms of ABC my exposure to many cross-cultural and international interactions. It is the learning from these conferences and forums on finance and economics that taught me to understand the differences and think alternatively from different positions of values or practices in dealing with matters of international essences. How shall we think differently but effectively, and how can we act differently in the market? This is the question I will seek for further answers in ABC classes.

The most stimulating aspect of ABC is that it readily builds on my college learning of finance and economics. ABC simply provides a reinforced version of my courses with the state-of-the-art techniques for financial analysis and seasoned guidance of faculties. I will bring to ABC what I learned from R University and work experiences, specifically in classes of Corporate Finance, International Finance and Investment Portfolios. I like particularly your approach that cases will be presented to guide students to test theories. I have been watching for years professor after professor presenting case after case, asking us to believe in theories, which is pale and weak. In ABC, I would like to share with my fellow students and faculty my understandings that key elements for a good financial expert is to develop one's own theories out of numerous tests, instead of sticking to certain rigid theory.

With an integrated and cutting-edged approach in financial teaching and learning, ABC will give me not just some formula or models, but more of a specific combination of accounting, economics, fiscal theories, public policies and international finance know-how.

3. <u>What is your career plan, short term or long term? Please be specific in telling the admission committee your goals and preparations for such plan. How ABC Master of Finance program can help you achieve such goals?</u>

I have a well-drawn roadmap for my career after the MS finance training at ABC. My first position shall be in the private sector, working for an established investment bank as a financial analyst. The scope of my analysis works shall cover areas of capital market analysis, stock pricing valuation and portfolio investment. In particular, I believe ABC's training will give me advantages to see through varieties of phenomenon in the capital market that are either induced or affected by the interactions between investors and managements. Behavioral study of financial entities in market has long been a fascinating subject for me. An advanced perspective towards multiple considerations in the market complicating the financial behaviors such as information, regulatory changes and contractual arrangements, will allow me to see the overall broad picture. After sharpening my skills as an analyst for two or three years, I shall move on the ladder so that my works can cover not only the sale side but the buy side of financial practices, where I can play a leading role directing international finance deals for different industrial sectors and corporations. Clean energy buyout, new bio-medical investment, cross-continental merger and acquisitions are fields in which I shall excel and make a difference.

To reach this goal, I have readied myself in several ways for the challenges. A student with college major in Finance, I underwent rigorous trainings in the finance fundamentals, including but not limited to macro/micro economics, accounting, corporate finance, investments and applied statistics. For the consecutive three years in BN University that is famous for its intensive curriculum hours and rigid exam system, I have achieved a GPA of XXX, and a finance course GPA of XXX. My fortes in advanced mathematics, with a particularly strong grasp of calculus and probabilities, enabled me to conduct graduate level researches on finance subjects. In 2009, my publication on a significant trade journal, entitled *Non-performing bank assets, Securitization and Security Pool Designs,* attested to my abilities in applying methods of quantitative analysis. In summer 2010, I joined the practice program of *Z Bank, H.K*, a Fortune 500 company, working at its consulting branch, where I led a team to finish various daily research projects and draft business plans for real clients. Starting this August, I also work 4 days a week in a major investment firm in Beijing, the *YH Securities*, where I take on more substantial responsibilities as a consultant, handling corporate advisory works, security analysis reports, and health care/ steel / automobile industry reports.

A quality graduate study is a must to complete my preparation for career. ABC is undoubtedly my top choice. To me, the most attractive aspect of ABC is its unique way of teaching and learning, *F.A.Ct (frame-analyze-communicate)*, which I believe can enable students more opportunities to discuss and exchange freely thoughts to develop their own perspectives. Compared with simple memorization of cases, ABC's way rejects the repetition of old solutions to a particular case but emphasizes on students' own approaches. Besides a unique way of learning, ABC attracts me with its diversified sources of learning, such as the Finance Club where world-renowned CEOs, CFOs and managers are guest speakers to discuss various finance issues in the global business world. I deem all these learning opportunities in ABC a resourceful and valuable second classroom. Furthermore, a crucial factor that drives me to choose ABC is its extraordinary alumni network that I've heard so much about. These exclusive resources are treasures to new business practitioners and financial professionals like us.

4. <u>OPTIONAL ESSAY. Share with the Admission Committee anything you wish to deliberate. If any part of your academic experience or personal background demands some explanations, you can also take this opportunity to do so.</u>

I excelled in many Mathematics courses for the past three academic years. Such courses range from Mathematics A1 to Mathematics A3. Mathematics A course is an integral part of advanced Calculus, e.g. definite integral & indefinite integral calculation. I took also AnalytVc Geometry and Vector Algebra, Functions of Variables, Linear and Curve Algebra, Surface Integrals, Infinite Series; and Advanced Probabilities as well as Matrix and Linear Space. What is more, I have particular strength in learning Probability Theory and Mathematical Analysis, Statistics, Accountancy and Econometrics. Further applying these mathematics know-how to real life modeling, I audited the graduate level seminar on

Mathematical Modeling and Financial Engineering for one full semester last year.

Winning the honor of First Prize of Provincial Mathematics Olympics as early as in my high school, I believe now I have put forward to a new height my mathematics and statistics skills. In July 2009, I was awarded the Second Prize in Mathematics Modeling Contest by the University for my extraordinary performance and leadership in the contest designing and drafting a 21-page paper in three days. The contest commission viewed my research paper with high appreciation as it made reasonable hypothesis by setting up options of practical mathematics modeling with aid of STAT and Matlab in such a short time frame.

Presented below is a brief introduction of the Abstract of my thesis, entitled "the AMC non-performing assets securitization." In the thesis, I give a full play to my mathematics and statistics skill, proposing that along with the process of our national finance market becoming more integrated into the global market comes a pressing need of developing products or solutions of securitizations for increasing non-performing assets. Within the current background and situation, I further propose that non-performing asset securitization requires some reforms and creations, especially in the development of an effective assets pool for commercial banks. My mathematical analysis combined with my perspectives on the current market situation has shown in the paper such needs for the non-performing assets securitizations are imperative for most domestic commercial banks here in China. I analyzed various factors of assets pool construction principles concerning non-performing assets securizations of commercial banks, finding out the speculated *minimum variance ratio of five-category asset* classifications of assets pool on basis of the model calculation and deduction of financial data.

5. Describe a situation where your professional ethics were challenged and how you came to terms with the situation. What did you learn from this experience?

I believe professionals are all faced with challenges or difficulties in work particularly when it comes to ethical concerns. Currently I am working for the AG Global Center in Beijing, in which Mr. G, one of my recommenders acts as the director. We also have one chief assistant who does not speak English here and sometimes acts very unprofessionally in the office, yelling to clients and condescending to other colleagues.

Two weeks ago he disappeared from work without notice to anyone and returned mysteriously. He then asked from another staff the work timesheet and self-corrected those absent days on it. I noticed that he sent the changed form to accounting office without going through the proper procedure. The number he fabricated was quite substantial as I could see from the fax copy. He then warned me not to disclose such facts because the salary matters are not issues discussable in the center. I was sure he would do something unfavorable to me once I reported this as he, in any capacity, is still the assistant chief here in the office. However, I asked myself whether I should let this pass and see the Center go through a crisis of financial integrity once the accountant or the head office in New York found out the truth about it. What is more, I asked myself whether I should submit to his threats and bluffing. Cowardice in face of atrocity is itself an accomplice. How should I face myself in the future work place if I know this and still turn my face against it pretending I know nothing?

As an intern, I did this with great risks. But I still picked up the phone and called Mr. G, our director in chief in Hong Kong. Who then quickly returned my call and inquired of all I know about this incident in a two-hour phone call. He praised me of my integrity and courage to protect the Center's image financial creditability. I also felt that acting honestly in work place will actually benefit many. Later that incident was resolved smoothly as the director in chief himself saw to its final clearing out the falsified account number and timesheet. The Center has since then become more professional in work fashion and colleagues are more congenial together as well. I still take caution of the assistant chief, as he must have known the reporting person is nobody but me. But I am not afraid at all and I trust I have done the right thing.

There are valuable lessons that I have learned from it and wanted to carry it further to ABC. First of all, be brave and also be prompt in action. I discovered the facts and made the move after a quick examination and evaluation. Then, the second most important thing is to be honest and truthful, not hiding anything from your client, co-workers or superiors. I have learned the lesson of reporting directly and communicating directly, avoiding any misconception or guessing in work as well. Finally, I have also learned the value of being steadfast in my own belief or tenet. A person with integrity is 100 times more professional than one without.

金融工程专业的申请文书样本

1. **Essay** *(Required for Full- and Part-Time Applicants)*

What are your reasons for undertaking graduate study in the field of computational finance? Please describe your future career plans and how they relate to your experience, your education and your proposed training at MC University. Describe your short-term and long-term objectives and how you plan to achieve them.

I believe a good Computational Finance program will eventually shape ones' career in this industry. Among the entire Finance Engineering programs that I have studied, MCU stands out prominently as it matches not only my career objectives but also my interests, experiences and talents mastered all these years.

The best part I like about financial modeling and computational finance lies in the power of quantitative methods integrated with information techniques to produce predictable and verifiable solutions to varieties and fluctuations of the financial market. This is the trend and this is also where the magic exists for computational finance in my views.

As a finance major student in R University, probably the best one in China in financial trainings and learning, I have a clear roadmap for myself even in my freshman year. I dream of being an expert with fine insights and sharp skills in investment, equity fund management, hedge fund operations and financial consulting with analytical advisory basis. Hong Kong and Singapore are in reachable range to my university and vibrant actions in the capital market are live shows here every day in or around the campus. In such a good stage, I have learned in-depth all fundamental fields of finance and economics, forming a strong and informed perspective toward theory, rationales, practices and skills needed in finance.

Possessing an instinct to analyze and integrate varieties of data, I have a knack to see through financial market fluctuations, CPI changes, foreign exchange rate movements and even the pricing of certain assets. I believe I possess the talents to feel and sense accurately and boldly that are crucial for an intrepid financial expert in the industry. As early as my freshman year in college, I took the programming course in C++ language, which was indeed intricate and mesmerizing. For the first time, I started to view quantitative analysis in an integrated way with computational programming, the power of which attracted me deeply ever since. Finance programming will rely on good instincts toward market actions for the maximum effects and application. My unique instinct shall allow me to stand on better positions than my peers. Bold but rational, sensitive but sensible, I dream to deliberately train myself to become more refined in aspects of financial analytical tools, model constructions and programming for specific investment targets.

I would like to practice in the financial industry for several years as an analyst or ground-level consultant after graduation from MCU, with a graduate finance degree that can allow me to better my talents and see more clearly where the true values of investment, fund management and asset combination lie in the daily ups and downs of the market. My internship with HSBC and an international fund management firm all affirmed in me that such trained insights can move my career higher up to a new level. In HSBC, I learned the values of pertinence, the fundamentals of quantitative analytical frameworks and the essences of various financial tools and products. Later in the fund management firm, I tried to apply modeling, portfolio structures, Black-Scholes stock pricing and programming basics. All these experiences are eye-opening events for me, to peek into the wonders of intricate process of verifying, rationalizing and standardizing the capital investments.

I like particularly MCU's unique curriculum, which highly matches my undergraduate courses such as theories of equity, bond portfolio management and statistical methodologies. MCU has unparallel strength in computational methods and training that I am longing to experience. Among all the computational programming courses I have looked at, MCU's training in this aspect is tremendously valuable in that it only teaches what the application calls for and what the market wants. MCU also places emphasis on cultivating professional ethics and social responsibility in financial engineers and computational experts. Such strength and tenor make me trust MCU stands out from other Finance programs.

2. **Essay** *(Required for Full- and Part-Time Applicants)*

Describe your background and preparation in the four concentration areas of the MSCF program—finance, computer science, math and statistics. In particular, please detail your background in calculus-based probability. If your only exposure to probability was as part of a course that combined probability and statistics, please list the probability topics covered by this course.

I believe my education background in finance speaks for itself that I have been well–armed of all necessary components for a continuing training in computational finance. I have excelled in many relevant finance courses as a preparation to my future career: *Finance, Finance Derivatives, Investment Theories and Strategies, Managerial Accounting, General Accounting Principles, International Economics*, etc. Performances at these courses in my transcript attest to my solid learning in finance and all related subjects.

Moreover, Mathematics and Statistics courses are my favorites, as I know the quantitative know-how will never get outdated in finance market applications. Without exception to any, I completed statistics and mathematics courses with exceptionally good grades. Core courses I have taken in college specifically dealing with Probabilities and Calculus are *Advanced Mathematics*, *Probability Theory* and *Mathematical Statistics*, and I excelled in every one of them. Calculus is the field in *Advanced Mathematics* that I devoted particular efforts to and achieved impressive results. I have extensive knowledge in calculus-1 and calculus-2 at college levels, well preparing myself for more advanced courses and application in work. In terms of training in Probabilities, I took challenging courses such as *Discrete and Continuous Distributions*, *Conditional Probability*, *Expectations*, *Time Functions*, *Joint Distributions*, and *Treatment of CLM*. Besides, I also ventured to study *Introduction of Stochastic Process*. In my perspective, probabilities study must go closely along with calculus as the latter speaks the basis for the application, innovation and adaptation of the former.

I sense this from very early on and continue to strengthen my knowing and understanding afterwards in both classroom and workplace. Time series analysis, matrix, probability combinations and probabilistic logics are all subjects comprehensively covered in my endeavors to improve my probability and calculus learning. This understanding took me further to apply what I have learned from the *Intermediate Finance* (Thomas E. Copeland), where I found immediate application of calculus based probability helps me understand the models, functions and results of various cases.

My strength in computer science and programming in specific started from my first year in college. A feat for a student majoring in Finance, I did not stop at satisfaction of learning pure finance theories or advanced calculus. I am an adept user of C++ and VB. As many of my peers in class lack interest in taking these daunting courses in computer programming or application, I found the subject both attractive and captivating. This area of competence, I believe, will be the win-or-lose factor in career of finance for the future. Quantitative methods must move forward with aid from programming technique and our adaptation to it is inevitable. This semester, I started to further learn the essentials for SAS/STAT systems and investment project pricing evaluation. The increased magnitude and difficulty involved in these courses prove to me the necessity to master well computer programming skills in finance. For me adventures like this will certainly continue on for this year, and I long to carry that forward to the exciting classroom of Carnegie Mellon.

3. <u>Please compose a personal statement to explain to us your plan, your academic capabilities, your potentials and any significant learning or working experiences in relation to your intended Master study in Computational Finance.</u>

PERSONAL STATEMENT

I am writing to demonstrate my abilities, interests, career development plan and the importance of a MS Computational Finance degree for my ambitions. Being a software engineer in S, Inc. China ("S"), I have accumulated substantial work experiences in software, system design and programming. Building upon my current self-studying for Chartered Finance Analyst, I want to take my career to a new height through your program. Before I joined S, I was a student of Electronic Engineering in R University of Science and

Technology ("RUS"), a top engineering school in China, acquiring a Major GPA of 3.64/4.

During my times at RUS, Mathematics and Statistics courses are my favorites, as I know the quantitative know-how will never get outdated in finance market applications. Without exception to any, I completed engineering level mathematics courses with exceptionally good grades. Core courses I have taken in college specifically dealing with Probabilities and Calculus are Advanced Mathematics, Probability Theory and Mathematical Statistics, and I excelled in every one of them. Calculus is the field in Advanced Mathematics that I devoted particular efforts to and achieved impressive results. I have extensive knowledge in calculus-1 and calculus-2 of engineering subject levels (the second most advanced level), well preparing myself for more advanced courses and application in work. In terms of training in Probabilities, I participated in challenging courses such as Discrete and Continuous Distributions, Conditional Probability, Expectations, Time Functions, Joint Distributions, and Treatment of CLM. Besides, I also ventured to study Introduction of Stochastic Process. In my perspective, probabilities study must go closely with calculus as the latter speaks the basis for application and innovation of the former. *Time series analysis, matrix, probability combinations and probabilistic logics* are all subjects comprehensively covered in my endeavors to improve my probability and calculus learning. This understanding took me further to apply what I have learned from CFA preparation materials, where I found immediate application of calculus based probability helps me understand the models, functions and various cases.

Besides my fervent interests in mathematics, I took the programming course in C++ language in RUS, which was indeed intricate and mesmerizing. For the first time, I started to view quantitative analysis in an integrated way with computational programming, the power of which attracted me deeply ever since. Finance programming will rely on good instincts toward market actions for the maximum effects and application. My unique instinct shall allow me to stand on better positions than my peers. I believe I possess the talents to feel and sense accurately and boldly that are crucial for an intrepid financial expert in the industry. A feat for a student majoring in Finance, I did not stop at satisfaction of learning electronics, circuits and system designs, even though they lay a good foundation for my future endeavors. I learned to become an adept user of C++ and VB(C#). I also found those daunting courses in computer programming or application both attractive and captivating. This area of competence, I believe, will be the win-or-lose factor in career of finance for the future. Quantitative methods must move forward with aid from programming technique and our adaptation to it is inevitable. With this belief, I started to further learn the essentials for SAS/STAT systems and investment project pricing evaluation. The increased magnitude and difficulty involved in these courses prove to me the necessity to master well computer programming skills in finance.

Carrying this strong foundation to S, I conducted and engaged in many system designs and operating software operations for insurance company, investment houses and broker-dealer clients. My work touched upon several key aspects of the financial engineering in real workplace, such as risk control, corporate management surveillance, financial data retrieving and processing, and client management database. I found not only my mathematics skills, engineer visions and programming expertise all come into play in one place. Attracted by the finance work, I started six months ago preparing for the CFA-LEVEL 1 test myself, through which I have learned with eager a lot of relevant finance courseworks as a preparation to my future career: *Finance, Finance Derivatives, Investment Theories and Strategies, Managerial Accounting, General Accounting Principles, International Economics*, etc.

I have tried hard and achieved good results for my work. Now, in aspect of my career aspiration, I am planning to pursue a career in financial analysis in top class investment banking in China. With the fast pace of growing economy in China, GDP rose at least 9% per annum. The numbers of well-structured Chinese companies to have fund raising in overseas stock markets, such as NASDAQ or Dow Jones of US and FTSE of UK are increasing. On the other hand, China is planning to develop a new stock market in Shanghai, an opportunity for foreign companies to have capital fund raising in China. In either repositioning and revitalizing companies by mergers and acquisitions, or restructuring and undergoing a business combination with capital rising, financial experts with the three key skills: (1) Finance know-how; (2) Math and Stat; (3) Programming and engineering will become elites in the market.

With the above trends, within next 5 years, my career in finance will work for an investment bank in China to serve with clients to analyze investment strategy, make out perfect portfolio, find money to run the business, make acquisitions, plan for their financial future and manage their cash flow and capital reserve. Responsibility can come fast and my problem-solving skills will put to work quickly in a real finance job. My target is to create value for my client, the company and myself. As Finance analytical works provide series of computations for estimation or valuation a company or a project, such as valuation of cash flow streams, valuation of bonds, valuation of stocks, capital budgeting decisions (NPV, IRR, payback), capital structure, limits to the use of debt, estimation of cost of debt and equity or WACC, any financial professional in the line of work must combine perfectly the three key components, finance, programming and math. So must any work on Investment Management or analysis on securities risk and return tradeoff, portfolio diversification, and capital asset pricing models and yield-curve mathematics, etc.

Computational Finance has been a successful innovation that provides well-balanced academic and applied training. MS Computational Finance will provide me with a thorough and extensive academic grounding that prepares all graduates to become successful business professionals. Gaining knowledge from MS Computational Finance through interactive lectures, real-life case studies and integrative projects, I can strengthen my skill-set for the three major components. The variety of applied courses offered in MS Computational Finance better prepares me for the job market and benefit from the good employment opportunities in one of top class's investment banks. The knowledge from your program also accommodates me in taking the CFA exams, which is a must to succeed in competitive world of investing and finance. I believe a better education of Computational Finance offered by your University and exposure, such as top professors, smart students, excellent campus and facilities will give me a perfect springboard to achieve my ambitions in the career of finance.

会计专业的申请文书样本

1. <u>A career you want to pursue after degree. Issues whether you are entering the business world for the first time, changing fields, or advancing in fields. Why you choose this accounting.</u>

Being an International Economics and Trade student in PK Institute of Foreign Trade, I took the Accounting courses in my third term of college. I like the major and want to continue my learning and practice in the field. I also believe Accounting is better and more promising major than the current one I hold. The sun is simply more shinning on the other side.

Hard work, fortitude and a little luck have allowed me to excel in almost every accounting course that I have been taking at college. Intermediate Accounting, Auditing Principles, Costs and Corporate Accounting are all fascinating and enjoyable to me. I also took ACCA courses, many of which introduced me to different accounting practices in western countries. This year, my internship with Shanghai HX CPA Co. Ltd further proved that I have the necessary talents and required skills to work effectively as an accountant. This training opportunity educated me and shaped me in many ways. I enjoyed life of being able to add values to clients and serve the society as an accountant more as it went by: verifying financial statements, reviewing tax payment documents, conducting procedures of auditing, and providing clients' consulting services. And the key point is to find meaning and enjoyment in my accounting work. On the basis of practice and deeper learning, I thoroughly understood what my goal is in the field of Accounting.

A Master's degree, in this sense, not only prepares me in terms of satisfaction of the necessary hour requirements for CPA and professional titles in the short run, but also trains me in basics of the accounting principles, practices and skills for my lifetime career. My career objective is clear and I am determined to reach the goal wit for CPA exam. In the last semester of the Master program, I shall apply to sit for the CPA exam. I want to first finish the Master's program in Accountancy with excellent grades and sufficient preparations as the first priority in my career plan. When I pass the CPA exam, I shall be working in the states for several years as CPA for an established firm or institution. Then, from the auditing side of work, I will be considering to change to the consultancy side of work, on basis of the accumulated experiences in practice these years.

2. What aspects of your chosen fields that made you decide to enroll in Master in Accounting program of DEF? Why it is the right one for you? Be specific.

When I was a freshman of college, I had a dream that one day I could work and lead an exciting life as certified accountant in challenging business world. To qualify myself for such a enviable post, I know well the important role that a quality Master in Accounting program plays in my career plan. DEF is exactly the place that I am destined to associate with, as its campus is promising with rapid developments, faculty far-sighted with canonical managements, and its curriculum passionate with professor's efforts. Among all graduate Accounting programs that I have studied, DEF stands out prominently as it matches not only my career objectives but also my interests, experiences and talents mastered all these years.

DEF is famous for its ability to produce excellent professionals in the industry and great Boston areas. Its graduates are highly appreciated and rated among employers according to the *Business Times* and the *US News*. Practical, honest and creative, are the words that have been given to DEF people. I want to be one of them and achieve the same height as they do in business.

In particular, I dream of being a CPA expert with fine insights and sharp skills in cost accounting, income taxation and financial consulting with analytical advisory basis. The DEF MSA curriculum organization is perfect for my career plan, especially for its professional courses such as *Financial Accounting Problem, Cost Accounting,* and *Federal Income Taxation* etc. I had plenty of practical problems to be solved and analyzed under your directions, and I am also looking forward to doing my accounting internship, more efficiently and more effectively, within DEF's great program in assisting students working for internships. Furthermore, location is another noteworthy fact that I choose DEF MSA program. Boston is my favorite city in US, because it embodies both the metropolitan magic and opportunities, and exciting social life and entertainment. I'll catch opportunity to chase my dream here in DEF. And I am sure DEF, one of the key training grounds of accountants and CPAs in eyes of many employers from Boston and New York, will be proud of me in the near future.

DEF's international reputation is on the rise. I knew a senior student who graduated from my college and is currently an accounting student in DEF. All I heard from him is compliment that this is a great learning place with diversity, vigorous style of study, sensible career services and international student community. Undoubtedly, this is the place where my career in accounting will set out with full power and full support.

3. After completing the MACCT program, what is your career objective and plan?

I have a clear career goal after MACCT, working as a top auditing professional in a major accounting firm or being the Chief Financial Officer for an established public company. Good accounting services can create and expand on existing corporate values, and I want to be one of those who master well the tools and senses of the industry. I see that a graduate degree in US with well-rounded training and preparation for the CPA exam and GAAP rules will definitely land me a better-paid and better-situated position in my career. A narrow learning of China's accounting principles or rules is far from sufficient. Therefore, I chose ACCA as my entry point to strengthen my professional training. From now on, studying in MACCT not only trains me professionally, but also prepares me well for future regulatory and practical requirements. My plan is to work in the states as accountant for several years before returning to China and Asia, where many companies listed in NASDAQ and NYSE will need talents like me who understand and practice the US GAAP.

E-filing is something I have particular expertise in, and I am a quick learner. My strength in mathematics and natural infinity to figures, numbers and charts also gave me a huge advantage in winning multiple math contests and excelling in exams. In 2007, I entered college and my understandings of accounting had been reinforced immensely as my studies in relevant college-level courses such as statistics, advanced algebra, economics and management accounting continued on. My first accounting class was delivered fully in English, which never daunted me but greatly encouraged me to delve into the subject fundamentals. Not a surprise, my final score at this challenging course was an enviable excellence.

Accounting is a line of work that goes beyond pages of textbooks or exams. My most significant accounting experience so far was working as a trainee accountant in the Auditing division of KBG Certified Public Accountants. This valuable internship that I still work on taught me the essences of real accounting works in daily life as a habit, not simply as a job. I also learn the importance to control your time and plan your energy at work, especially for our accountants in handling immensely substantial amount of figures, numbers and data. These in my eyes are like blood to our clients, and we should take them on with utmost carefulness and sense of obligation. Besides the several major projects in KBG that I am in charge for serving the real estate companies, I was often called upon to do many time-sensitive and minor tasks, such as fillings at the close of the quarterly season and conducting primary work on raw income/revenue of specific accounts.

Nowadays the international business environment has raised new criteria for accounting professional working in a global framework. I also want to use what I learn from the MACCT to be more socially responsible to all, to help others and to create values for others. In the same time, I will let the world and China know better of Tulane and our Freeman school. I believe the more professionally qualified I am, the more capable I become in service to the public.

人力资源管理专业的申请文书样本

Every year MN College's MLHR program admits a select group of talented students with demonstrated potential to become successful business leaders in an increasingly competitive, global environment. Briefly summarize your educational and professional accomplishments to date. Why do you want to earn a MLHR degree in general and a Fisher MLHR specifically? Include your goals (including career goals) post–MLHR and your plan for achieving them. *(recommended maximum 1,000 words)*

Globalization has been a fact for nowadays corporations and the business community. The core competence for a corporation or an organization to secure an edge in the market is to best utilize the most valuable asset within its own framework: the human capital. Just as the business community urgently calls for such Human Resource expert, I need to align myself both conceptually and practically with such needs in the global marketplace. I choose the MLHR program at S University as a spring board to reach higher for my future career.

My career goal is to become a top expert in Human Resource Management, serving clients of all lines of work, having particularly strong know-how and hands-on in areas such as compensation and benefit design, work task evaluations, and workplace relationship, and inter/intra organizations relations. A cross-border awareness and comparative perspectives toward modern HR theories and practices are among the key skills that I have clearly in mind to develop and train for myself.

As an undergraduate student in K University of China, I have done sufficient preparations for my pending graduate studies in Human Resource management and employment relations. K University prides itself in strengths of Economics, Law and Business Administration, where I excelled in almost every course of my undergraduate years with my distinct performances in a class of 90. The vigorous economics program and related courses have armed me with a solid basis of fundamentals, such as *Macro/Micro-economics*, *Econometrics*, *Statistics*, *Business Management Theories*, *Accounting* and also *International Finance*. However, my college major in Economics did not blindfold me to a single academic discipline, while I ventured further beyond my curriculum to touch upon various courses in *Organization Behaviors*, *Fundamentals of Human Resource Management*, *Psychology* and *Sociology*, etc. I view them all as necessary building blocks for a successful career as a HR professional in the age of globalization.

Learning of HRM or ECON courses in classrooms did not show me the full picture of reality, even though they did impart in me the central principle that human beings are not just particles of a giant machine in the organization. Since this July, I have won the rare opportunity to work as a consultant trainee in *M, Inc.*, the largest US human resource consultancy firm with substantial presence here in China. Guided by experienced HR veterans in M, I was involved and introduced into many sizable projects, such as the BMW (China) incentive and benefit scheme design plan 2010, and the multi-million dollar project of work and employee relation improvement for several public companies. Different factors in actions, such as increased diversity in workplace, distinct patterns of reporting and conflict resolution and shifting roles of employees and employers, all seemed to me so complicated yet fascinating. In particular, I was drawn to these several magnetic fields: employee incentive and benefit design and inherent management and assessment issues inherent in organizational relationship.

Never before have I become so enlightened of the essentials in real Human Resource works: an organic composition of business accounting, statistics applications, Human Resource dynamics and personnel training routines & development. They all come into play in a fully dynamic fashion. I have also peeked into the regulatory side of HR work, the compliance, filing procedure, social insurance. Excited with the work content and its prospects, I found myself more and more attached to this discipline. Practice, read, learn and practice. I followed this study habit, not only consulting diligently professionals and colleagues in M, but returning sometime to the University libraries and professors for more clarification on issues that I found critical but complex. My industriousness helped me draft multiple work reports on workplace diversity and incentive plan design, as well as some academic thesis on relevant Human Resource fields. I derived immense joy when I applied my economic perspective and behavioral analysis to certain issues in work, as in many times I would have many different ideas and proposals of actions that later proved to be both innovative and effective. Isn't it the field deserving your life time devotion? I asked myself, and the answer is a firm yes as my studies of Human Resource and organizational relations and work in M continue further.

I have come thus far and so close to my dream, as companies such as M have extended to me an enviable offer of position as a HR consultant in the Beijing office after my graduation. However, I decide to press forward, as I can see in myself some deficiencies of trainings in several key aspects of Human Resource management. To secure a good footing in my career, I need a quality graduate program in Labor and Human Relations, and the MLHR at S provides me exactly such. In MLHR of S University, I need to enhance my HR understanding more comprehensively to cover public policy rationales, psychological reasoning, labor law and union interaction and employment & recruitment. I also need to keep abreast of all the intricate personal and organizational issues central to our practice as HR professional. What is more, I need a great toolbox that contains all the systematical analyzing methodologies, evaluation criteria and effective means to administer and realize the designated or specific Human Resource work tasks. The purpose of study in MLHR is to have my own frameworks and approaches to analyze the diverse organization practices, employment structures and Human Resources management strategies.

In S, I trust that the seasoned guidance of MLHR faculty will make me knowledgeable in terms of comparative analytical methods, interdisciplinary views toward human factors in workplace, and economic statistics for multi-national organizations. The program will definitely prepare me for a consolidated understanding, in both the *Macro* structure and the *Micro*' facets of the most updated Human Resource and organizational relation. With such a trained vision for the big picture and guided thoroughness specialized in the strategic, operational and behavioral sides of the human resource management, I believe I will reach out faster and easier to my ultimate career goal as a HR expert.

Be it a position in a major established consulting firm like M or an in-house position of employment relation for a corporation, I can see my career after the S as a promising and well-paying one.

市场营销和物流专业的文书样本

1. <u>Describe how a Master of Supply Chain Management degree from the B School of Business will complement your educational and professional background to help you achieve your career goals.</u> (500 word maximum)

Today's supply chain management touches every function of global commerce in global sense. I have been fascinated by both the content and prospect of being a supply chain professional, working to process, control and strategize the flowing of goods and supplies globally.

My short-term objective is to complete with top marks the Master degree in Supply Chain Management in B School, and after my graduation work for a logistics consulting firm or company that focuses on Import and Export optimization and inventory design works in Northeastern part of the States. Fortunately, the top-ranked MSCM program of B School is career-oriented and student-centered. To prepare the students of the institute more competitive in the world with business and technology closely integrated, MSCM program of B School was organized together with the engineering college. Therefore its curriculum was more practical, consistent with the current demand for the personnel in supply chain management.

Moreover, because of the superior fame of the program, its excellence allows the graduates to have broader scope of job choices, and also provides many valuable practicing and career opportunities. Especially for the overseas students, as far as I am considered, the network is significant. The alumni of MSCM program have an advantageous network of more than 40,000 business school graduates, with half a million alumni around the world. While at the same time, B School got abundant sponsors and these companies were built on the basis of its network. Moreover, after completing the first term of 14 weeks of MSCM coursework, well equipped with the prerequisite knowledge, B School will offer me with a valuable chance to enter a firm where I put the knowledge right to practice and consult on an organizational challenge. This summer paid job will definitely help me in getting progress in the study of business with some real sense of commerce, not to mention for international students such intern opportunities in America is always rare and precious. Especially, this project is completed in the form of team. For this reason, before entering the business world, I could better train my spirit of cooperation and teamwork. Meanwhile, develop my potential to the utmost extent.

My career plan, though not fully in shape, does have its roots in my own projection of the future work of supply chain management. In the long run, I wish to establish myself as a leader in the field with the topmost knowledge and skill-set to serve clients with multinational deals and cross-border business needs. As I see it, supply chain works must go global. In B School, firstly I want to learn methods to predict accurately clients needs, ways to manage effectively orders and inventory and also perspectives and approaches to deal with global logistics challenges as a leader. B School will definitely satisfy me in this, with its systematic procedures of leadership development training, including personal leadership assessment, team-building courses and team dynamic training and so on, together with its emphasis on the multinational cultures and innovation.

2. <u>Tell the Admission Committee about a time when it cost you to maintain your integrity and what you learned from the experience. Who was affected besides yourself? Was there anything you might have done differently? Would you make the same decision again if given the chance?</u>

At the end of 2009, the Department of Economic Management held a model international business negotiation competition. The organizing committee requires every team to record the negotiation progress into video and deliver it to the teacher. We performed in a formal way from the clothes to the negotiation form. As the team leader, after the teacher assigning this task, I convened a meeting immediately. Different from other teams, our team did not decide the topic at the beginning. We thought at first that if we need to film the progress, we need the hardware such as video camera, clothes borrowed from fellow students, and most importantly a meeting room. So we contacted with the teacher and scheduled the usage time by applying. Afterwards, we were busy in preparing for the competition for many days with thousands times of rehearsal. When only the last filming part was lacking, we went to film according to the application time. After arriving at the meeting room, we found that some other team was using it.

I was shocked and went to negotiate with the team leader of that team, saying we had already booked the conference room, while she did not cooperate with the words arrogantly: "So what, you may ask the dean, she has already permitted us to use it." When I asked the teacher who agreed to our application, the teacher, to my surprise again said he did not remember we had applied. Then, our team member helped him in remembering every word on that day, he had no choice but to tell the truth. He said: "There is no good solution for it, since the leader of that team is the granddaughter of the dean. And the dean promised himself the usage of this room. You have to find another way."

At that time, it was very urgent since the next day would be the deadline for delivering the final video. Worse still, at the end of December in Beijing, it was really cold and everyone just wore shirts and suits to be formal. We, eight girls, were standing there, feeling really desperate. Everyone was very angry including me. They all said that we should go straight for the dean for an argument. However, after my consideration for a while, I decided to find another room for the filming. At the beginning, they did not accept that, feeling that I was afraid of teacher's criticism and it was compromise. While I explained to them that the resting time was limited and it would only cost more time in quarreling with others. Because it was Sunday, it was already impossible to borrow the library building as well as the office building for the second time. All of a sudden, I thought of the teachers' rooms in the teaching building. When I asked the supervisor of the classrooms I was disappointed again. Fortunately, I ran into a professor who taught me when I was a freshman. Although almost a year had passed, he remembered me clearly over my expectation. I told him my problem and he promised to let us use the teacher's room for resting. The teacher's room was not equipped with air conditioner but it was the only room we could use. Although we were cold, and it was over 10 o'clock, we filmed the whole negotiation process in that situation.

Later, the judges asked every team to play our video before giving the final scores and would publicize the results after a few days. In the end, we successfully got the champion with the teachers' comment that: "Although the negotiation process was very simple and a little bit plain, but it won with the advantage on its negotiation etiquette and insights absolutely complying with the regulation, while the works of other teams were empty without substantial content." At that moment, all of us cried.

I kept thinking that if time flew back, would I choose to argue with the team in against to injustice? I thought, probably not, I would not just appear more grand in others' eyes, and choose to challenge the long existing substantial rules in China—power, and the power could change everything. Moreover, I believe, if I went to the president of the school, he would not stand on our side. Could he choose to support us instead of other teachers? If he did not support the teacher, where would the dignity and pride of the dean be? Facing such situation, arguing would only put us in a much troubled situation and offend the teachers. Instead, thinking of another solution would not be the best, but would be the most suitable choice.

管理学相关专业的文书样本

1. The IPA personal statement is divided into three questions, each with a word limit. You will compose your responses to each question and then upload your responses as a single

document. Please follow the instructions below very carefully.

2. Please use 12 point font and choose a common font such as Arial, Calibri, or New Times Roman.

3. Please double space your responses.

4. Please type each question in bold font into your document and then follow the question with your response.

5. Please pay attention to the word limit on each question.

6. The document you upload is final. Once the statement has been submitted it may not be changed at a later date.

Personal Statement/Essay Questions for Spring 2011 and Fall 2011

First Question (500 Word Maximum)

1.What distinct impact do you hope to have on the world in the future? Please be as clear as possible about your future goals, the policy/public service issue(s) you are passionate about, and your personal motivation(s). Be sure to include details regarding the features of IPA that you believe are integral to helping you in your pursuits and what skills you need to develop to achieve a lasting impact.

In my eyes, any change in Macro economic policy of major countries, even as small as adjusting only 0.01 deposit reserve ratio, will cause a major earthquake in the international capital market. Players of stock market who are sensitive to these indices will profit handsomely, while the unknowing groups of people will simply observe the dwindling of their numbers in accounts. Bankers will then adjust the loan ratio or credit policy according to such policy shifting and changes, thus impacting on the investment needs by the general Public, which has also chain effects on the economy of that country. The Butterfly Effect does exist, and one index could alter the landscape of the whole nation's preference or tendency in consumption, trade and international economic exchanges.

We must think more broadly and also more deeply of all these factors in the "chain of actions," for a clear picture regarding the soundness of economic policy, financial planning or even banking/trade policy changes. Money is the chips to play and policy is the dealer who distributes and regulates the desk in the house.

I love the studies of international economics and finance from a macro perspective, as the whole process of national econ policy design and implementation is not only delicate and complicated, but fascinating and intriguing. My aspirations in life are simple but noble, changing the world with my own limited abilities and skills. In a public institution, I can achieve for many better welfare and living through my expertise in macro economics. In a private business job, I can contribute to the company's growth and prosperity with my in-depth international economics and finance perspectives.

Until today, the Federal Reserve has employed almost every means in its pocket to handle the recent credit crisis, subsidy, government taking over and institution reforms, not to mention the large amount of new financing tools such as reverse auction and innovative liquidity. Such tools, along with discounts or commercial bill financing, indeed enhance the liquidity in the market. But this policy actually transfers from future times the inflations onto the economy in present times in order to relieve the debt crisis of US. I see now a prospective inflation expand not just across North America, but also to other major economic entities. Should a macro economic or finance policy deal only with current concerns or pressing issues? Or should the policy magnitude, timing, and implementation be considered in a balanced scheme?

This is what I want to achieve and impact on the world, and this is also where IPA can help me to grow more competent in face of challenges: to peal off the layers of varieties of politics, economics and trade relationship and subtlety. IPA at C University carries C tradition to focus on practice and realistic approaches in academics. Its location is perfect as NYC provides a natural lab for our econ/finance policy testing. I like particularly your track of concentration on international finance as it prepares me for careers that require knowledge of capital markets, banking and public policy. Building on my already strong finance, mathematical and practical know-how, IPA's program will complete my toolbox to realize my career goal.

Second Question (300 Word Maximum)

2. Describe a conversation or experience that challenged your beliefs or caused you to reevaluate your perspective on life.

This summer, I have been working as an intern at the International Account Management Office of our Bank of China, the central bank here in the country. Even though I beat other 120 applicants to win this position, I was assigned to a desk job of file organizing, releasing notices and doing simple policy and market research for the operation team.

My quantitative skill is not just good, but superb good. And my finance and economics backgrounds are equally strong. Why put me to deal with errands! I started to hold a grudge here even though I was doing my job diligently and attentively. However, gradually, I found that my post was actually quite important in this giant machine that regulates and operates all of China's most important, life-and-death economic decisions and policies. My second task was to draft a simple notice of changing the commercial bank's credit evaluation policy for realty owners with more than two properties in a particular month. That three line notice took me three hours to draft. And I had to call by telephone one by one, all the 25 commercial banks in Beijing and 32 foreign banks as well for such a notice.

I was quite exhausted after placing all the calls. While such a simple notice went out with great impacts, different banks, when receiving instructions from the central bank, have shown different reactions and also very different mechanisms to receive and implement such instruction. I started to see more clearly how the People's Bank operates, regulates and monitors the banks and financial institutions, and feel the real power of policy change and its swift impacts on the economy and our society.

My post was no longer a simple-minded work, but an important function in the whole chain of action that moves, changes and works every day. I learned to become more broad in vision, and more attentive in action after such a valuable experience this summer.

Third Question/Response (200 Word Maximum)

3.Please share any additional information about yourself that you believe would be of interest to the Admissions Committee. Please focus on information that is not already reflected in the other parts of your application or might not be clear in the information submitted.

I excelled in many Mathematics courses for the past three academic years. Such courses range from Mathematics A1 to Mathematics A3 as integral parts of Advanced Calculus, e.g. definite integral & indefinite integral calculation. I took also AnalytVc Geometry and Vector Algebra, Functions of Variables, Linear and Curve Algebra, Surface Integrals, Infinite Series; and Advanced Probabilities as well as Matrix and Linear Space. Also I have particular strength in Probability Theory and Mathematical Analysis, Statistics, Accountancy and Econometrics.

In July 2009, I was awarded the Second Prize in Mathematics Modeling Contest of the University for my extraordinary performances and leadership in the contest designing and drafting a 21-page paper in three days, which made reasonable hypothesis by setting up options of practical mathematics modeling with aid of STAT and MATLAB in such a short-time frame.

In the thesis entitled "The New Securitization Trend for Mortgage Related Financial Products," I gave a full play to my mathematics and statistics skill, proposing that along with the process of our national finance market becoming more integrated into the global market comes a pressing need of developing products or solutions of securitizations for increasing non-performing assets. I analyzed various factors of assets construction principles and derivatives used in major commercial banks, finding out the speculated minimum variance ratio of five-category asset classifications of assets pool.

媒体管理等专业的申请文书样本

1. Statement of Purpose

Value is the key to the industry of public service and consultancy. If an industry can not create value to the society, the industry has no reason to exist. For the past twenty years, Public Administration studies have evolved from a branch in policy analysis and communication to a full-blown line of work that creates, adds and changes the values to our society. My career is to become one of top-notched professional in public relations, public service and policy consultancy. Such a learning motivation and development goal has grown inside me ever since I entered the university with a systematic exposure to the theories, practices and trends in the field. By all means, it is a mesmerizing and constructive art, as many disputes and issues are essentially rooted in the people's communications barriers associated with their vast cultural, economic and political differences. A strategic and well-planned public relation campaign could bring about enormous economic and business values to corporations, organizations and the community.

Driven by this passion and appreciation about the public administration, I have been actively seeking opportunities to increase my training in the industry and hone my skills. Starting from September 2010 to present, I have been working as an intern in the department of Crisis Public Relations in *H & J*, one of a leading PR companies in the world. I started as the manager of digital media for a RMB 3-million project, and managed the whole process of content production, dissemination planning, supervision over the public opinion direction, and regulation of suppliers' work. Success in this sizable project won me another opportunity to work on a major network PR company, where I held meetings with their directors to discuss the packaging and propagandizing program and took charge of every detail independently. Then I became the maintenance personnel for media relations communicating with the Shanghai media outlets on a regular basis and tried to get the opportunity to distribute news dispatches. So far, my dedication and professionalism had earned high praises from the superiors, clients and colleagues.

While working as an external PR consultant, I also had a chance to work very closely with some high-profile Chinese corporations, which gave me a lot of valuable insights as to how PR work could create value to real business and even Chinese economy. *H and T Brew* are the two of H & J's largest customers in China, and I was fortunate enough to be part of the projects and actively involved in a wide range of PR activities. I took charge of the English daily and weekly for these two companies, participating in bidding preparation, monitoring daily news and conducting some maintenance. Furthermore, I looked for related materials and completed topic analysis which was affected by public opinion in media in many times. Other than the regular maintenance assignments, I also involved myself in some strategic work, including interviewing clients and writing press releases, which entail a lot of knowledge and skills that I could rarely obtain from classroom. I particularly enjoyed the creative and strategic aspects of these projects. The PR internship was not just an eye-opening experience to me, but more like a real adventure into the wonders and charms of the real engagement of PR industry.

My interests and commitment of the industry were sparked off. What accounts for an effective and beneficial public policy consulting practice? What are some key factors and means that we could utilize for a campaign or promotion to change people's perception about a corporation and an issue? How could we make a public campaign more educational and valuable to the society as a whole? These questions intrigued me and have helped me decide to further pursue my study in the PR and communication field. Though I am not a veteran practitioner, I believe I have obtained sufficient passion and commitment that a determined PR professional would have.

I make this decision not on impulse. I study hard at TS University of China, especially on the theoretical fundamentals. As a return, I got excellent grades after 3 years because my overall GPA is 3.62/4.0, and Major GPA is 3.70/4.0. I majored in Broadcasting and Television Journalism and particularly excelled at the core courses such as Media Operation and Management; Public Relations; Public Survey Methodologies; TV Editing; Television Planning; News Commentary; News Reporting and Writing; Management and Journalism theories. I also learn well in varieties of subjects of economics, political science, business administration and corporate finance subjects. These courses are highly related with public relations and public administration and prompted me to join the class discussion actively. Testing theories, reviewing experimental settings and testing again, I gradually learned to combine effectively what my practice know-how with textbook teaching, to see why finance, politics, sociology come into play with public administration and policy studies.

The more I learn and practice, the stronger feeling I have that most of achievements in the media realm are rooted in research results from America or other countries. The special national conditions of China simply can not perfectly align with them. An urge to learn more and stand tall, has become an acute need for me at this stage. In CIPA of D University, I have opportunity to study public policy, fiscal policy, social and international studies in a truly global perspective. I also choose CIPA for its strong emphasis on cross-disciplinary approach, as I have the necessary academic backgrounds in quantitative and economic know-how, and also the strong command of communication and journalism theories and practices. Here in CIPA, political processes are formulated, de-structured and analyzed and fiscal, social and political basis for government and organizational actions are studied with visions of market economy. This is exactly what I need for a graduate program. I also became fascinated by D University's strong Human Resources management theory, public and private organizational behaviors and management studies. If I have to decide to write a thesis for MPA program, that will definitely be within CIPA's best grasp: Fiscal Policy, Policy Studies, International Development Studies and Social Policy. I will use my competence in quantitative methods and practical experiences, I will definitely make a valuable addition to your program in policies studies, corporate communication and others.

Just as the global forum "Finance" said, China has a lot of famous entrepreneurs, but few experts in public service and advisory industry. I hope I can be such expert without regret in learning, without limitation in practice and without hesitation to pursue dreams. Armed with the expertise gleaned from your program and guidance, I am confident I can do more than what I have now in the booming China's emerging industry.

Time changes our concept of value, so does the public service and consultancy industry to the society. I think I will press forward with such passion unchanged, to create values, benefits and changes in a greater proportion with my own talents and skills.

2. Plan of Study

The criteria I set for my future career refer to what I called P.I.C., the three quintessential in perfect integration: P for passion; I for intelligence; C for convergence. As my experiences and learning accumulate through times, I have come thus far to the firm belief that Public Relations is a perfect career that has every element of P.I.C. in work.

Someone may enjoy a rather easy life, but what I want for my life is one that presents constant and endless challenges, busy while productive and fast-pacing but full of passion. Passion, for me, means the cornerstone of all successes. PR industry gives me such a passion as it is both highly practical and eventful. Every time when you have a new case at hands, challenges of varied sorts will knock on your office door. In the crucial process of transforming contents to marketization of media, PR industry plays the ultimately crucial role to connect and coordinate. From content production to the very end of consumption, PR is everywhere.

Driven by this passion and appreciation about the public relations, I have been actively seeking opportunities to increase my training in the PR industry and hone my skills. Starting from September 2010 to present, I have been working as an intern in the department of Crisis Public Relations in H & J, one of the leading PR companies in the world. I started as the manager of digital media and took charge of the whole process of content production, dissemination planning, supervision over the public opinion direction, and regulation of suppliers' work. While working as an external PR consultant, I also had a chance to work very closely with some high-profile Chinese corporations, which gave me a lot of valuable insights as to how PR work could create value to real business and even Chinese economy. H and T Brew are the two of H & J's largest customers in China, and I was fortunate enough to be part of the projects and participated in bidding preparation, monitoring daily news and conducting some maintenance. Other than the regular assignments, I also involved myself in some strategic work, including interviewing clients and writing press releases, which entail a lot of knowledge and skills that I could rarely obtain from classroom. I particularly enjoyed the creative and strategic aspects of these projects. The PR internship was not just an eye-opening experience to me, but more like a real adventure into the wonders and charms of the real engagement of PR industry, which makes me certain that the PR industry is the well of passion to me.

Another important element is "I"—intelligence. My passion and commitment of the industry were sparked off. However, passion does not speak every golden word in the industry, and one successful professional must always rethink, reflect and recharge his/her own power base in order to meet new challenges. Though I am not a veteran PR practitioner, I believe I have obtained sufficient passion and commitment that a determined PR professional would have. Thus, I decided to further pursue my study in the PR and communication field. In other words, I must empower my own element of "I."

I make this decision not on impulse. I study hard at TS University of China, especially on the theoretical fundamentals. As a return, I got excellent grades after 3 years. I majored in Broadcasting and Television Journalism and particularly excelled at the core courses such as Media Operation and Management; Public Relations; News Commentary; News Reporting and Writing; Management and Journalism Theories. These courses are highly related with public relations and prompted me to join the class discussion actively. I combined effectively what my practice know-how with textbook teaching, to see why finance, politics, sociology come into play with PR studies. Moreover, I learned how to cooperate with others, which is also one of the makings of a good PR consultant.

The more I learn and practice, the stronger feeling I have that most of achievements in the media realm are rooted in research results from America or other countries. The special national conditions of China simply cannot perfectly align with them. An urge to learn more and stand tall, has become an acute need for me at this stage. G University's Master of Professional Studies in Public Relations and Corporate Communications stands out from other program, as it can teach me a comprehensive knowledge of Marketing, Public Relations and Communications. Strategic Communication is the point of focus in G University on teaching me how to use effectively communication in a strategically sound fashion. It is a comprehensive footing in strategy, digital communication, and integration informed by a truly international perspective that will move me forward in the PR industry. I am also fascinated by the works in G University's Center for Social Impact Communication. Following closely what happened recently in the Center's G University's Africa Interest Network, I think my experiences of international interactions, exchanges and extensive international visits will definitely provide assistance to the Center. Besides, what I like particularly about G University is its ample opportunities as the school has substantial relationships with many organizations that facilitate us to obtain internships, placements or opportunities.

When it comes to C—convergence, it is decided by the changing market needs. As convergence becomes a trend in nowadays globalized world, business entities will all entangle with cooperation with other industries and professions. In media industry, convergence involves both a change in the way media is produced and a change in the way media is consumed. And in PR industry, such trend will find its best vehicle. By all means, it is a mesmerizing and constructive art, as many disputes and issues are essentially rooted in the people's communications barriers associated with their vast cultural, economic and political differences. A strategic and well-planned public relation campaign could bring about enormous economic and business values to corporations, organizations and the community. Sensing and knowing such prospect for PR industry, I am confident that my choice of such a career is correct and justified. I am aspiring to learn more and practice more in the field under your training for an in-depth knowledge and proficient PR skills.

P.I.C. is also an abbreviation of picture. I believe that with the passion in bone, intelligence in mind and convergence in business, I can create values, benefits and changes in a greater proportion with my own talents and skills.

后 记

在这本书的写作过程中，申请商科的学生仍旧在一如既往、异常踊跃地和我预约时间咨询。有时我感到一种沮丧，因为单单凭我的能力和精力，不可能帮到每一位学生，这种感觉非常强烈，尤其是一些学生埋头准备考试不闻窗外事，到了暑假才在我这儿听说实习很重要、文书很重要这些话，对他们这些完全没有思想准备的学生相当于泼冷水。于是他们开始着急上火和郁闷。还有的例外，开始无所谓，慢悠悠地说，没事，中国学生的东西都是编造的，我也可以变出花样来。部分家长也是如此，觉得自己的孩子上了上海交大或者北京化工大学，就不把这些美国院校放在眼里，上来就牛气地说：张老师，我的孩子不上哈佛的金融硕士就浪费了，您一定要帮忙！于是我又开始重复地说一样的话：对不起，您应该先了解，哈佛不设金融项目硕士，只有博士。

我常说的一句话是，要让自己或孩子成功留美，首先一定要让自己成为半个留学专家。为什么现在留学市场这么混乱，这么多无良的中介能够如鱼得水，这么多雷同的、不专业和错误的信息在网上大肆传播？为什么这么多学生和家长轻易就被一些刚入门的毫无经验的"老师"蒙蔽？原因很简单，骗子就欺负那些不懂行的，不骗你们骗谁？这本书如果有什么意义，我觉得就在于此。

我原先想得很美好，想把这些专业的学校信息全部列出来，每一个学校，甚至每一位老师或每一篇文书。但是估算了一下，按照我的想法成书，这本书恐怕要超过1 000页！于是作罢，只能挑选一些主要的来写了。

即便如此，工作量也很大，这里我要感谢博创留美升学辅导的王老师、邵老师、唐老师、魏老师和翟老师，他们对书籍的写作付出了许多努力和汗水。也要感谢中国人民大学出版社的几位老师，我知道自己的中文写作已经变得很怪异，不好意思麻烦你们要忍受一下我那些奇怪的句式和用词，今后我一定努力改正和学习！一定要把中文学好！我有这个信心，请大家监督我的学习表现。

张 旭
2011-10 于北京